STAR WARS
THE
MANDALORIAN

THE MANGA

ADAPTED BY
YUSUKE OSAWA

Based on the series created by
Jon Favreau and written by Jon Favreau,
Dave Filoni, Christopher Yost,
and Rick Famuyiwa

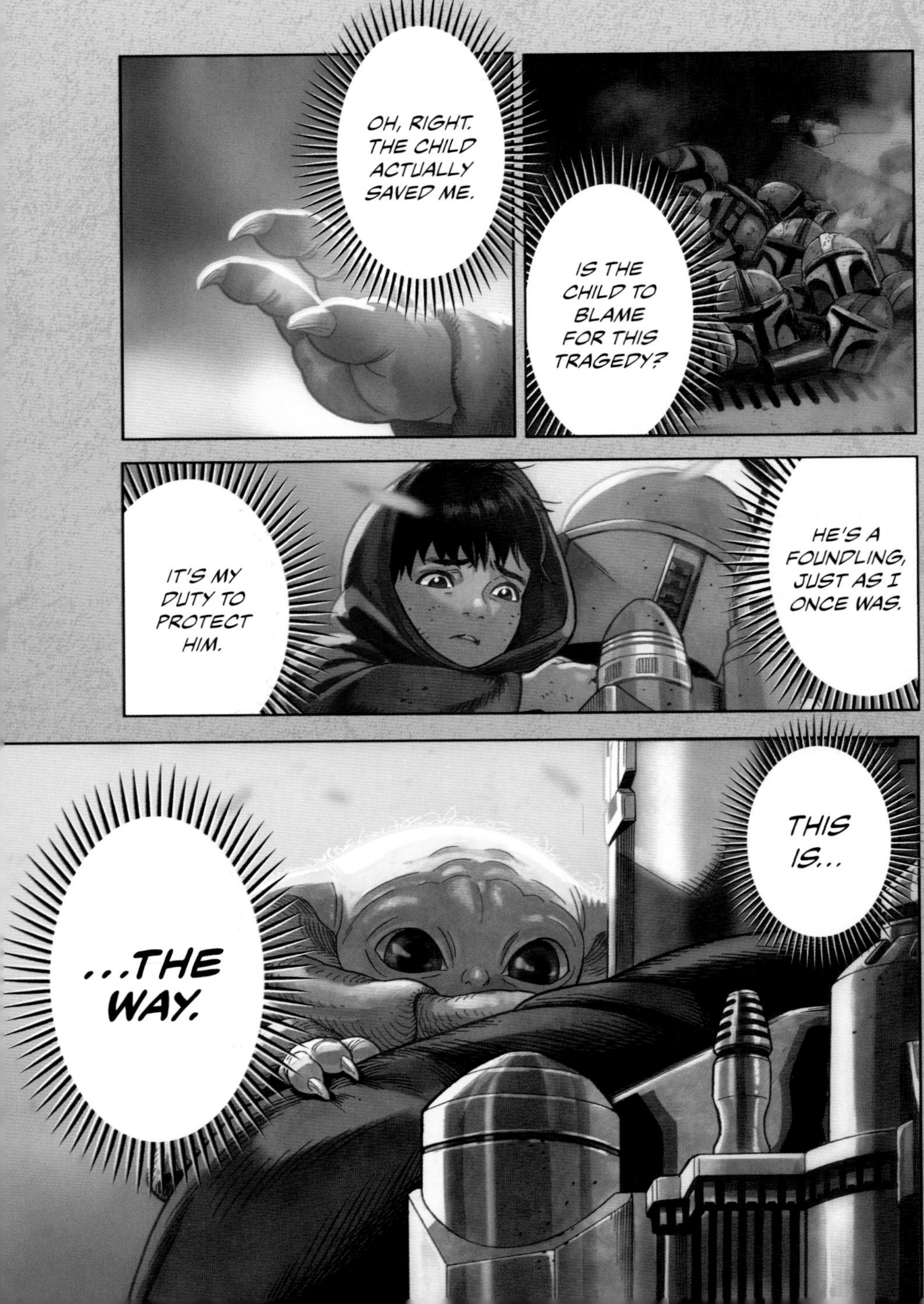
IS THE CHILD TO BLAME FOR THIS TRAGEDY?
OH, RIGHT. THE CHILD ACTUALLY SAVED ME.
HE'S A FOUNDLING, JUST AS I ONCE WAS.
IT'S MY DUTY TO PROTECT HIM.
THIS IS...
...THE WAY.

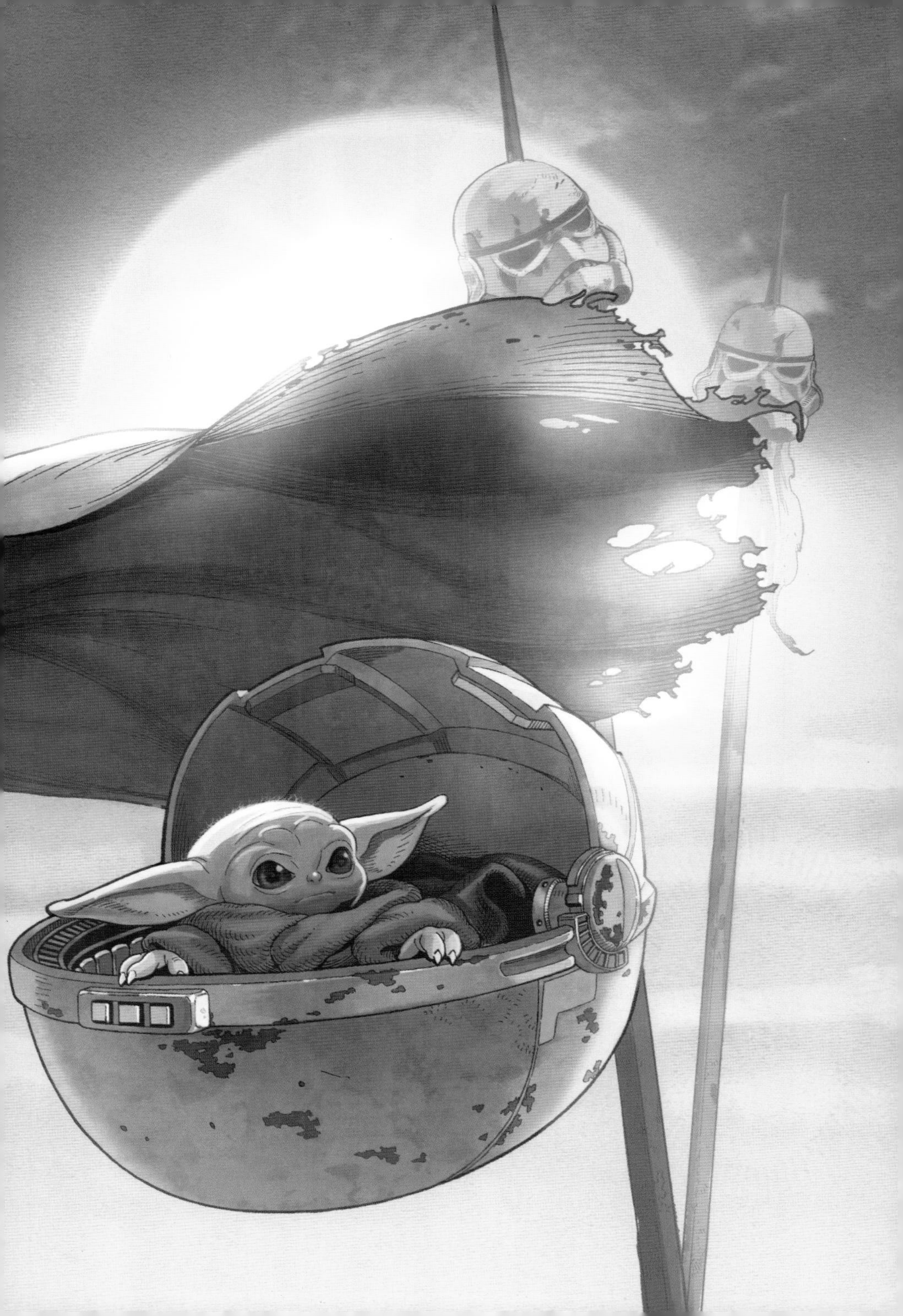

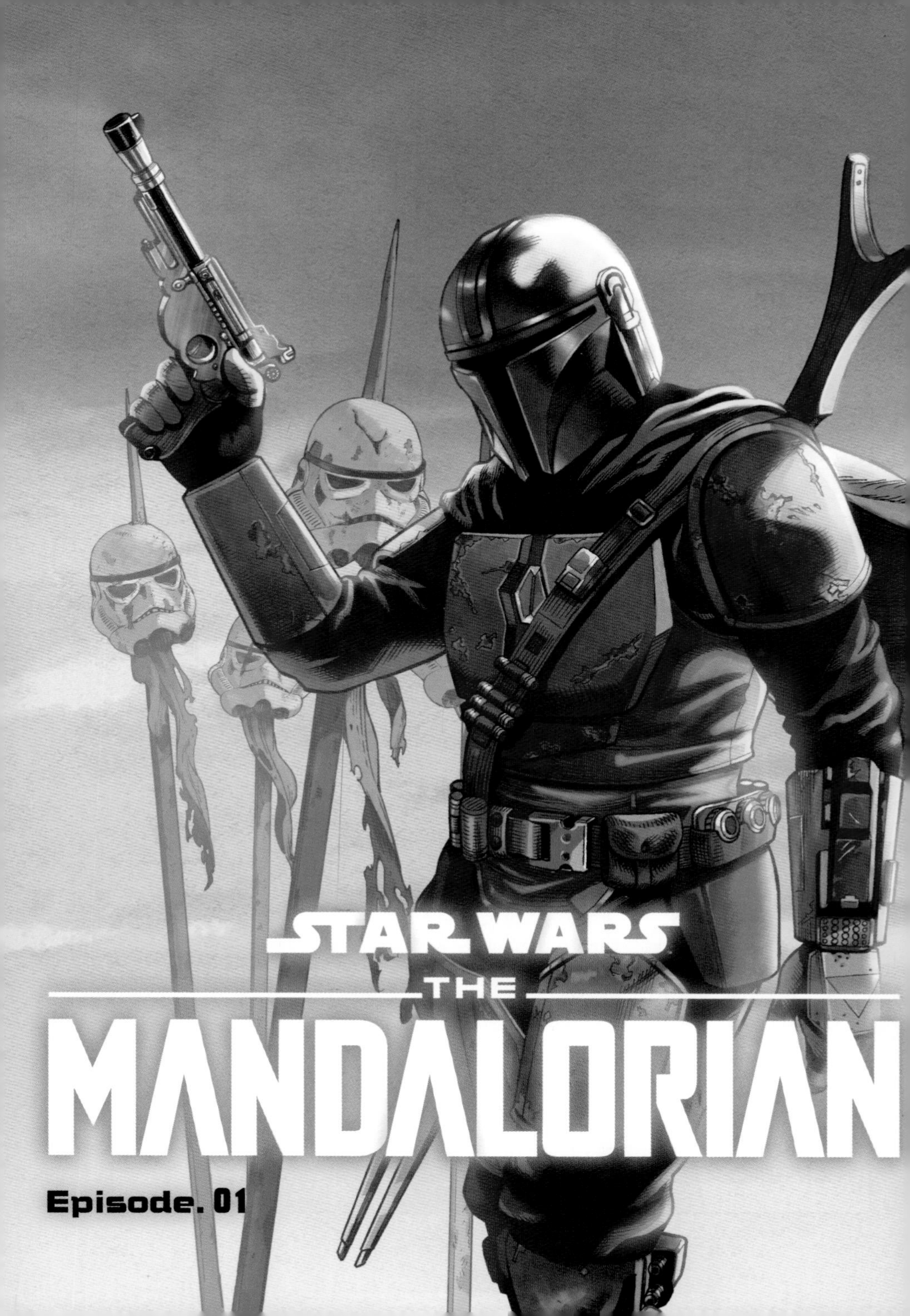
STAR WARS
THE
MANDALORIAN
Episode. 01

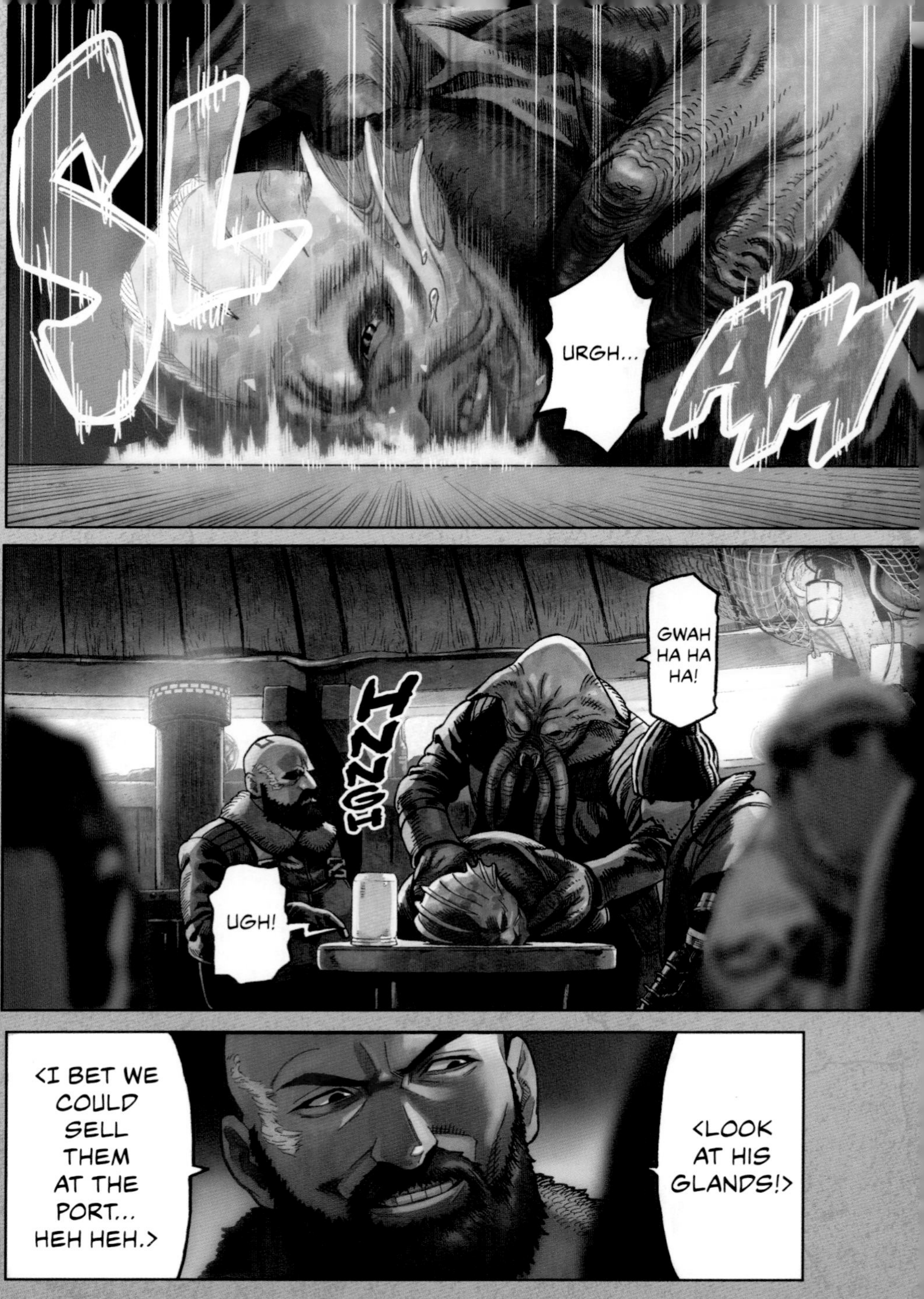
SLAM
URGH...
GWAH HA HA HA!
HNNGH
UGH!
<LOOK AT HIS GLANDS!>
<I BET WE COULD SELL THEM AT THE PORT... HEH HEH.>

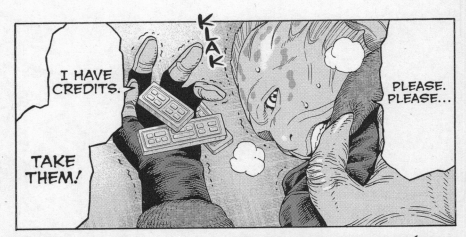

KLAK
PLEASE. PLEASE...
I HAVE CREDITS.
TAKE THEM!
YANK
!
SKWEEEZ
<HE'S YOUNG. THE MUSK WILL BE SWEET...>
<AND NOW FOR THE REAL PRIZE...>

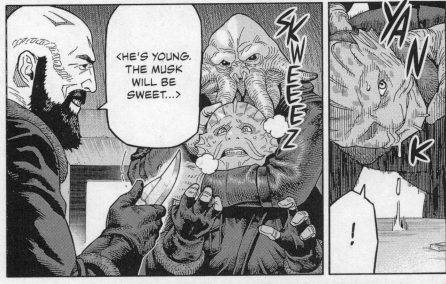

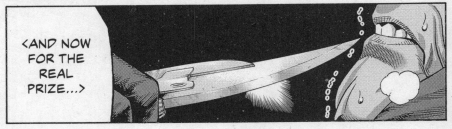

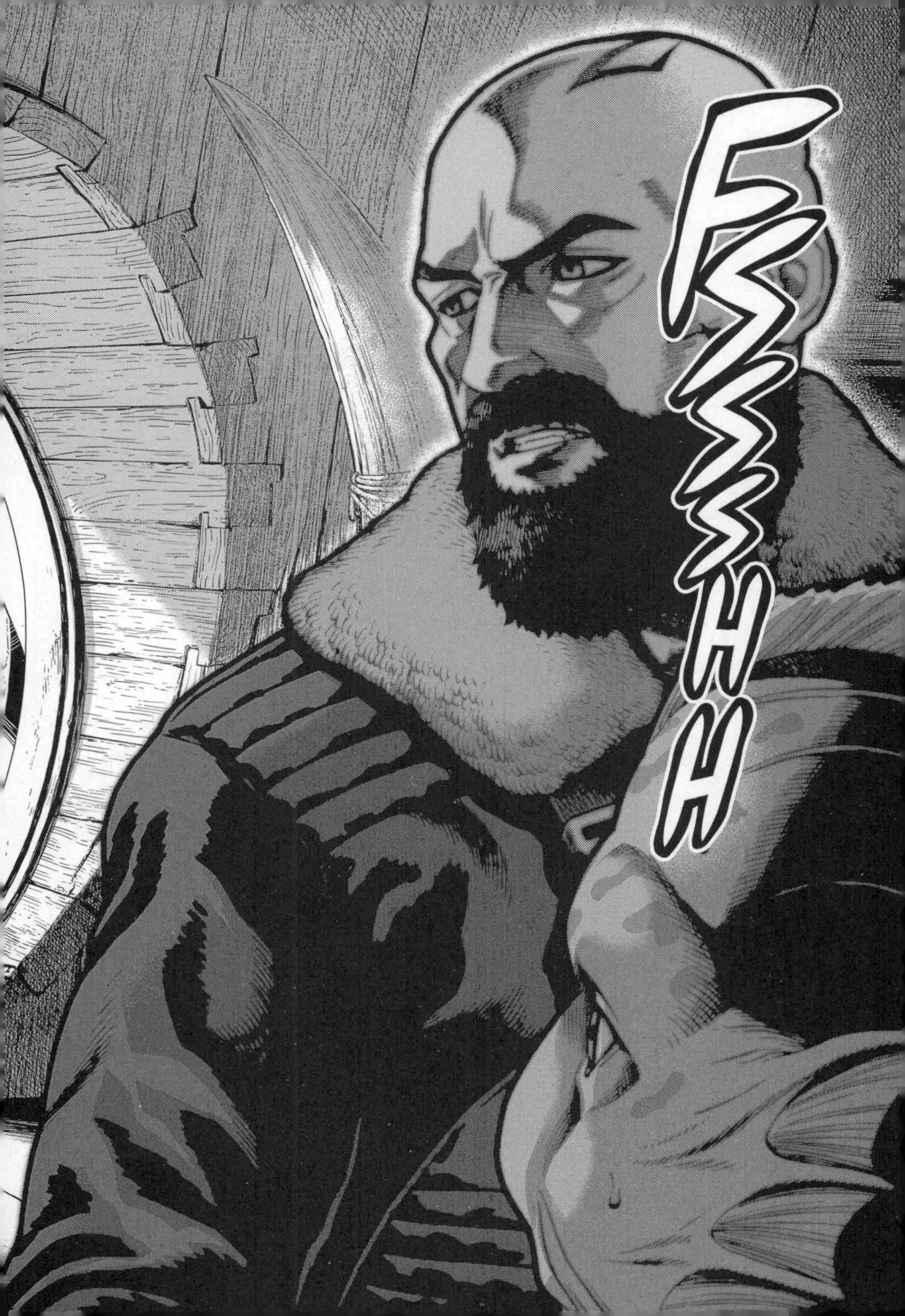
FSSSSHHH

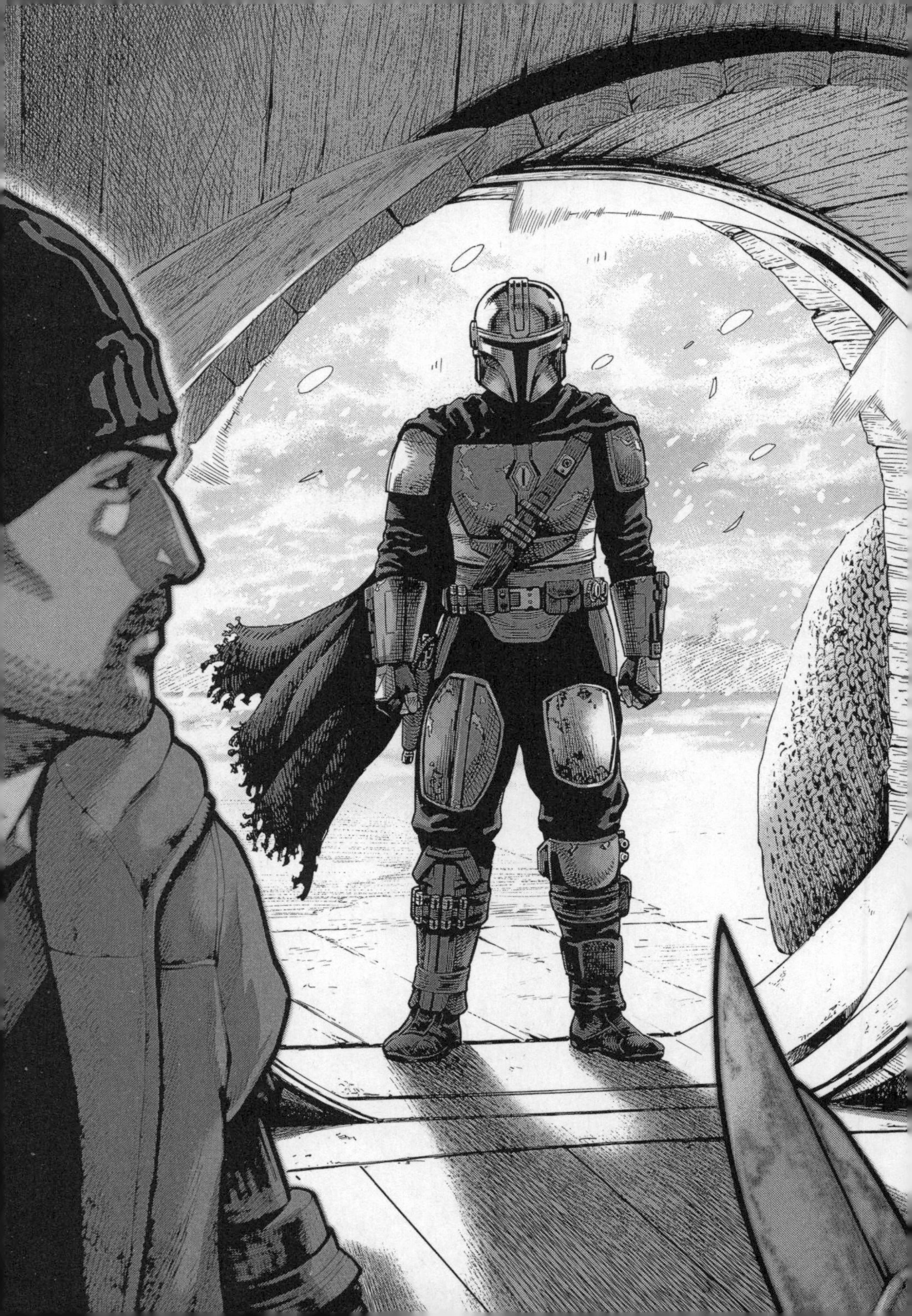

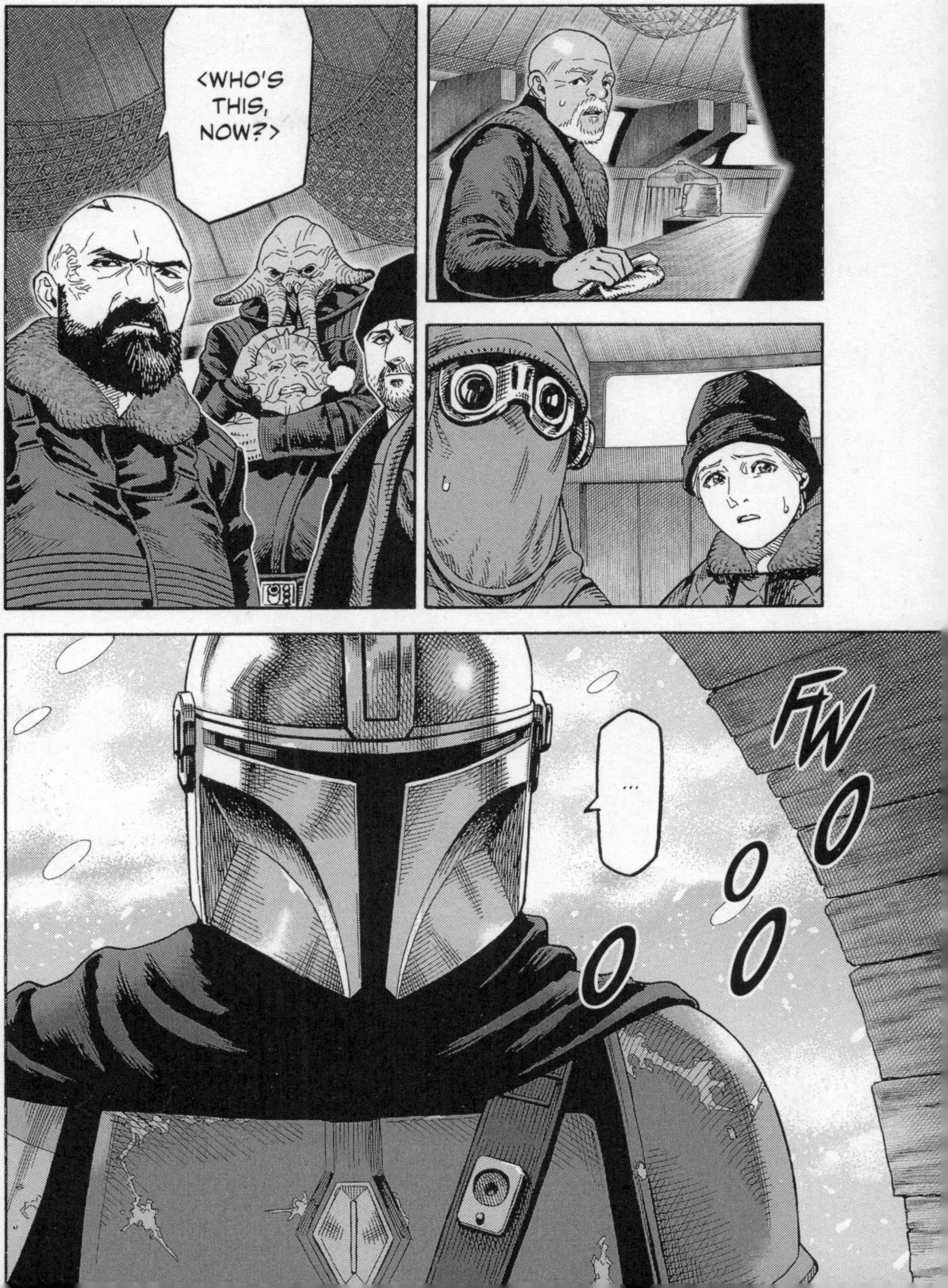
<WHO'S THIS, NOW?>
FWOOOOO
...

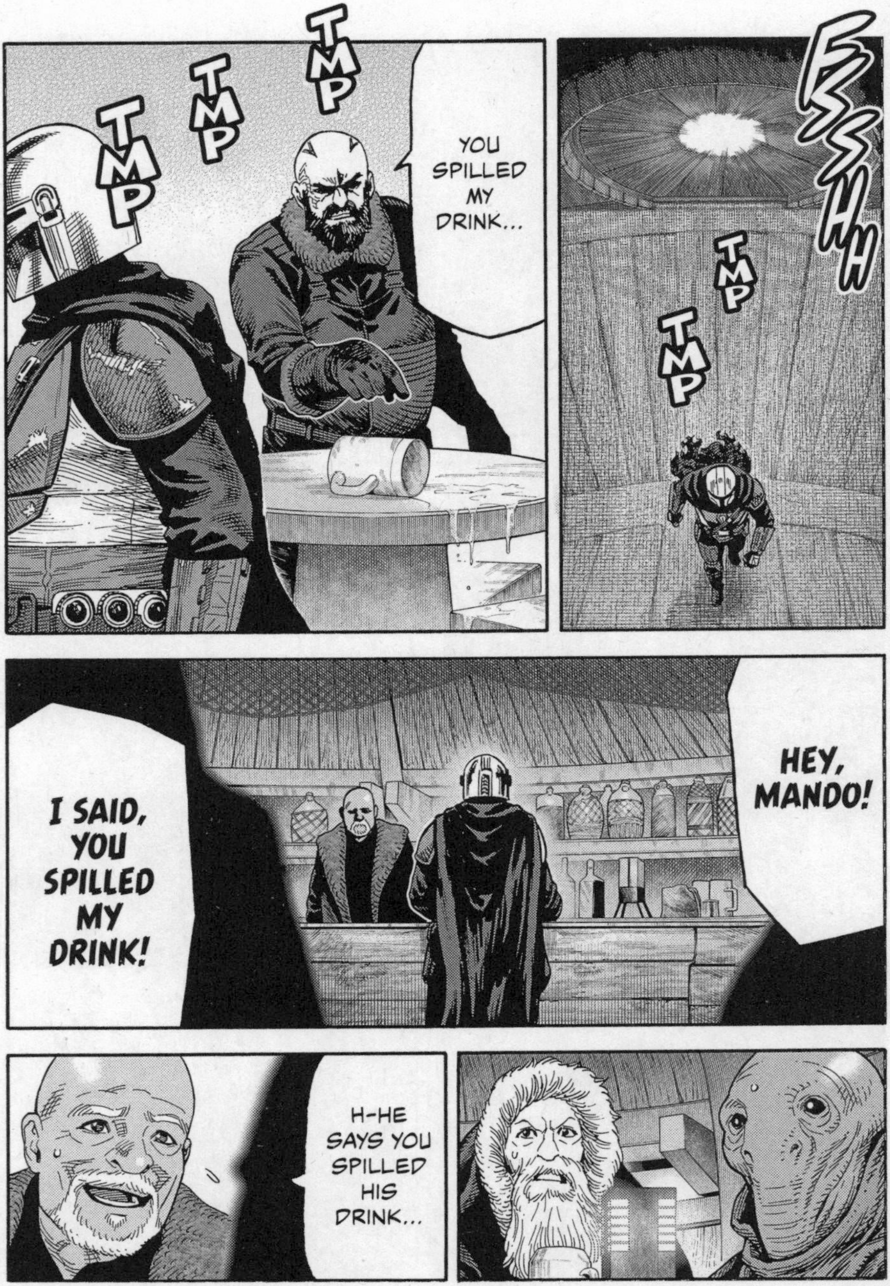
FSSHH
TMP
TMP
TMP
TMP
TMP
YOU SPILLED MY DRINK...
HEY, MANDO!
I SAID, YOU SPILLED MY DRINK!
H-HE SAYS YOU SPILLED HIS DRINK...

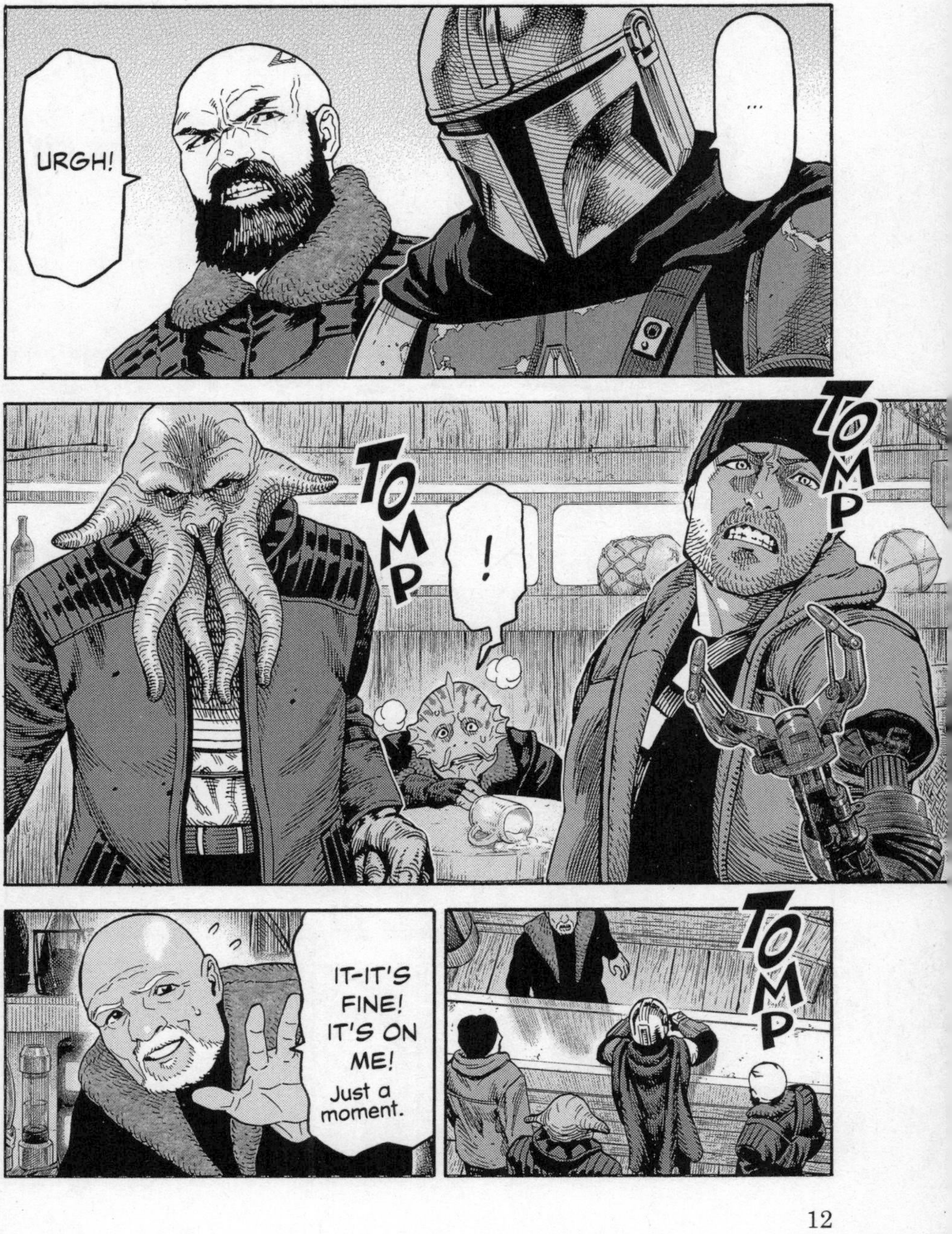
...
URGH!
TOMP
TOMP
!
TOMP
TOMP
IT-IT'S FINE! IT'S ON ME!
Just a moment.

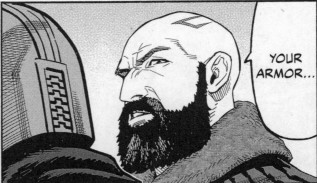

YOUR ARMOR...

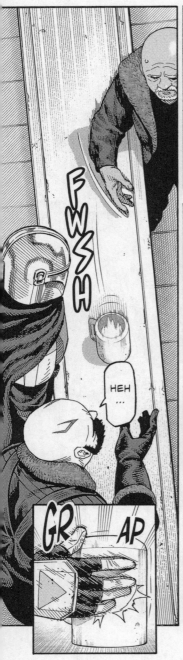

FWSH

HEH...

GR AP

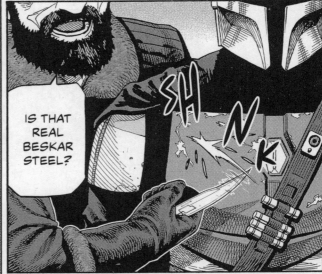

IS THAT REAL BESKAR STEEL?

SH NK

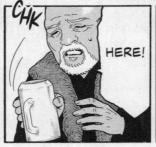

CHK

HERE!

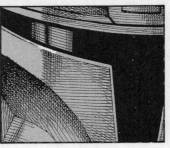

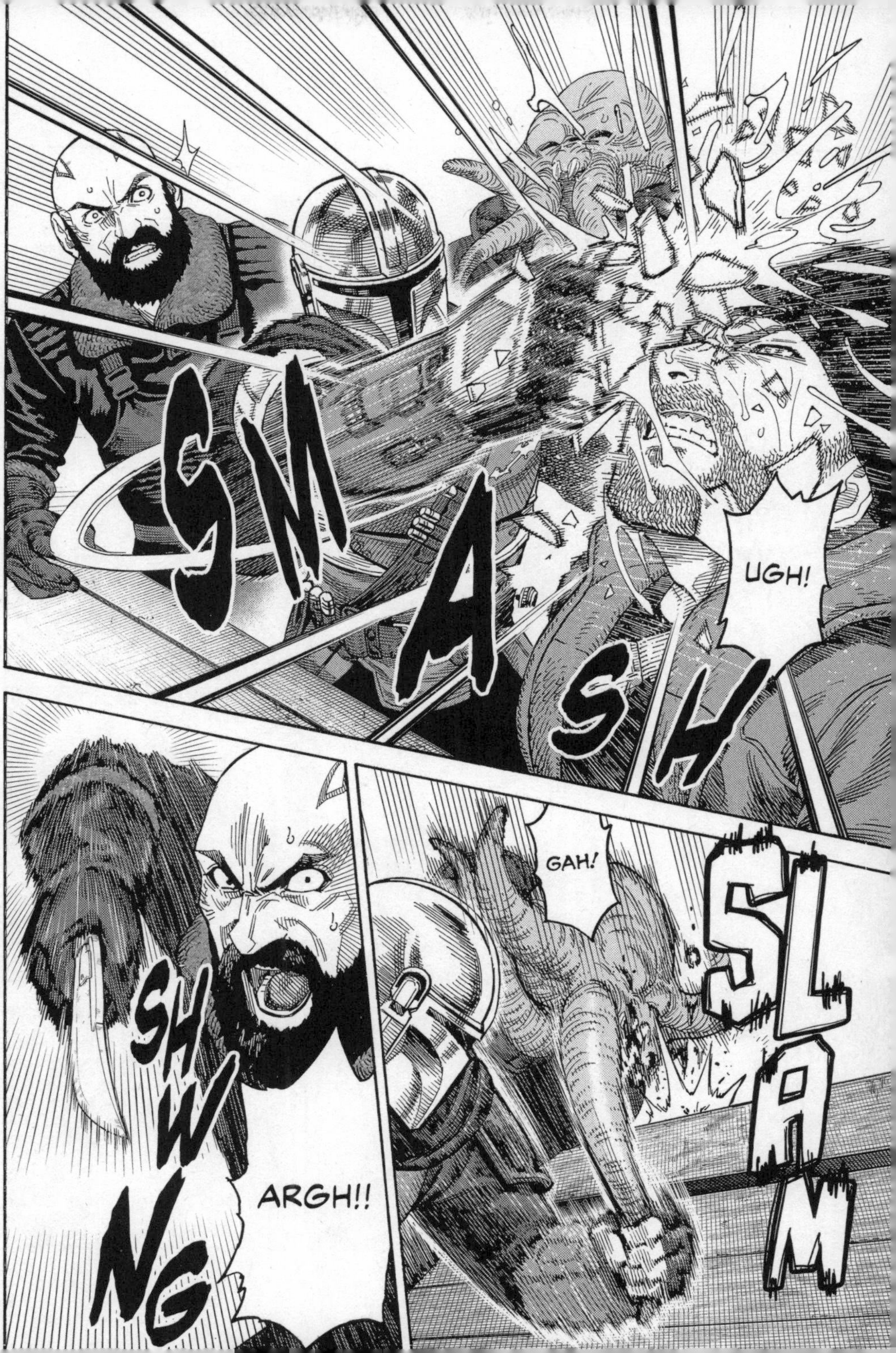
SMASH
UGH!
GAH!
SLAM
SHWNG
ARGH!!

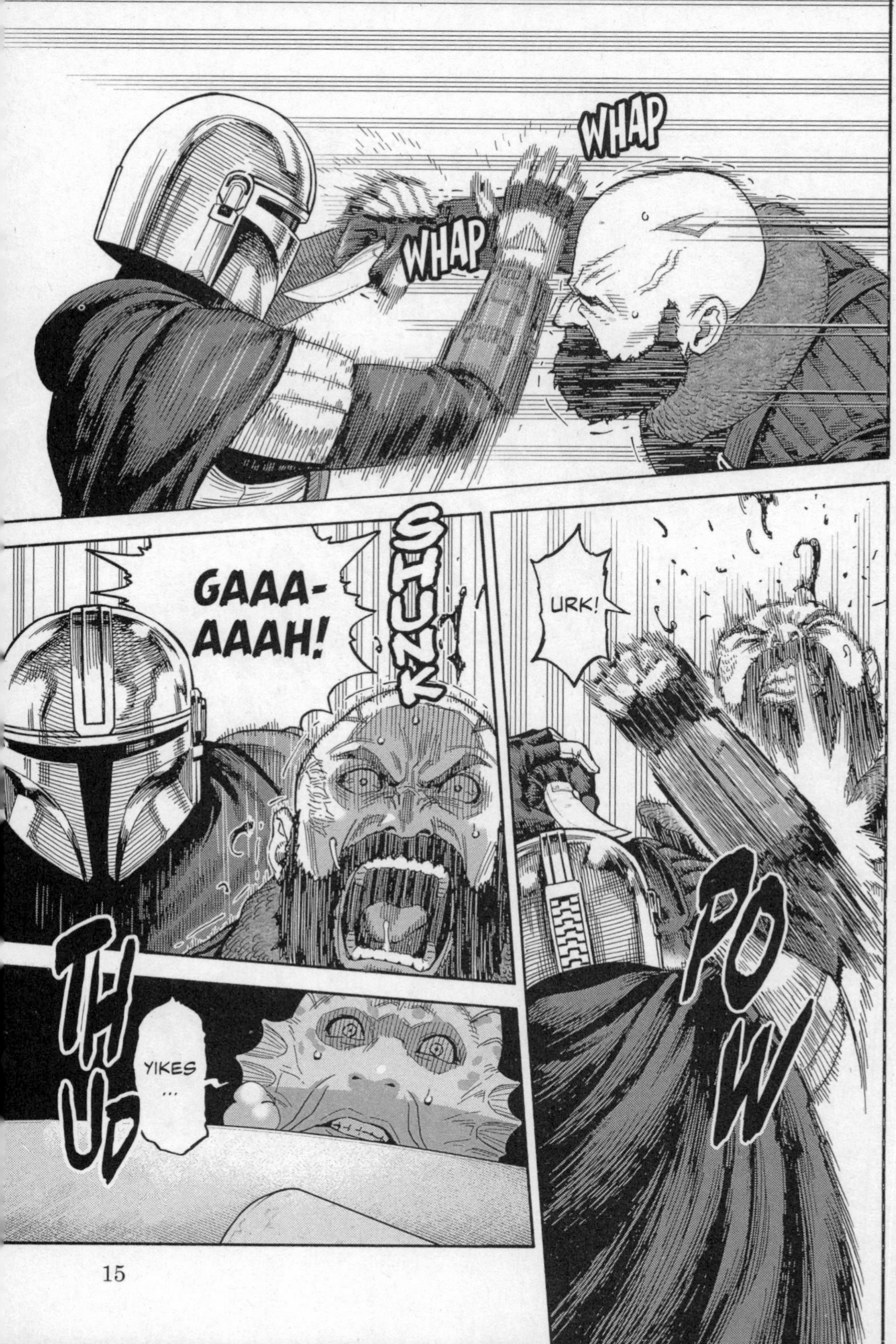
WHAP
WHAP
URK!
POW
GAAAA-
AAAH!
SHUNK
THUD
YIKES
...

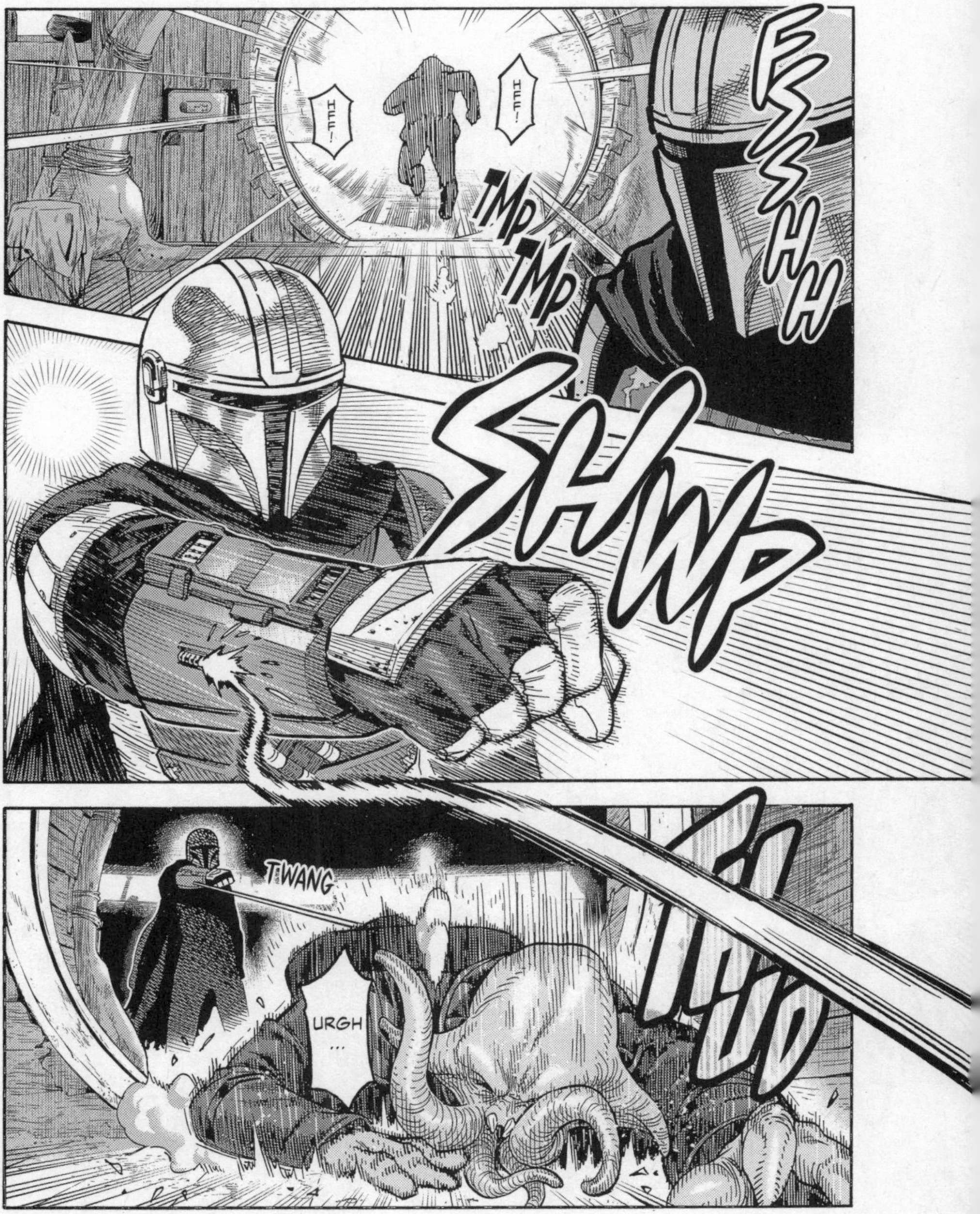
FSSHHH
TMP TMP
HFF!
HFF!
SHWP
TWANG
URGH ...

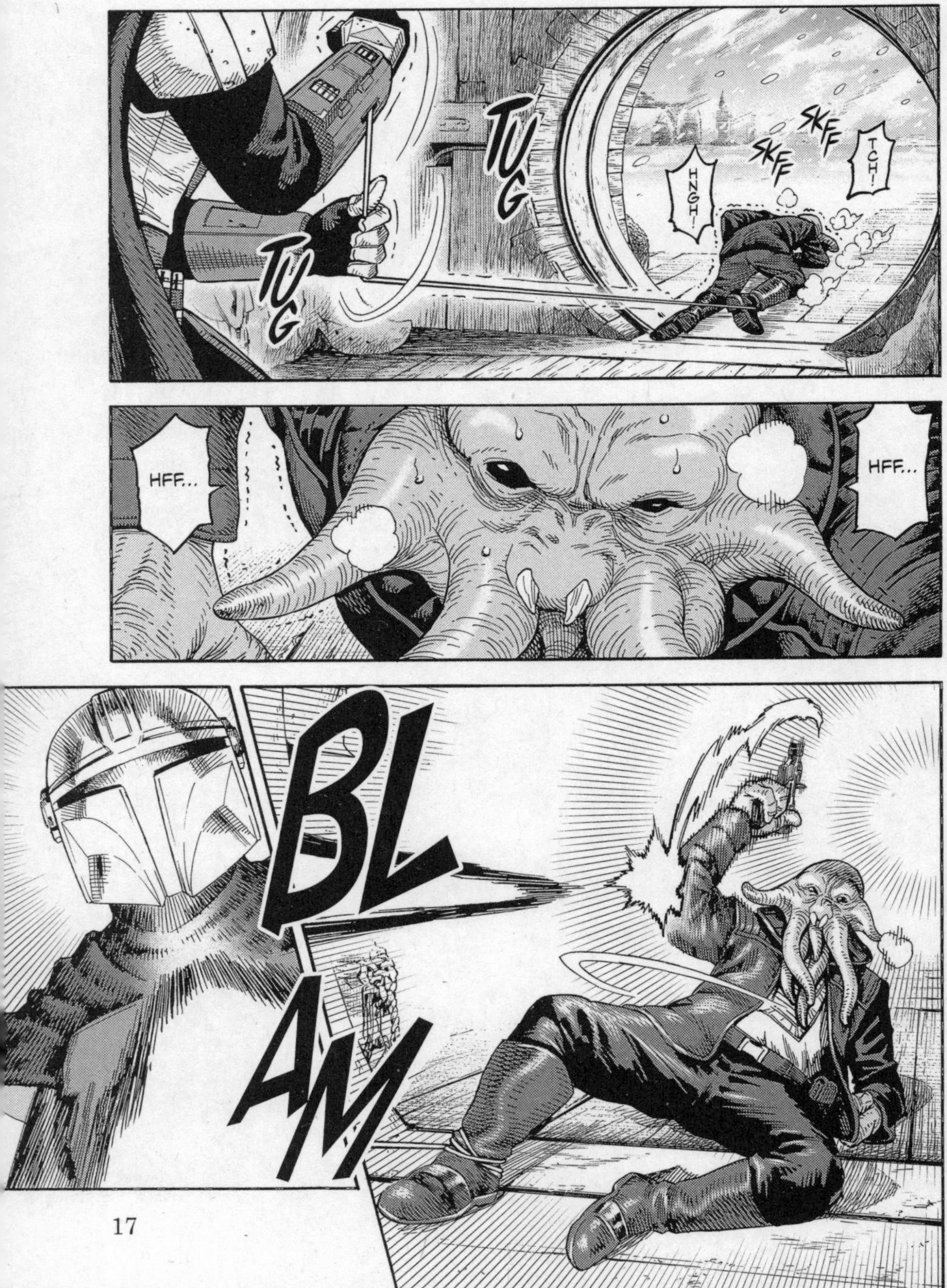
TCH!
SKFF
SKFF
HNGH!
TUG
TUG
TUG
TUG
HFF...
HFF...
BLAM

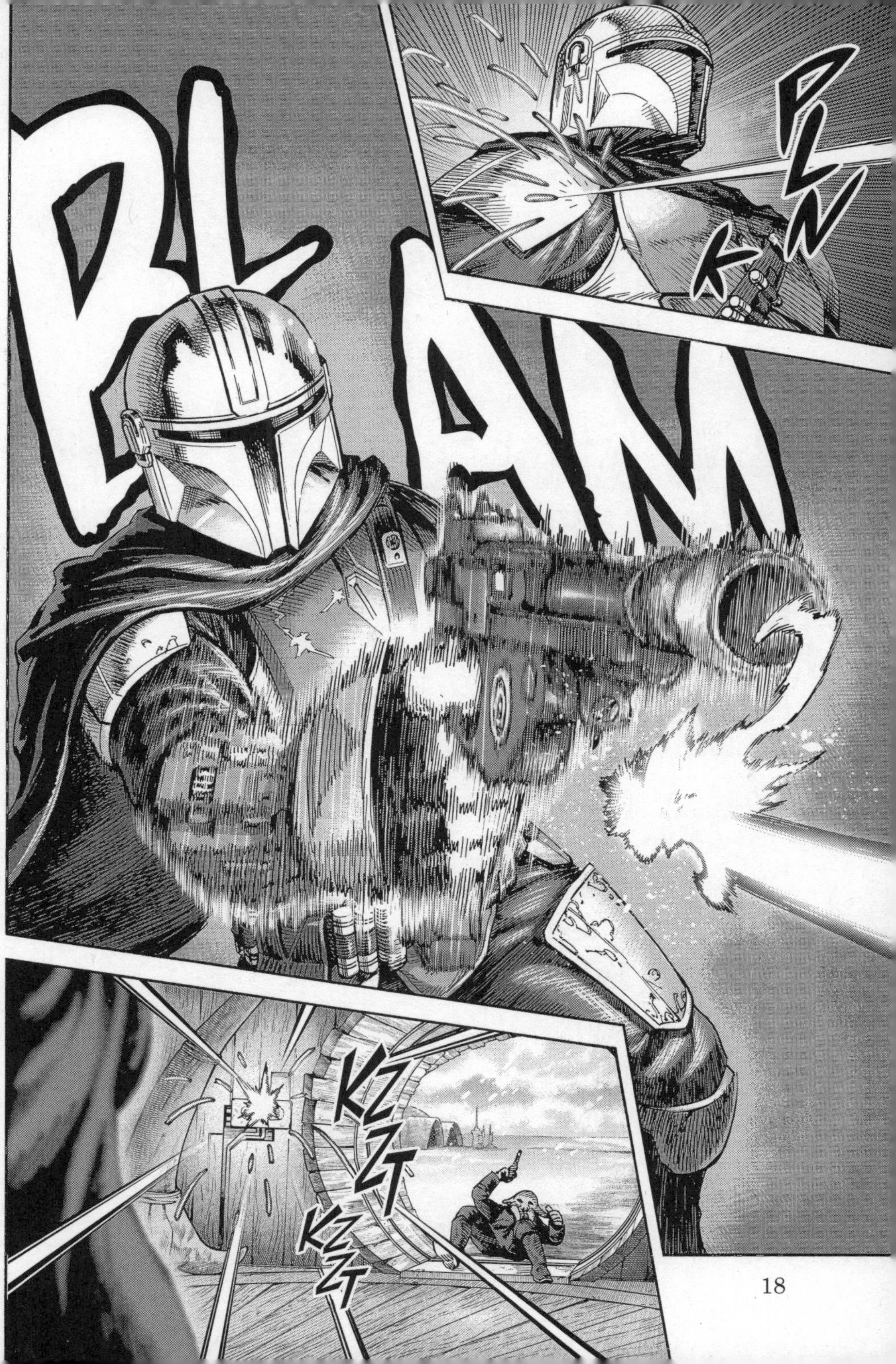
PLINK
BLAM
KZZT
KZZT

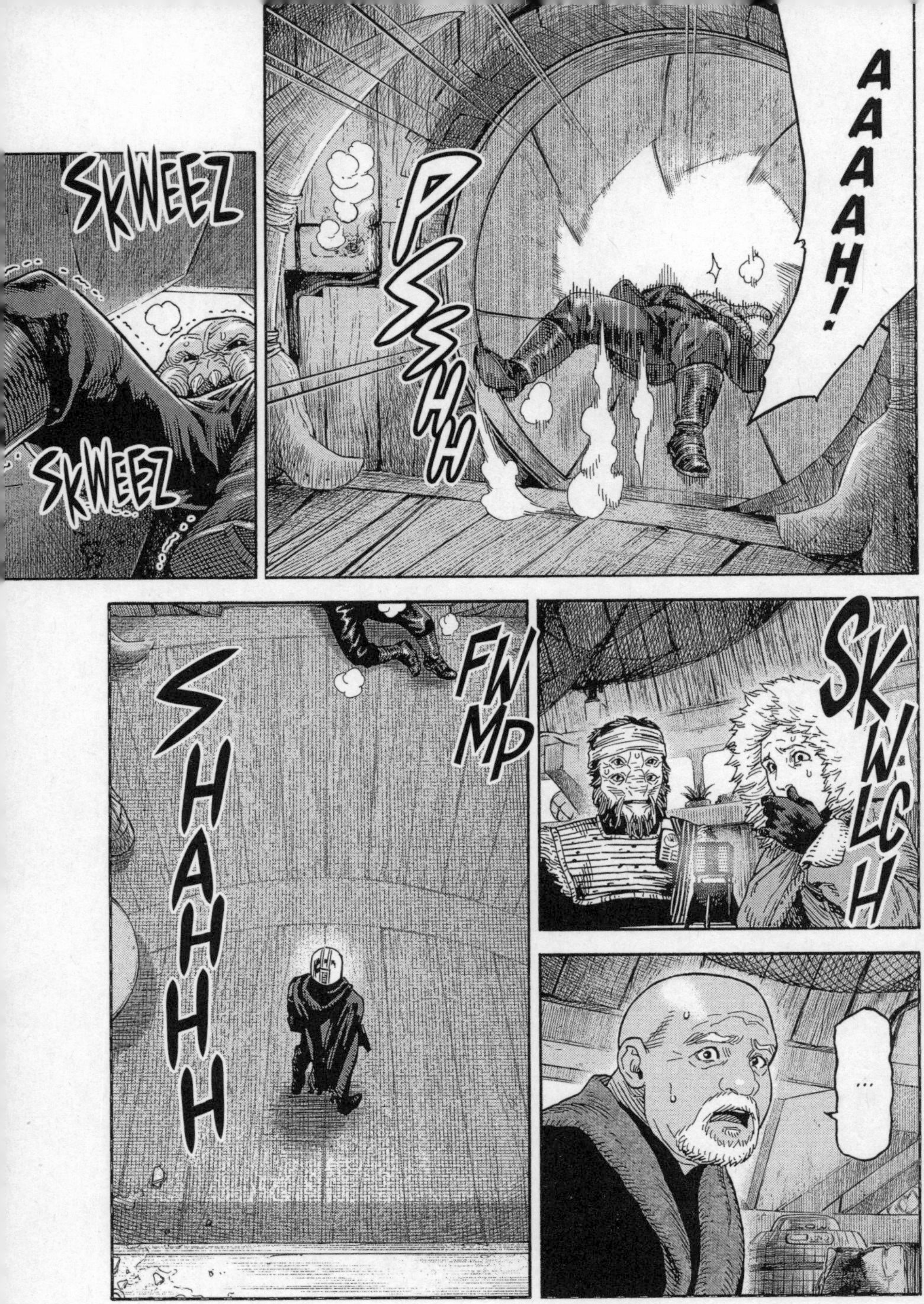
AAAAAH!
PSSHH
SKWEEZ
SKWEEZ
SKWLCH
...
FWMP
SHAHHHH

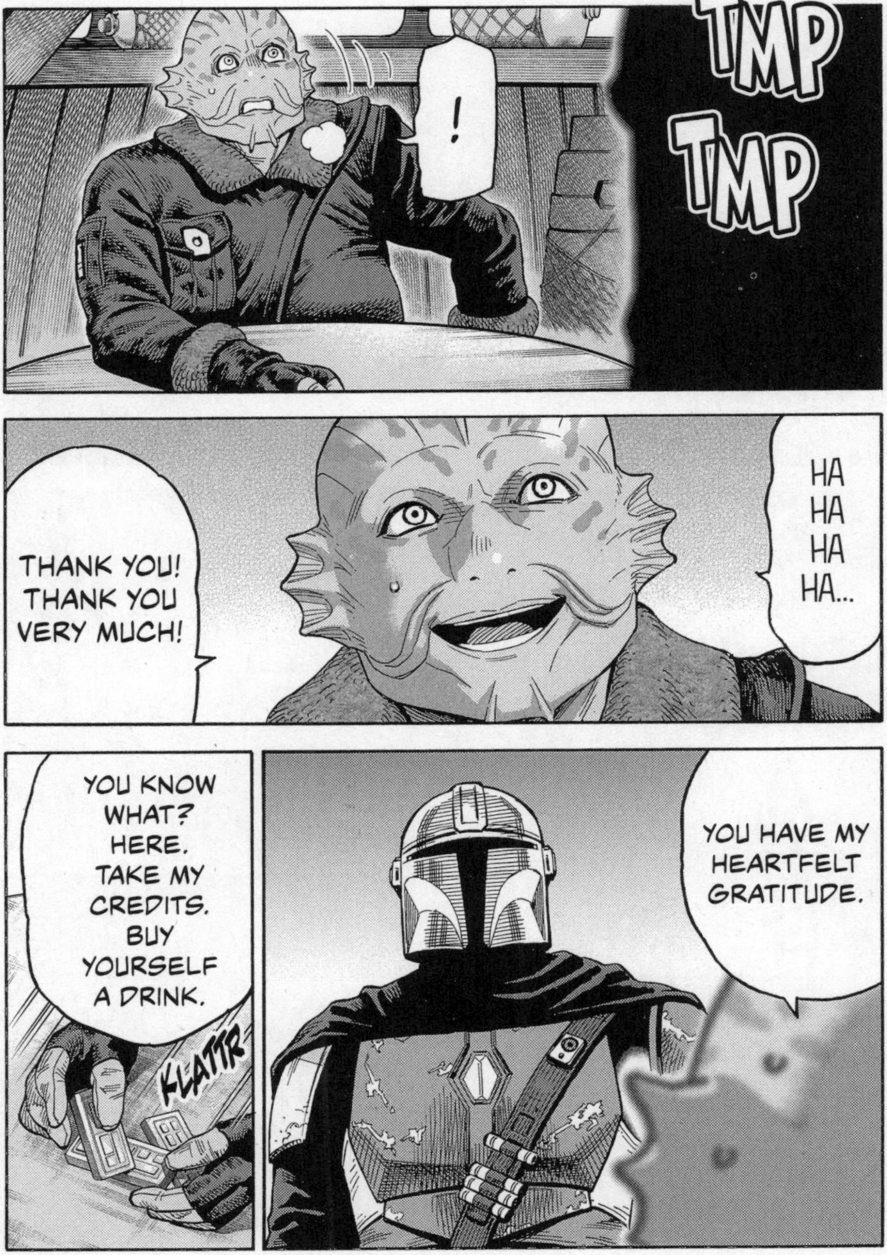
TMP TMP
!
HA HA HA HA...
THANK YOU! THANK YOU VERY MUCH!
YOU HAVE MY HEARTFELT GRATITUDE.
YOU KNOW WHAT? HERE. TAKE MY CREDITS. BUY YOURSELF A DRINK.
KLATTR

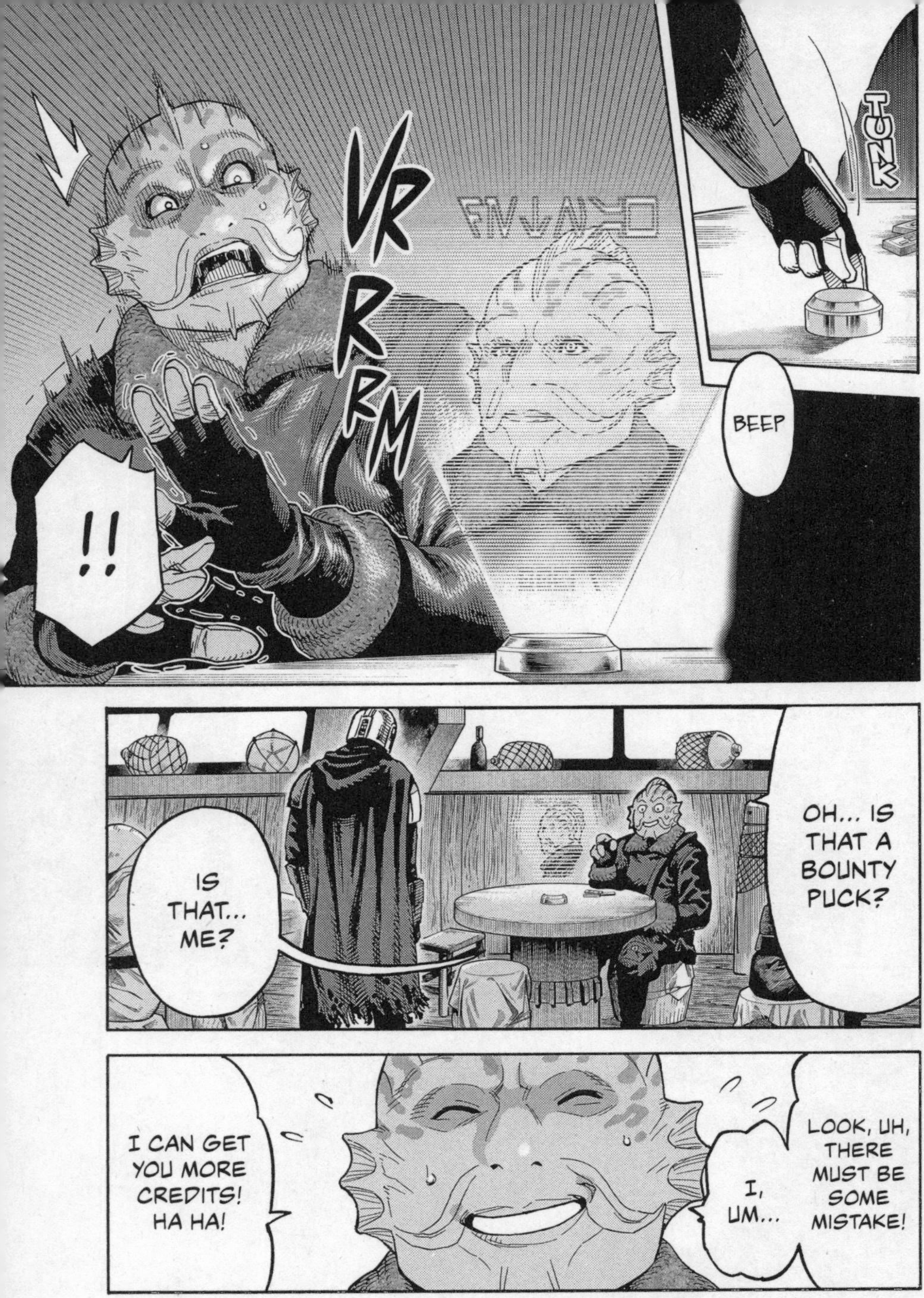
TUNK
BEEP
VRRRM
!!
OH... IS THAT A BOUNTY PUCK?
IS THAT... ME?
LOOK, UH, THERE MUST BE SOME MISTAKE!
I, UM...
I CAN GET YOU MORE CREDITS! HA HA!

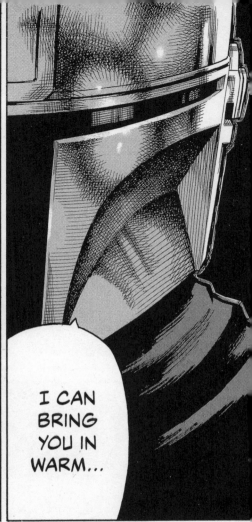

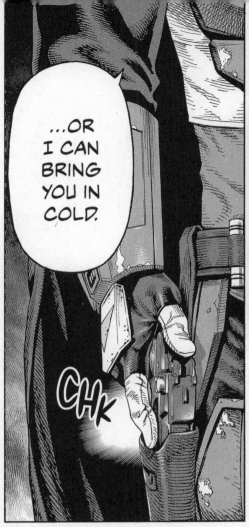

...OR I CAN BRING YOU IN COLD.

CHK

I CAN BRING YOU IN WARM...

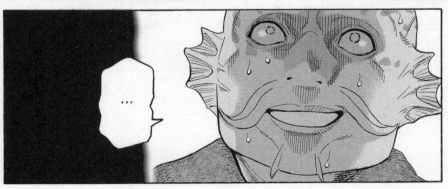

...

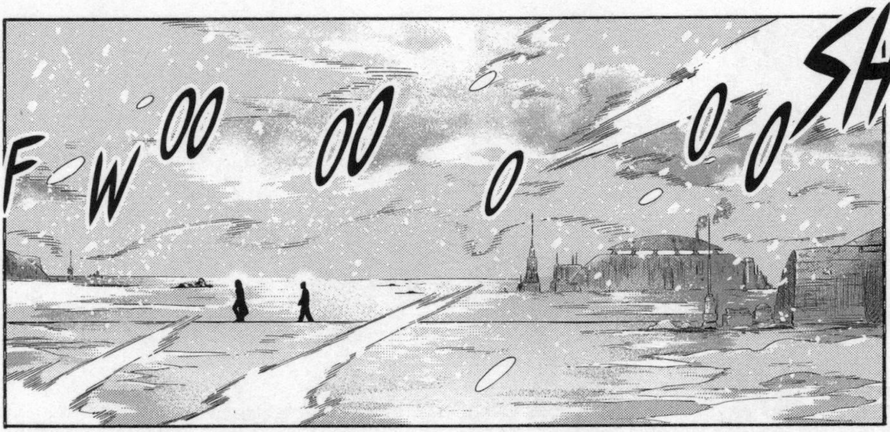
FWOOOOOOOSH

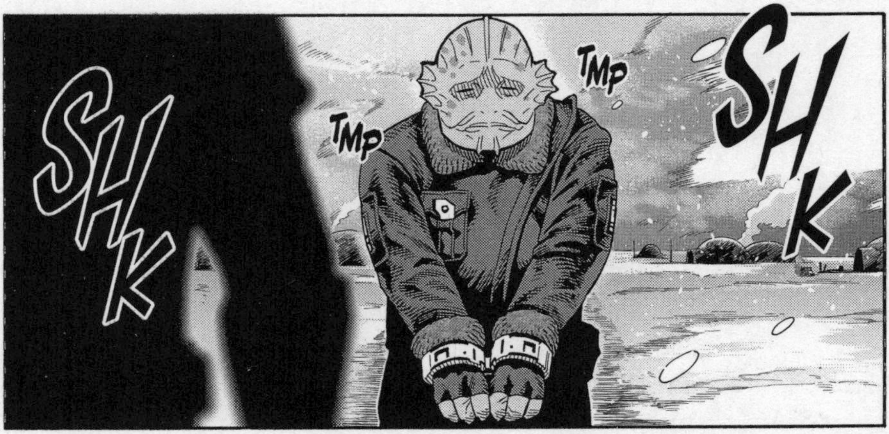
SHK
TMP
TMP
SHK

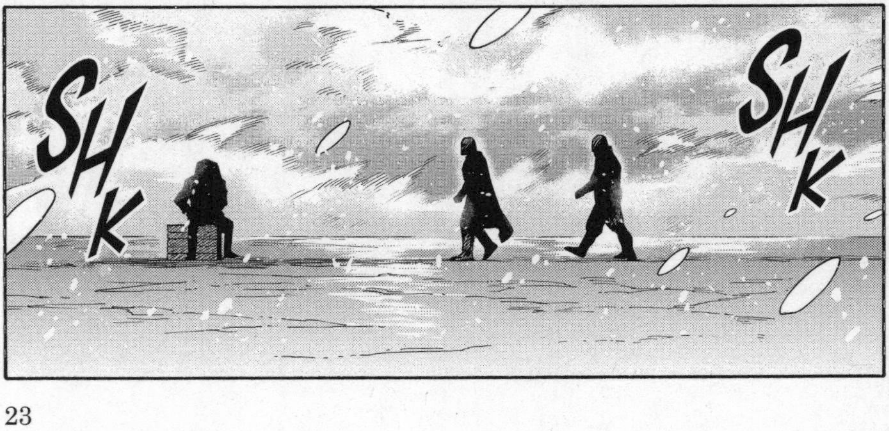
SHK
SHK

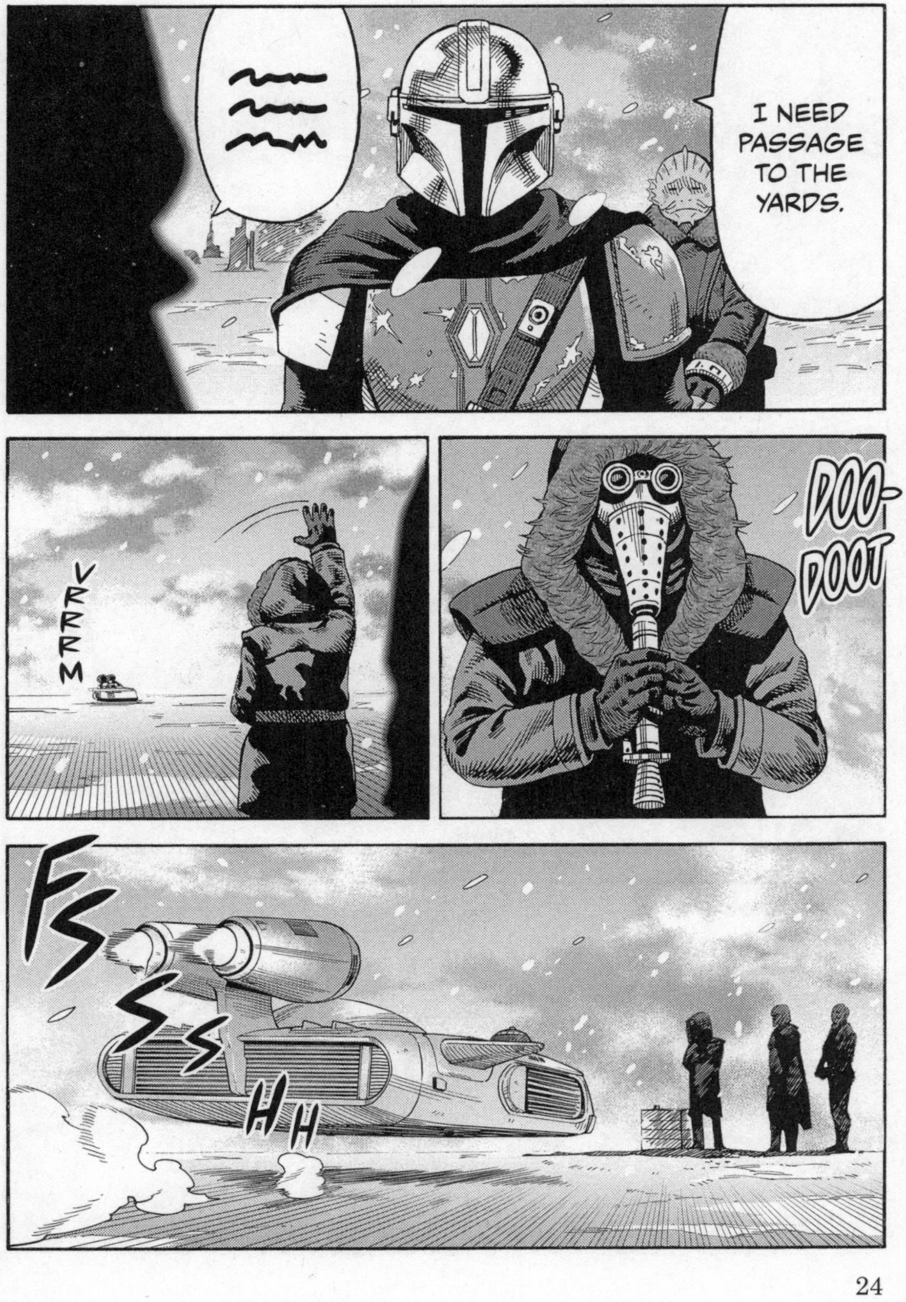
I NEED PASSAGE TO THE YARDS.
DOO-DOOT
VRRRM
FSSSHH

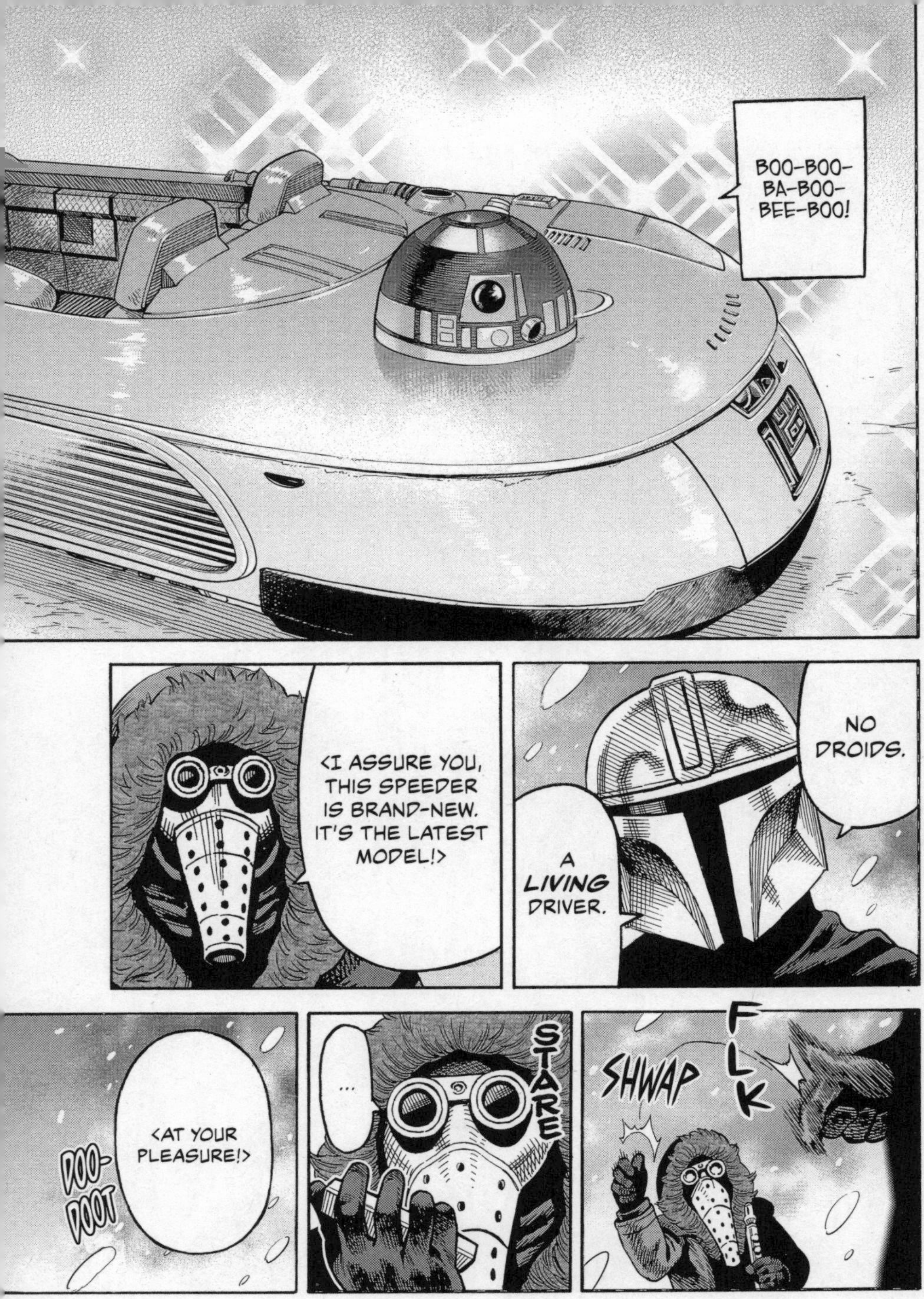
BOO-BOO-BA-BOO-BEE-BOO!
NO DROIDS.
A LIVING DRIVER.
<I ASSURE YOU, THIS SPEEDER IS BRAND-NEW. IT'S THE LATEST MODEL!>
FLK
SHWAP
STARE
...
<AT YOUR PLEASURE!>
DOO-DOOT

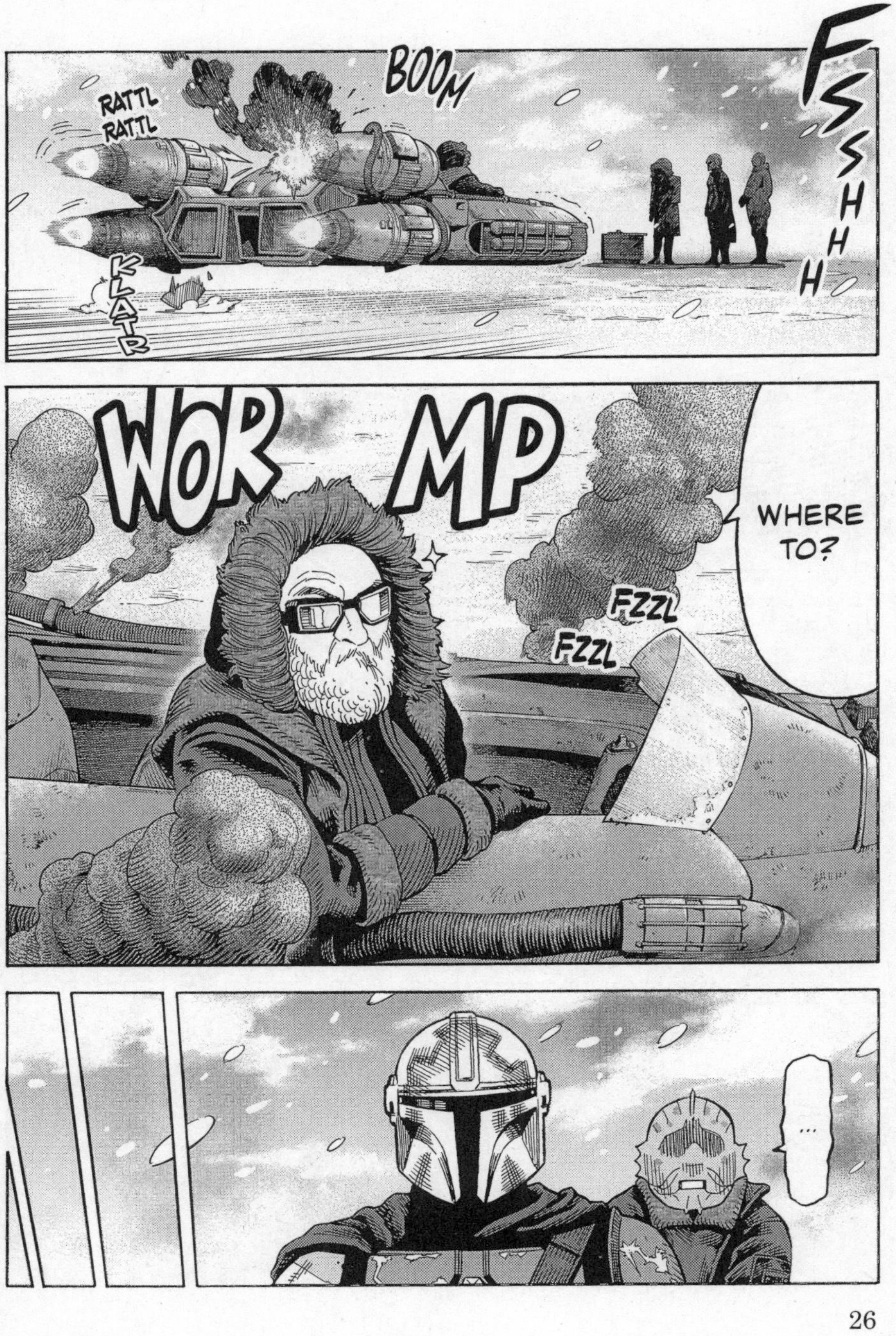
FSSHHH
BOOM
RATTL RATTL
KLATR
WOR MP
WHERE TO?
FZZL
FZZL
...

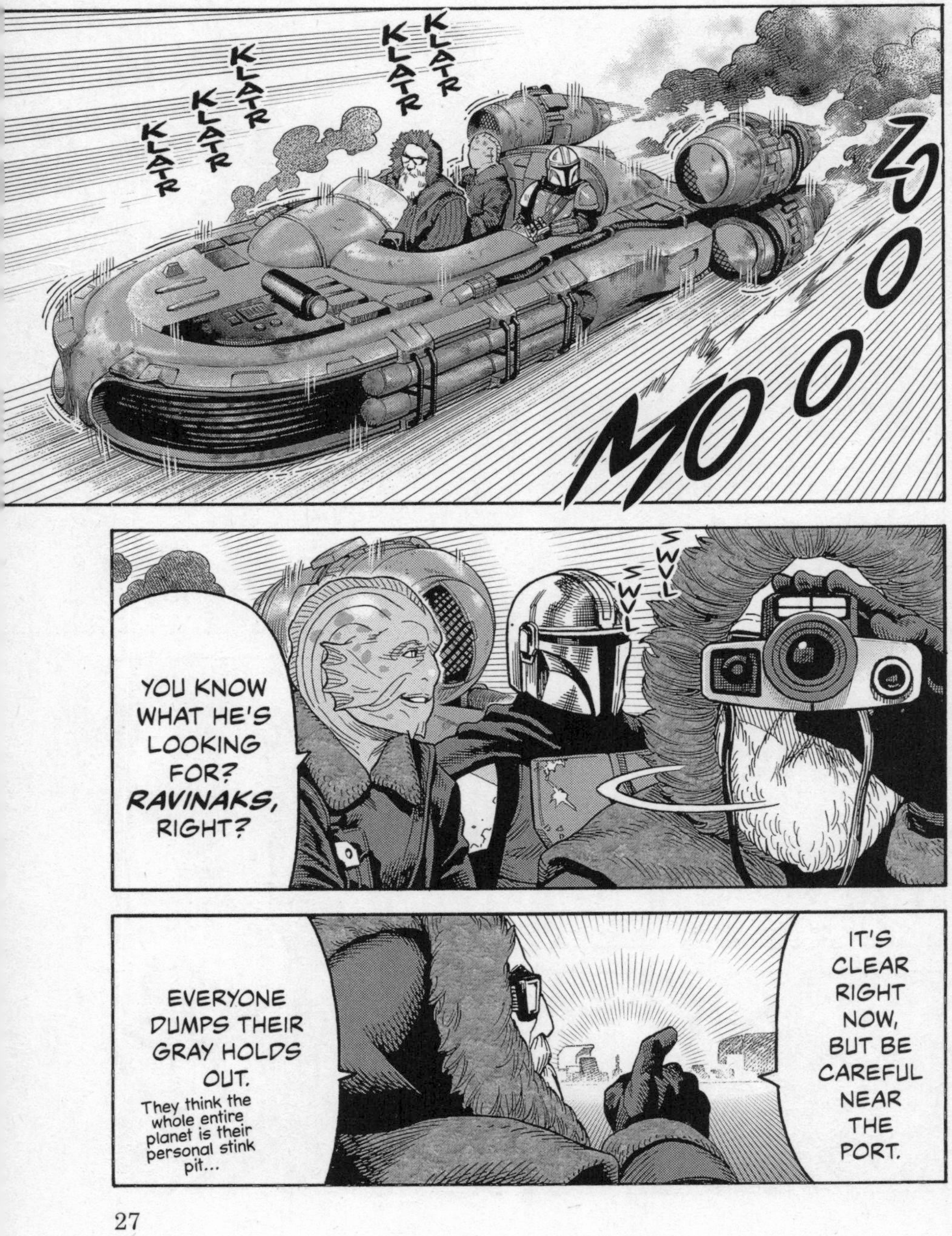
KLATR
KLATR
KLATR
KLATR
KLATR
ZOOOOOOM
SWVL
SWVL
YOU KNOW WHAT HE'S LOOKING FOR? *RAVINAKS*, RIGHT?
IT'S CLEAR RIGHT NOW, BUT BE CAREFUL NEAR THE PORT.
EVERYONE DUMPS THEIR GRAY HOLDS OUT.
They think the whole entire planet is their personal stink pit...

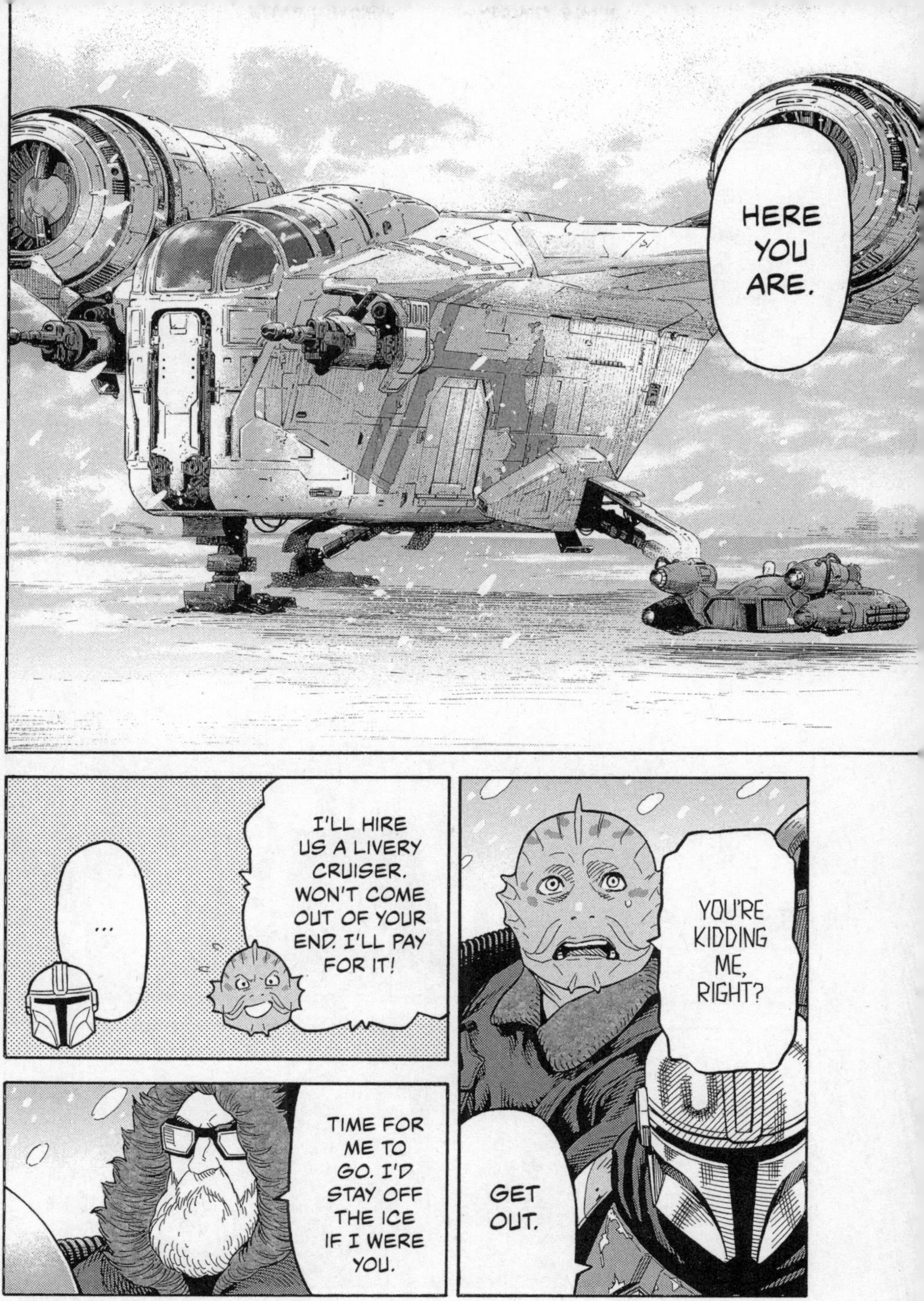
HERE YOU ARE.
YOU'RE KIDDING ME, RIGHT?
I'LL HIRE US A LIVERY CRUISER. WON'T COME OUT OF YOUR END. I'LL PAY FOR IT!
...
GET OUT.
TIME FOR ME TO GO. I'D STAY OFF THE ICE IF I WERE YOU.

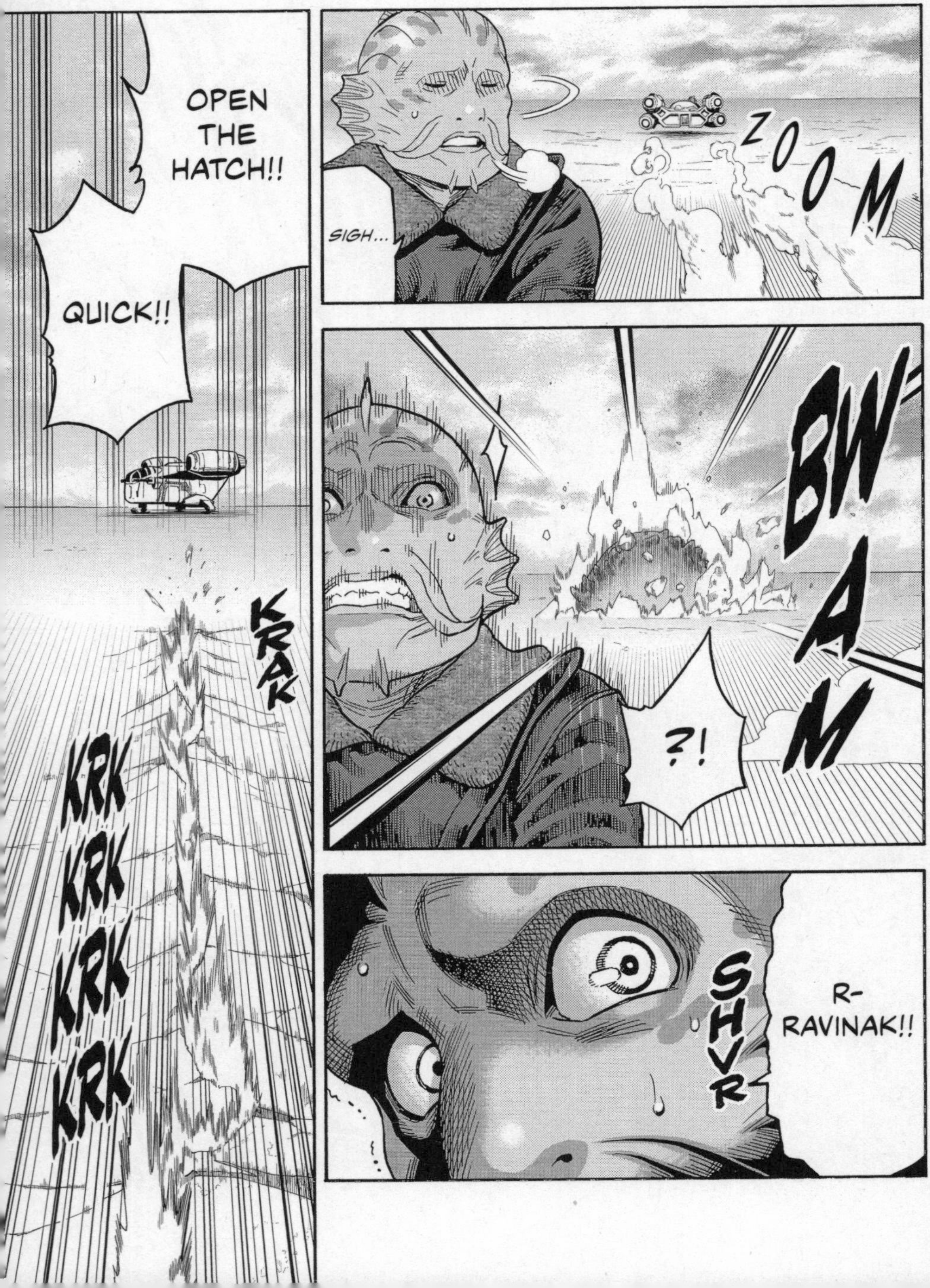
ZOOM
SIGH...
BWAAM
?!
SHVR
R-RAVINAK!!
OPEN THE HATCH!!
QUICK!!
KRAK
KRK KRK KRK KRK KRK

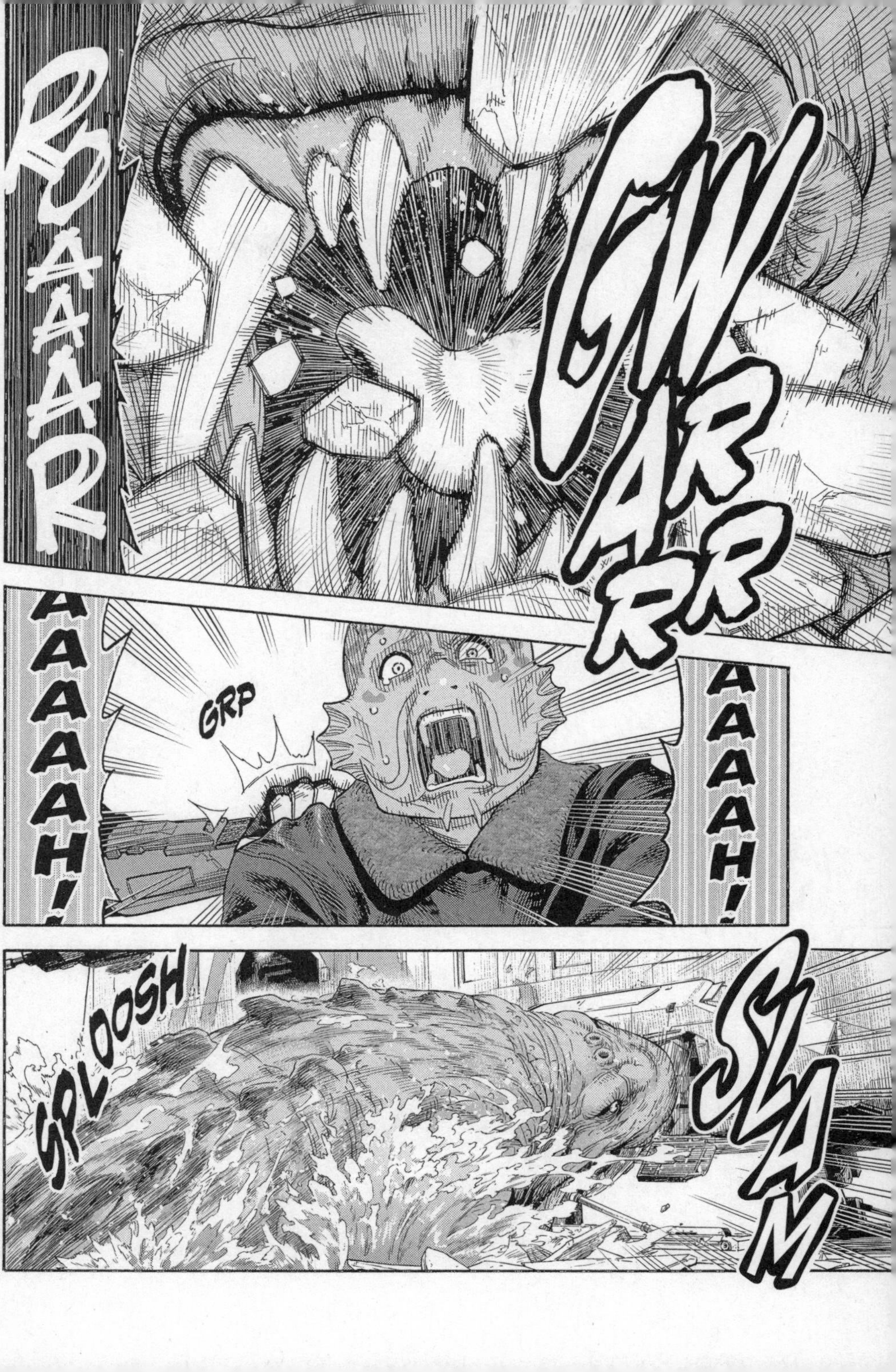
GWARRR
ROAAAR
AAAAH!
GRP
AAAAAH!
SLAM
SPLOOSH

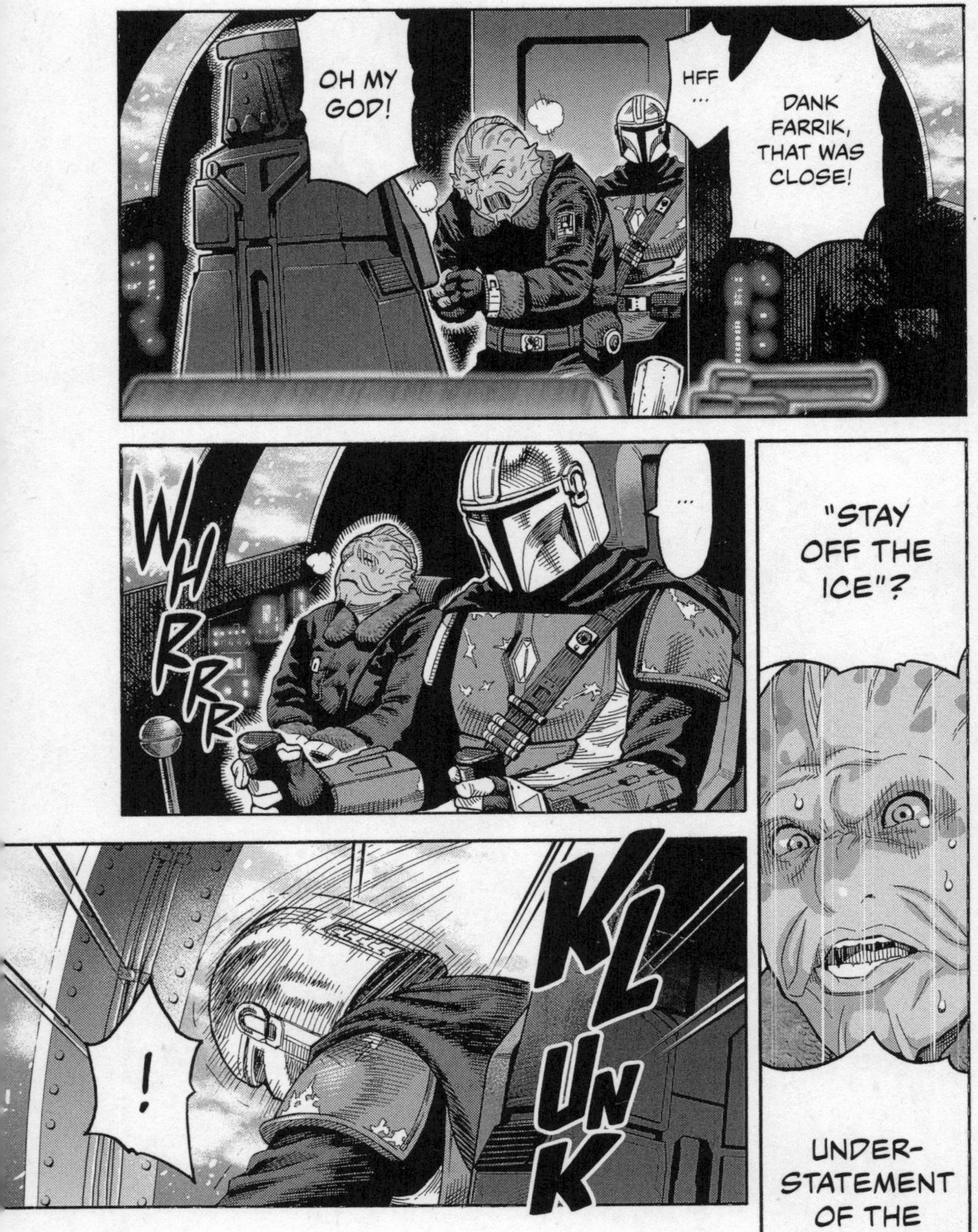
DANK FARRIK, THAT WAS CLOSE!
HFF ...
OH MY GOD!
"STAY OFF THE ICE"?
UNDER-STATEMENT OF THE MILLENNIUM!!
...
WHRRR
KLUNK
!

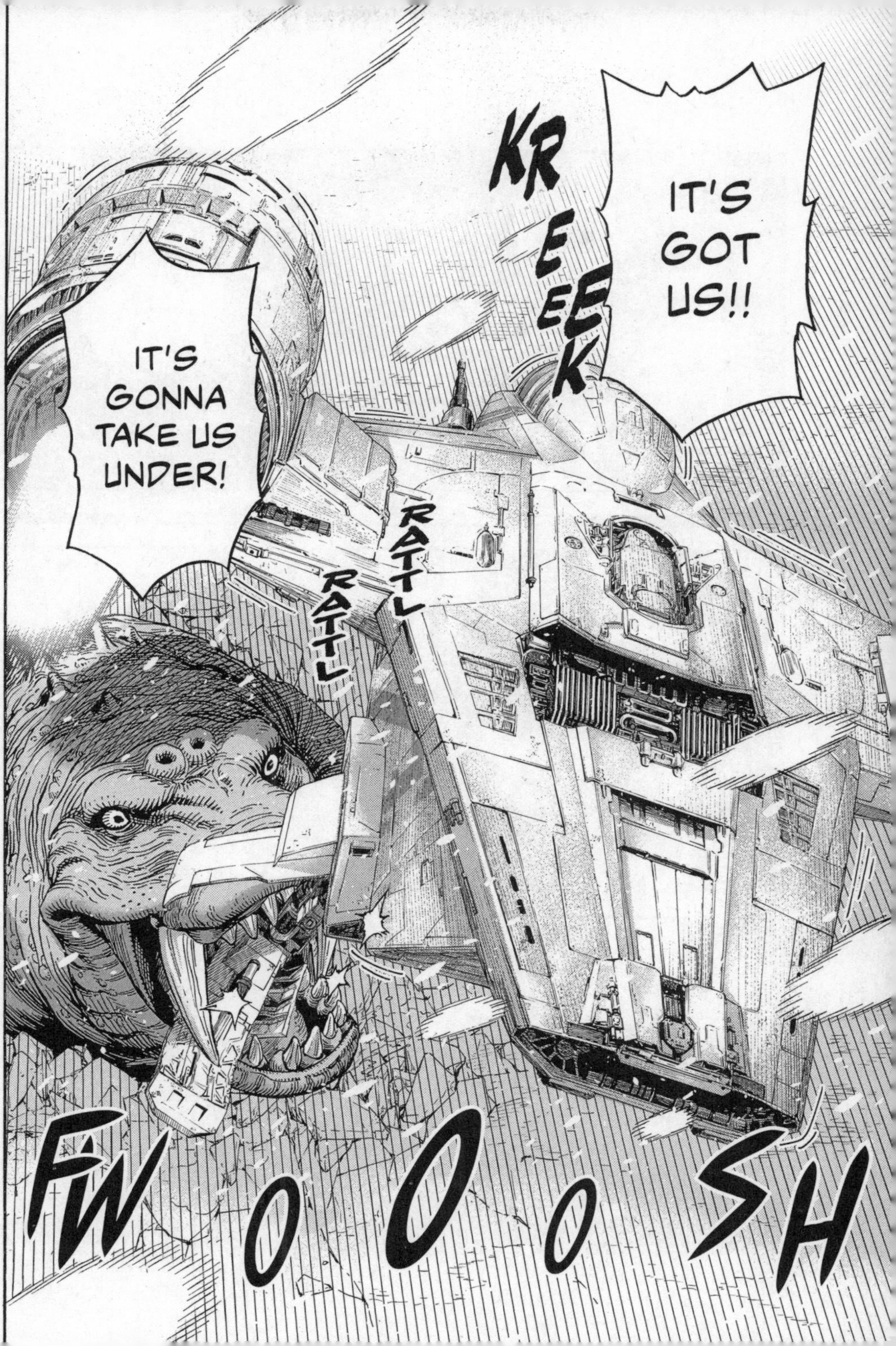
IT'S GOT US!!
KREEEK
IT'S GONNA TAKE US UNDER!
RATTL
RATTL
FWOOOSH

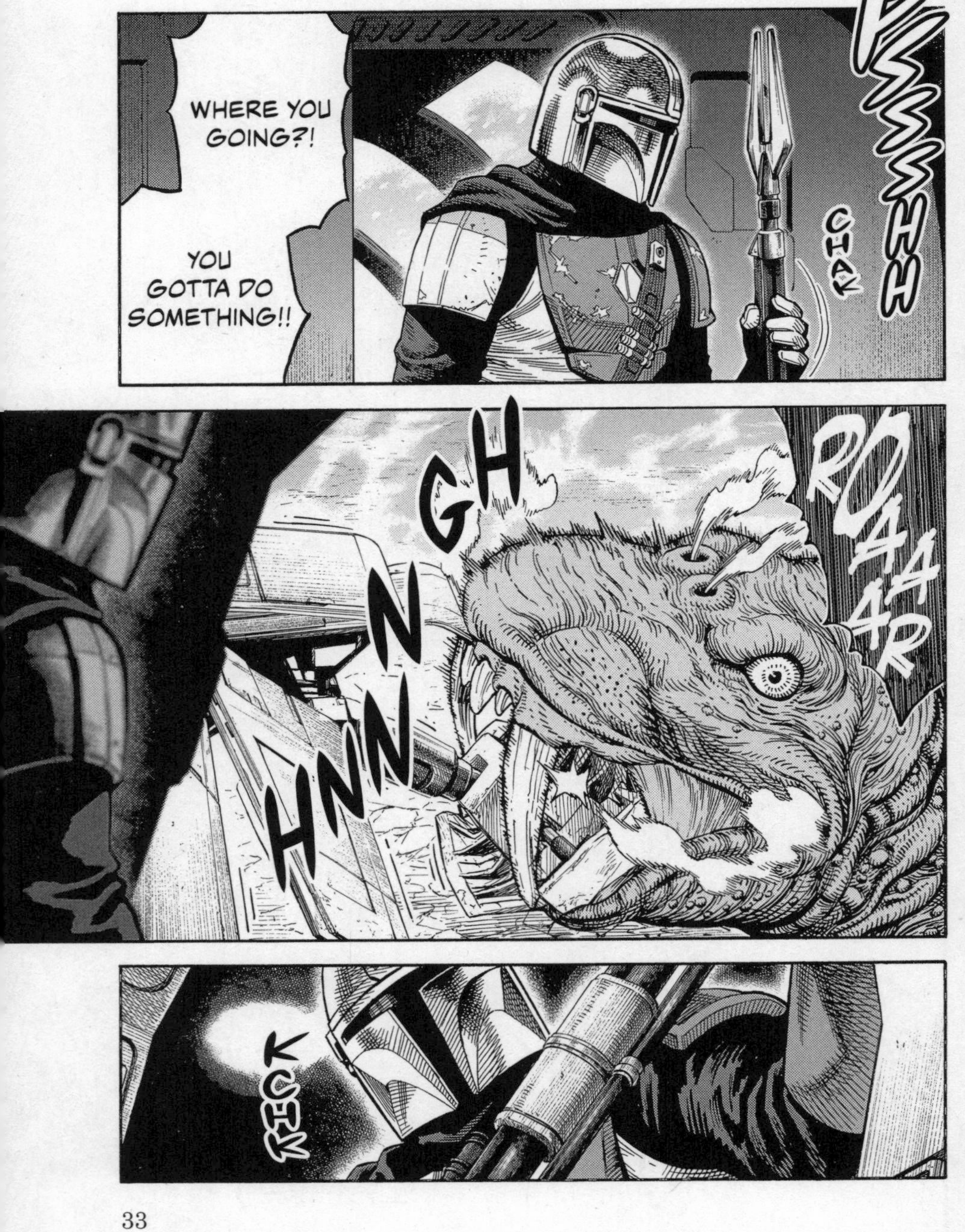
PSSSHH
CHAK
WHERE YOU GOING?!
YOU GOTTA DO SOMETHING!!
ROAAAR
HNNNGH
KCHK

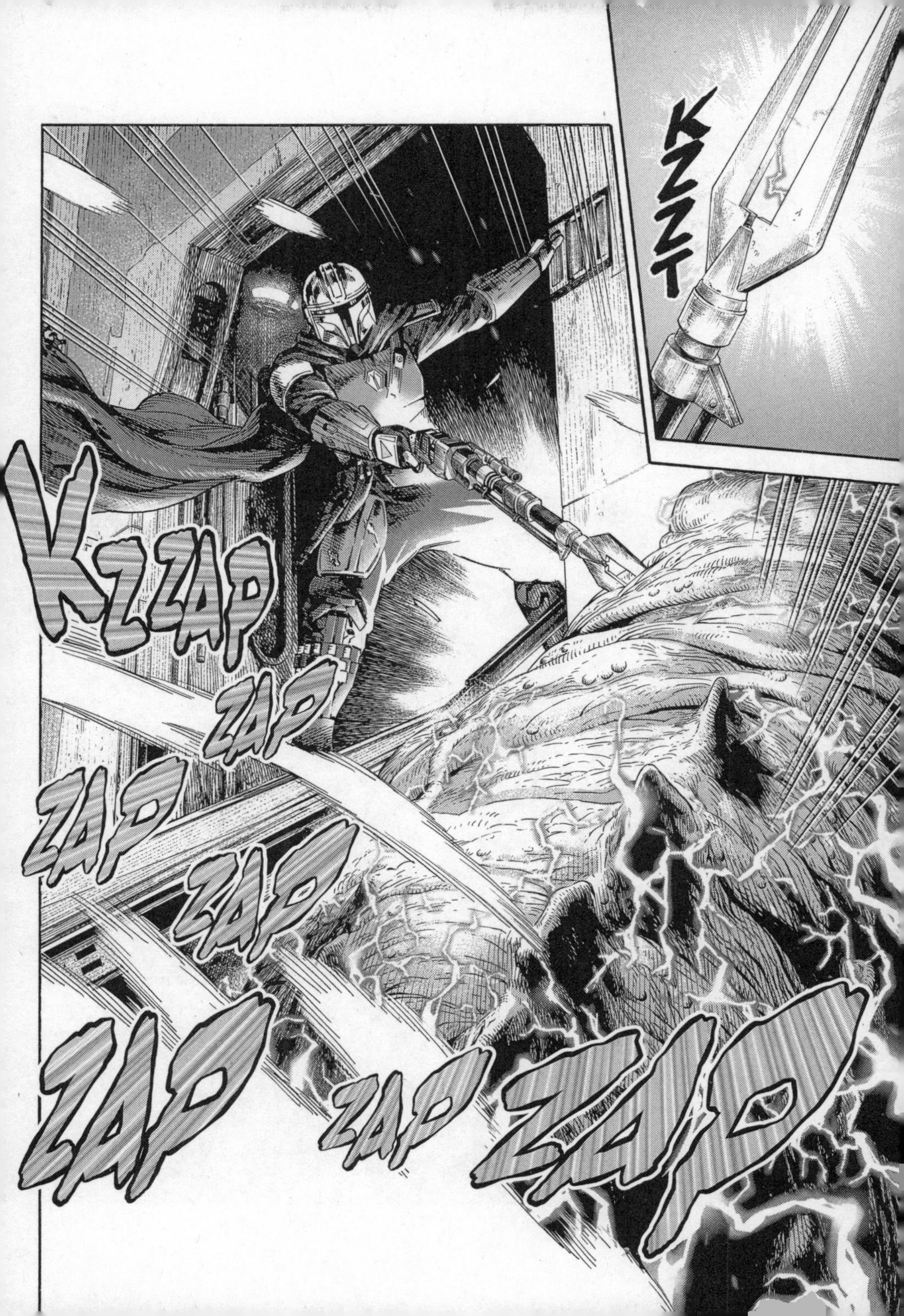
KZZZT
KZZAP
ZAP
ZAP
ZAP
ZAP
ZAP
ZAP

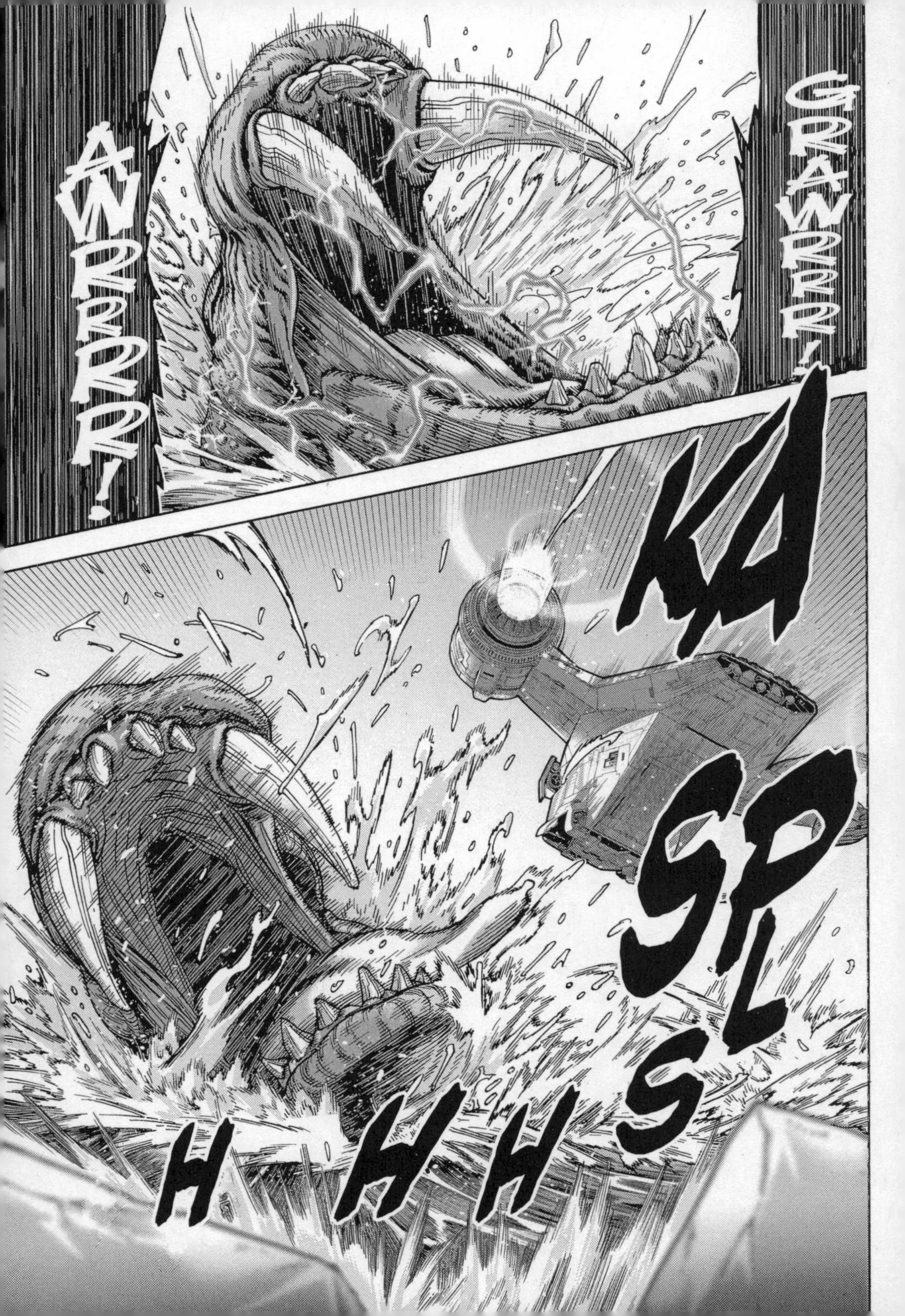
GRAWRRR!
AWRRRR!
KA
SPL
SHHHH

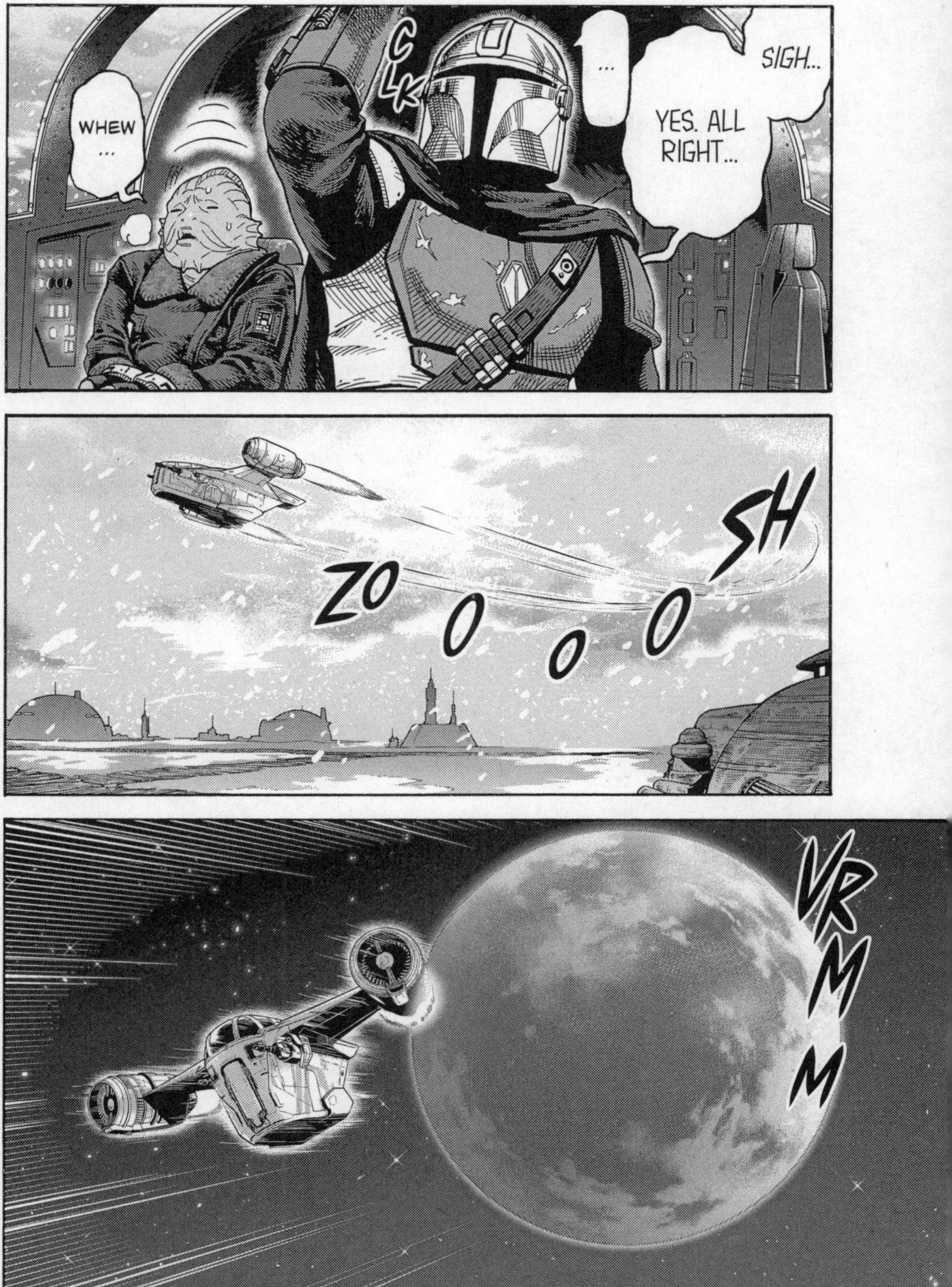
SIGH...
YES. ALL RIGHT...
...
CLK
WHEW ...
ZOOOOOSH
VRMMM

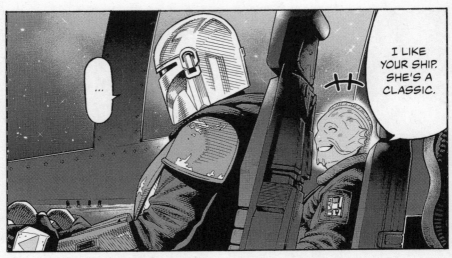

I LIKE YOUR SHIP. SHE'S A CLASSIC.
...
A RAZOR CREST, AM I RIGHT? PRE-EMPIRE?
...
I HAVE A LOT OF CREDITS, BY THE WAY. HOW MUCH ARE THEY PAYING YOU?
...
IS IT TRUE THAT YOU GUYS NEVER TAKE OFF YOUR HELMETS?
...
SIGH...
BOY.

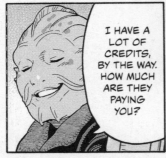

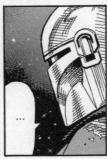

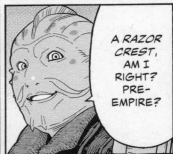

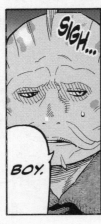

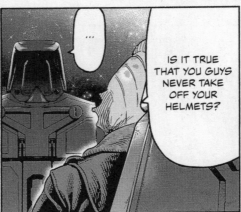

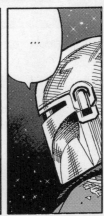

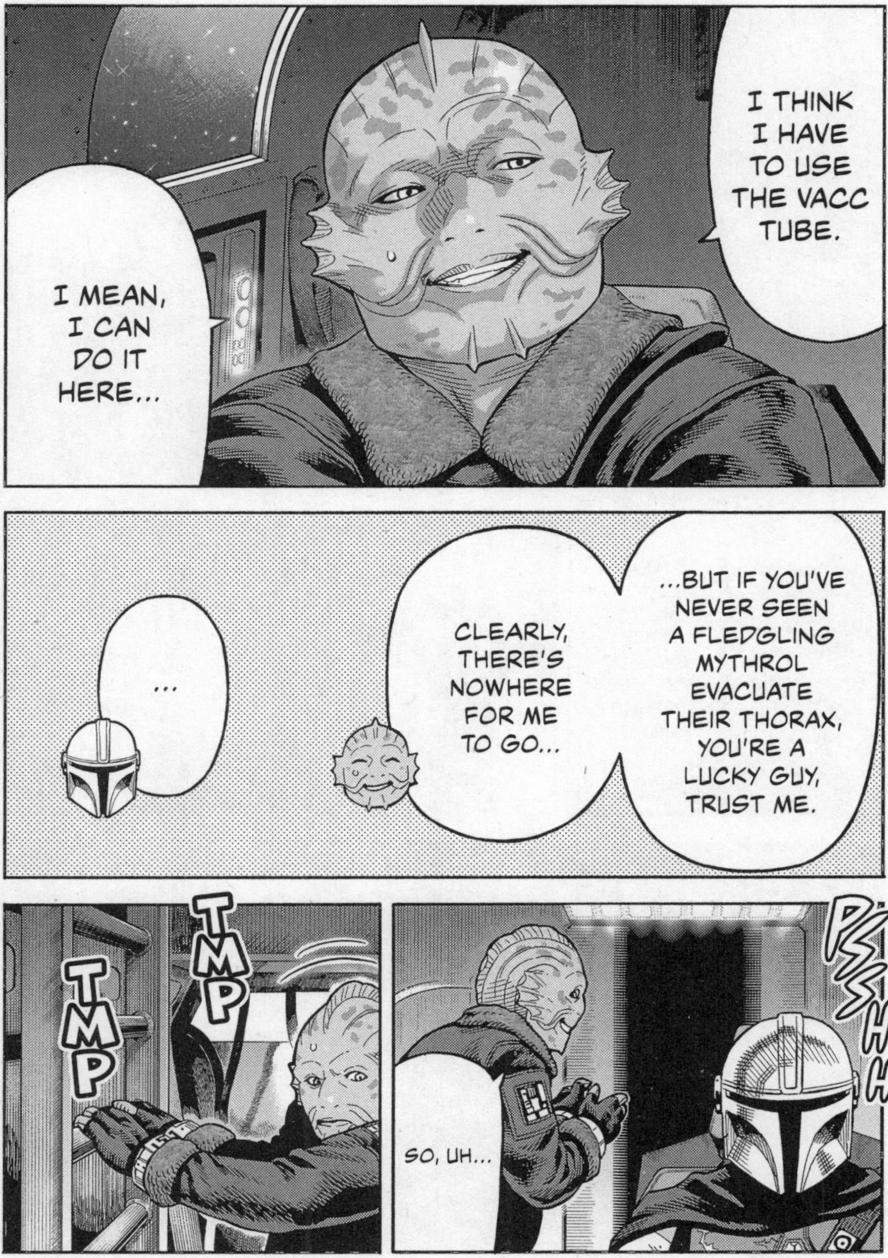
I THINK I HAVE TO USE THE VACC TUBE.
I MEAN, I CAN DO IT HERE...
...BUT IF YOU'VE NEVER SEEN A FLEDGLING MYTHROL EVACUATE THEIR THORAX, YOU'RE A LUCKY GUY, TRUST ME.
CLEARLY, THERE'S NOWHERE FOR ME TO GO...
...
PSSHHH
SO, UH...
TMP
TMP

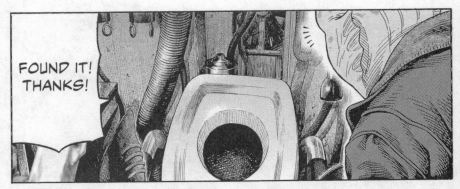

FOUND IT! THANKS!

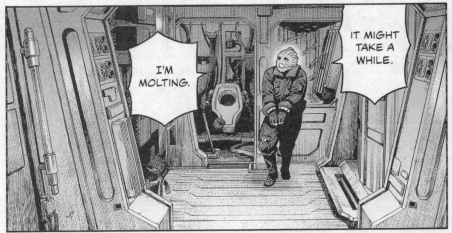

I'M MOLTING.

IT MIGHT TAKE A WHILE.

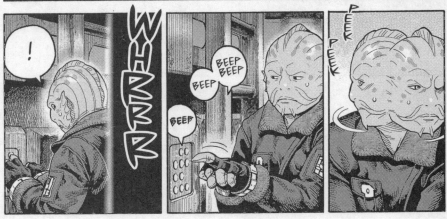

!

WHRRRR

BEEP

BEEP

BEEP BEEP

PEEK PEEK

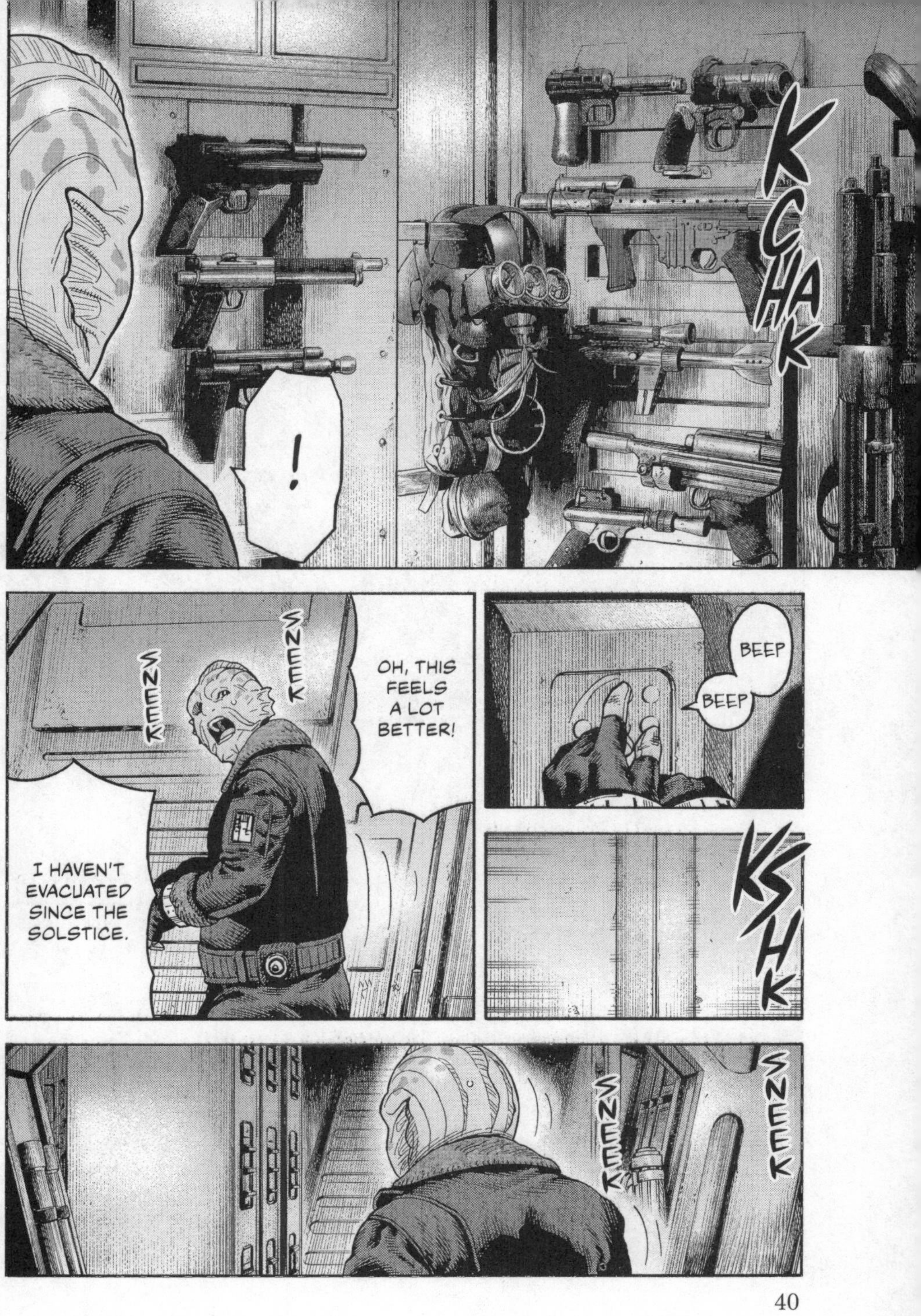
KCHAK
!
BEEP
BEEP
KSHHK
SNEEK
SNEEK
OH, THIS FEELS A LOT BETTER!
I HAVEN'T EVACUATED SINCE THE SOLSTICE.
SNEEK
SNEEK

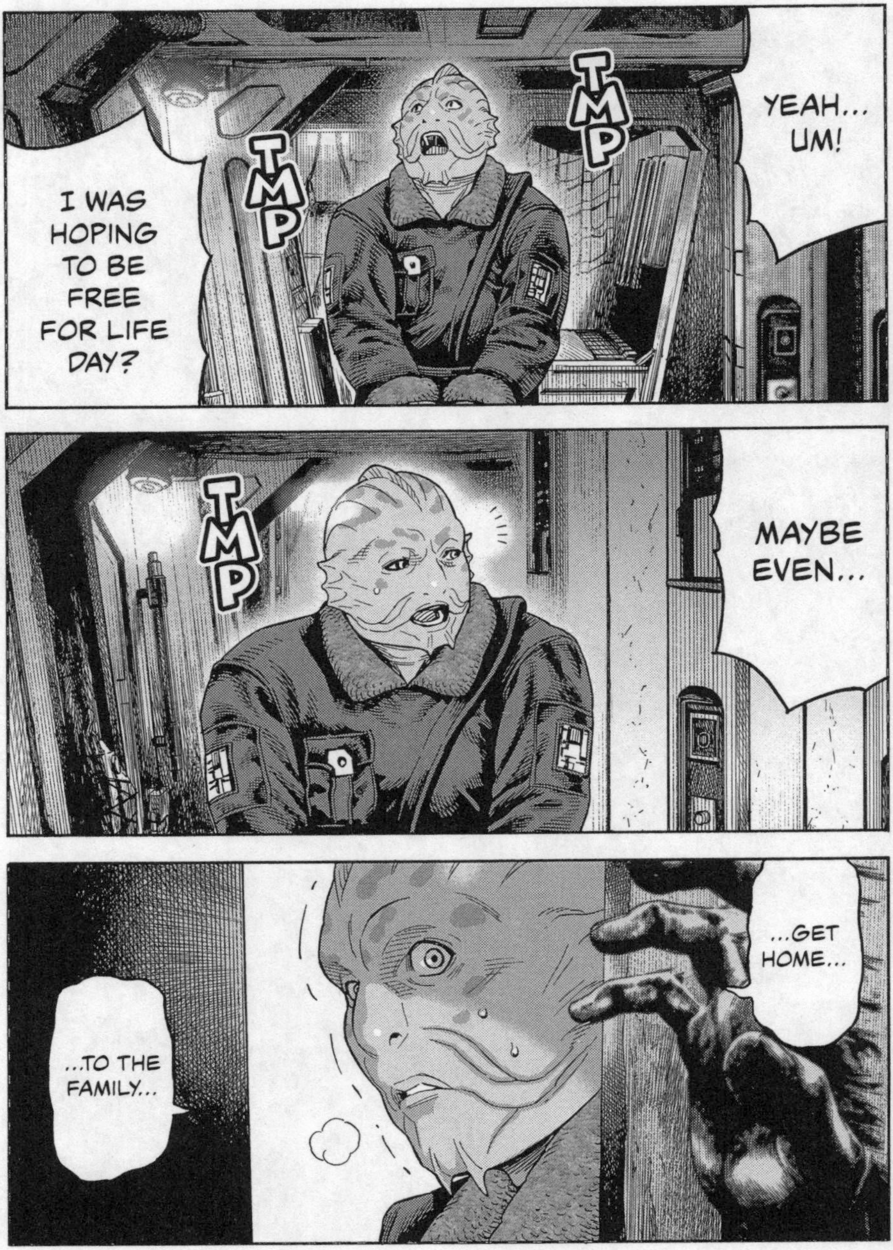
YEAH... UM!
TMP
TMP
I WAS HOPING TO BE FREE FOR LIFE DAY?
MAYBE EVEN...
TMP
...GET HOME...
...TO THE FAMILY...

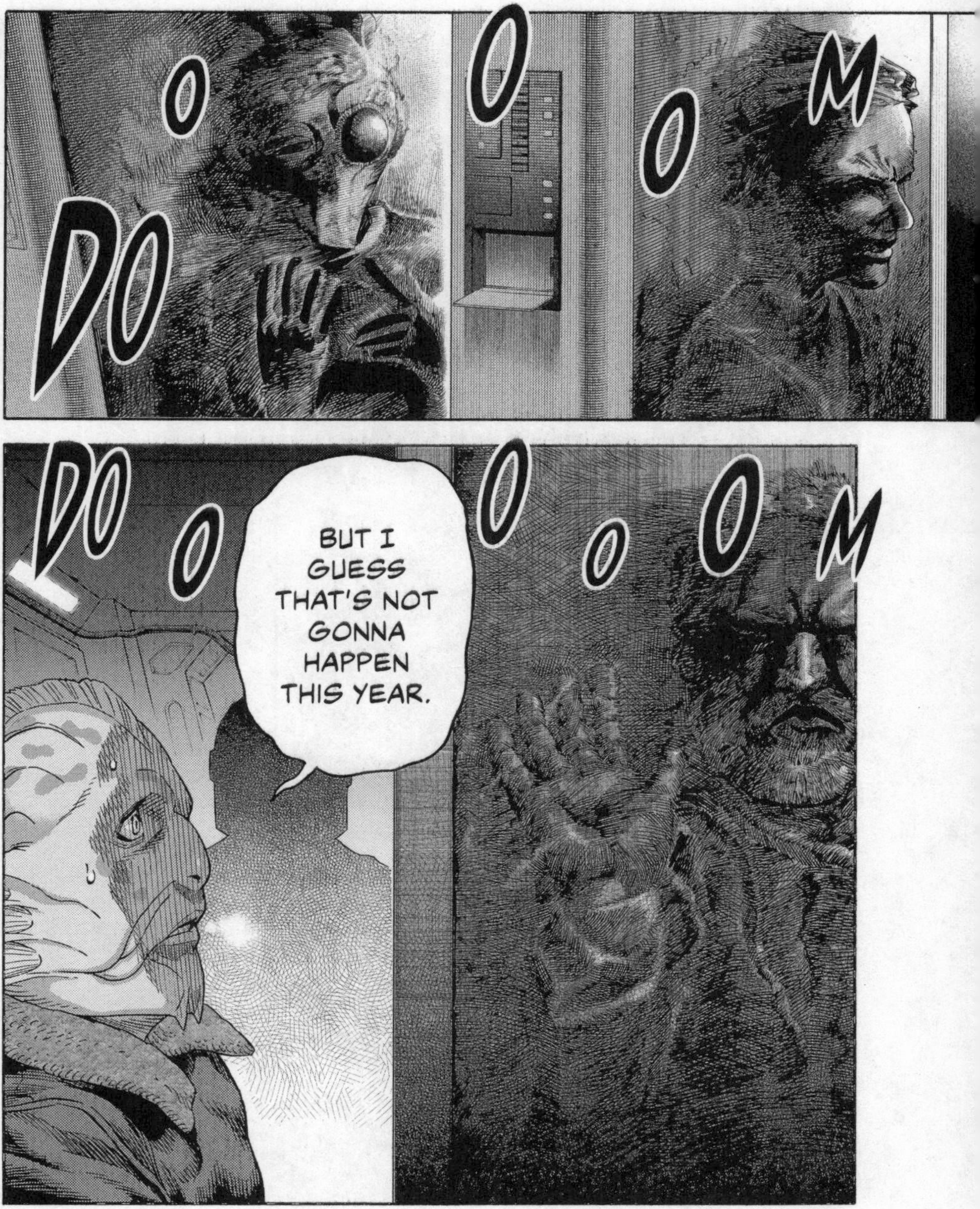
DOOOOOM
DOOOOOM
BUT I GUESS THAT'S NOT GONNA HAPPEN THIS YEAR.

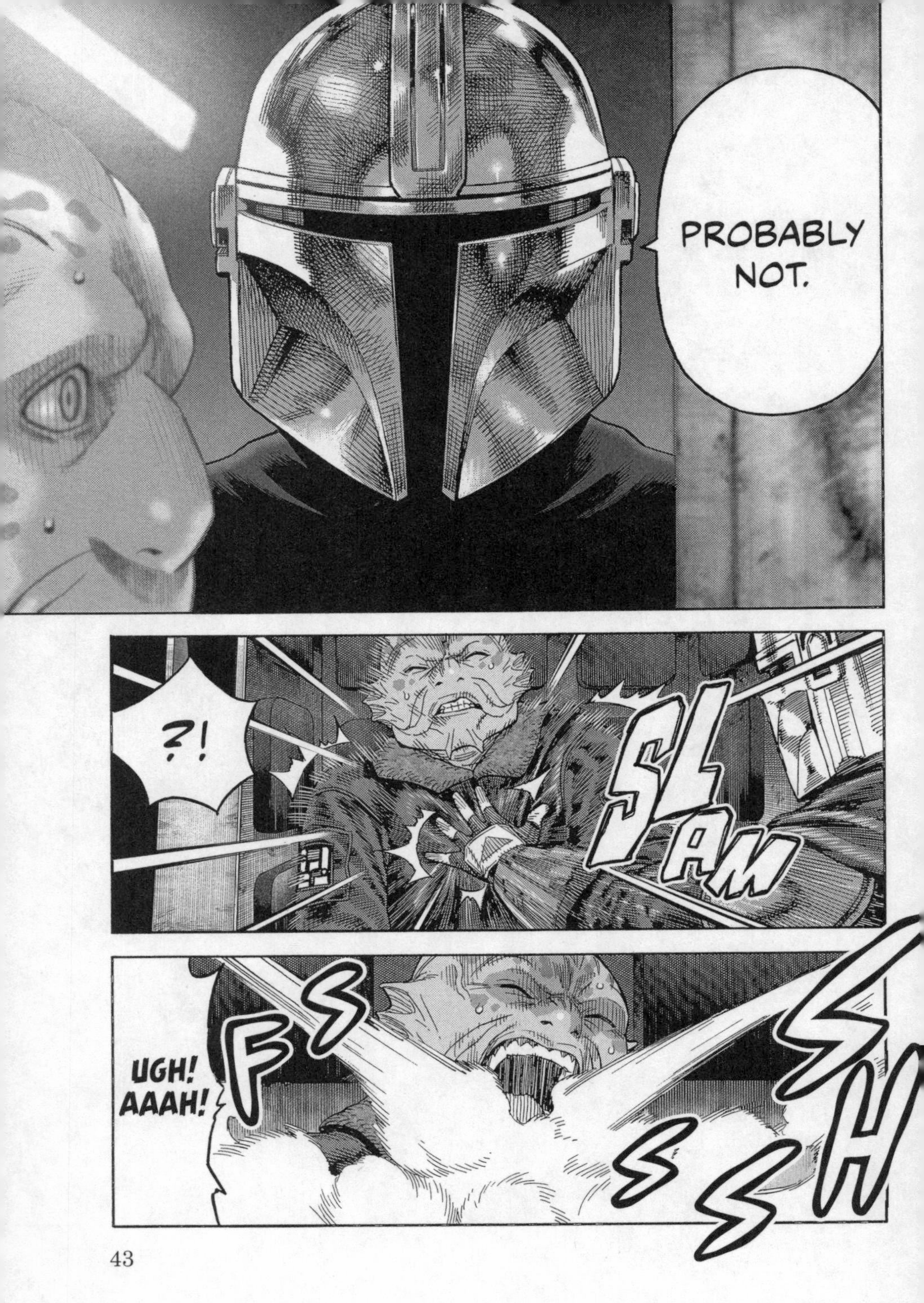
PROBABLY NOT.
SLAM
?!
SSSSH
FS
UGH! AAAH!

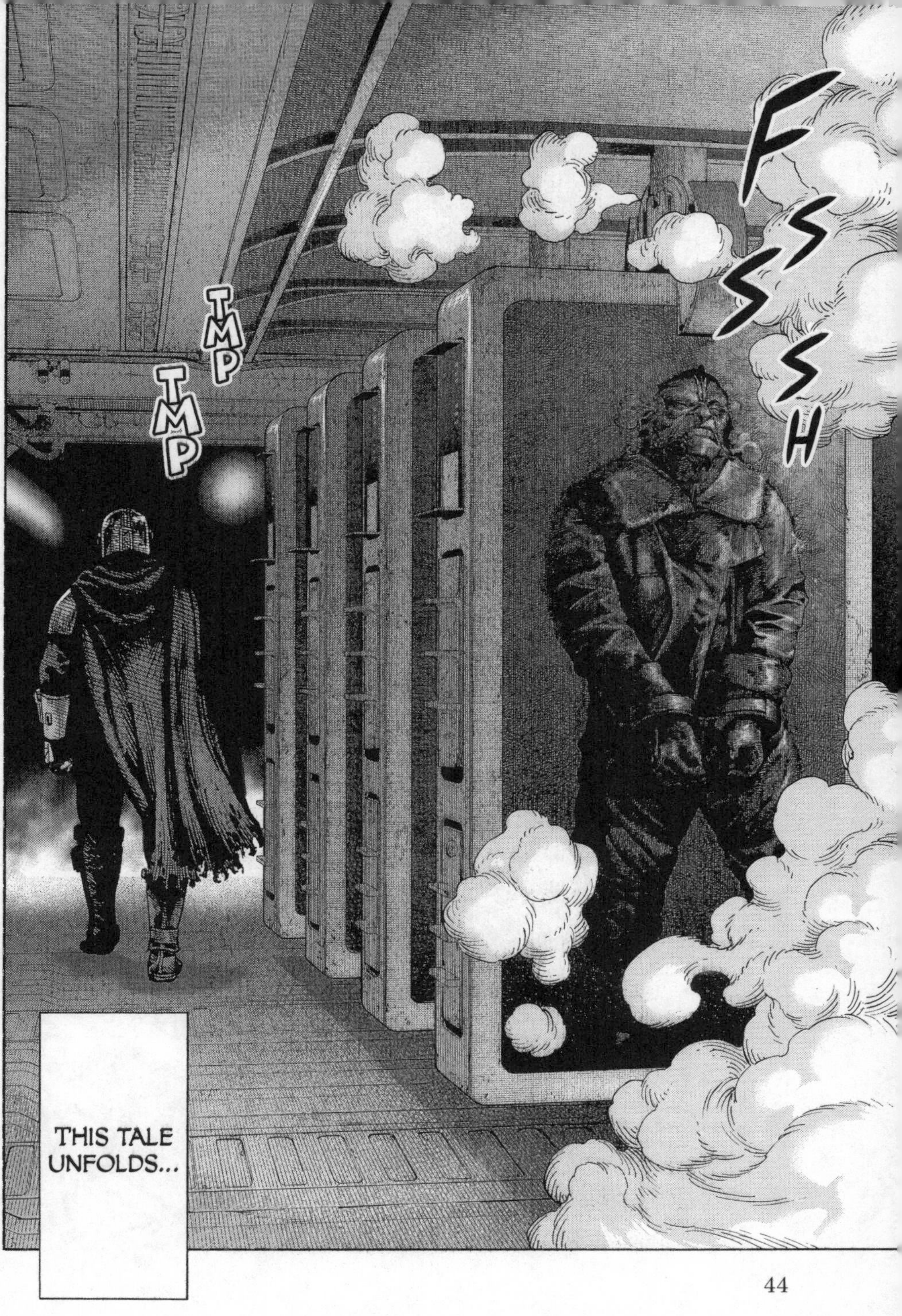
FSSSH
TMP
TMP
THIS TALE UNFOLDS...

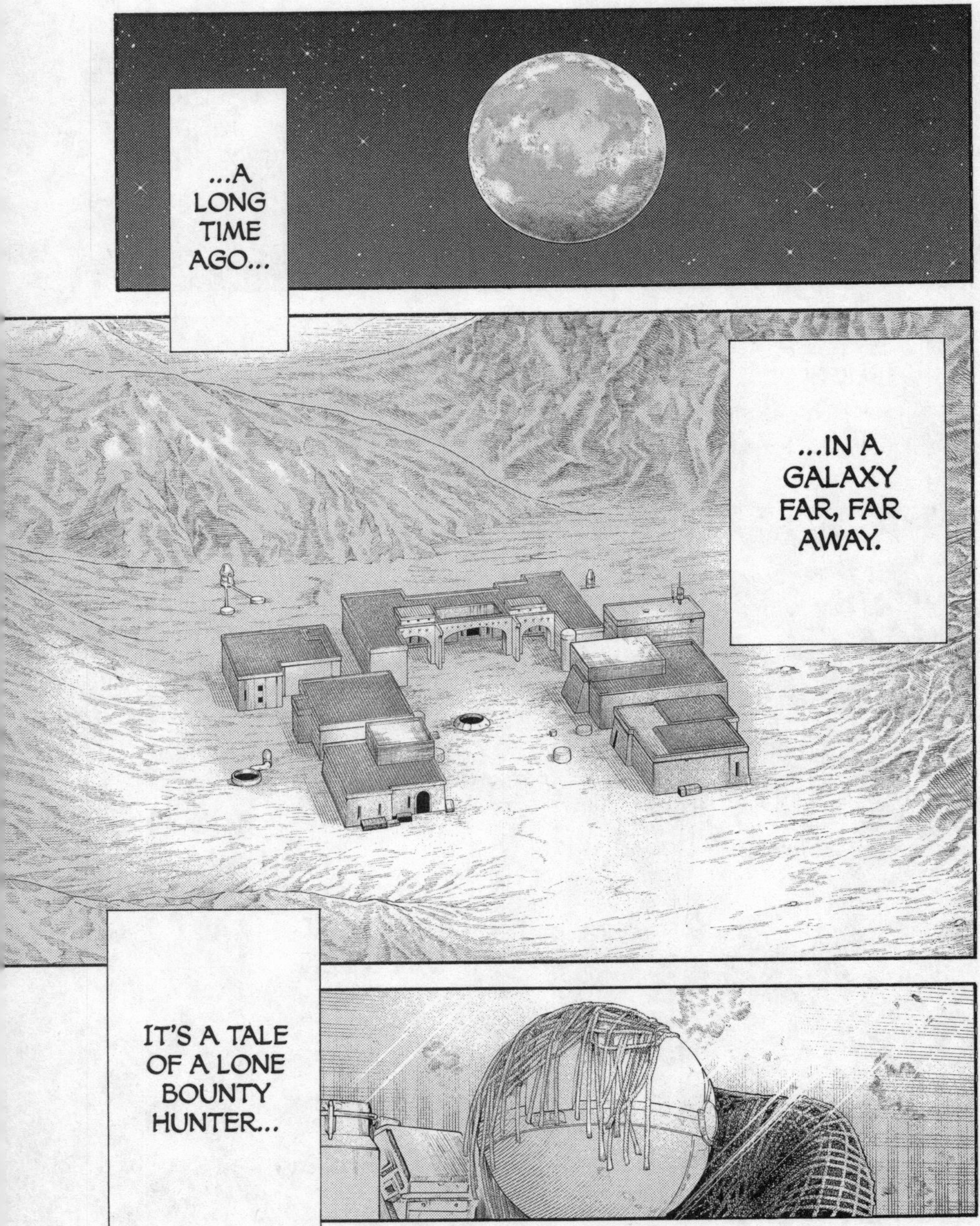
...A LONG TIME AGO...
...IN A GALAXY FAR, FAR AWAY.
IT'S A TALE OF A LONE BOUNTY HUNTER...

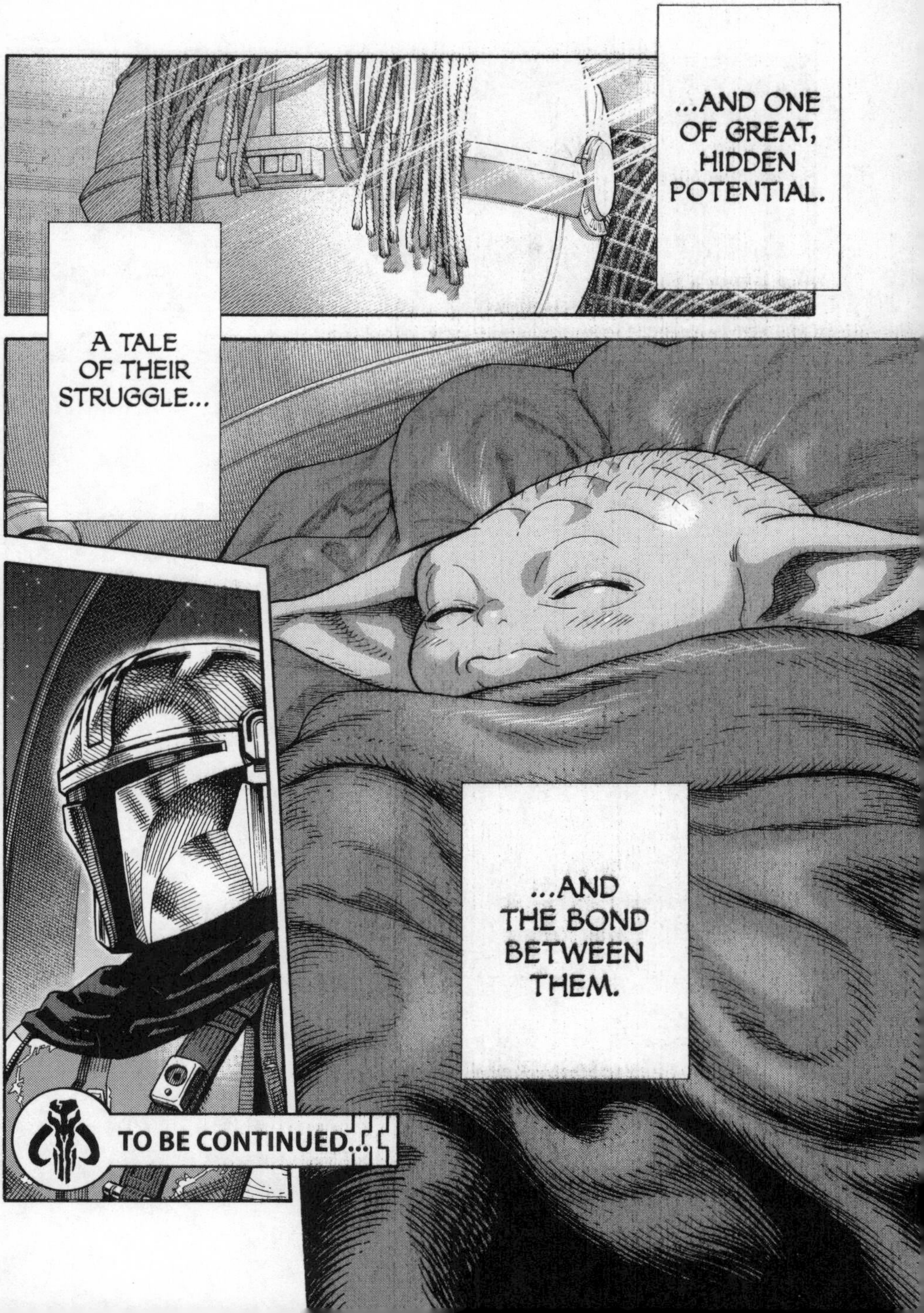
...AND ONE OF GREAT, HIDDEN POTENTIAL.
A TALE OF THEIR STRUGGLE...
...AND THE BOND BETWEEN THEM.
TO BE CONTINUED...

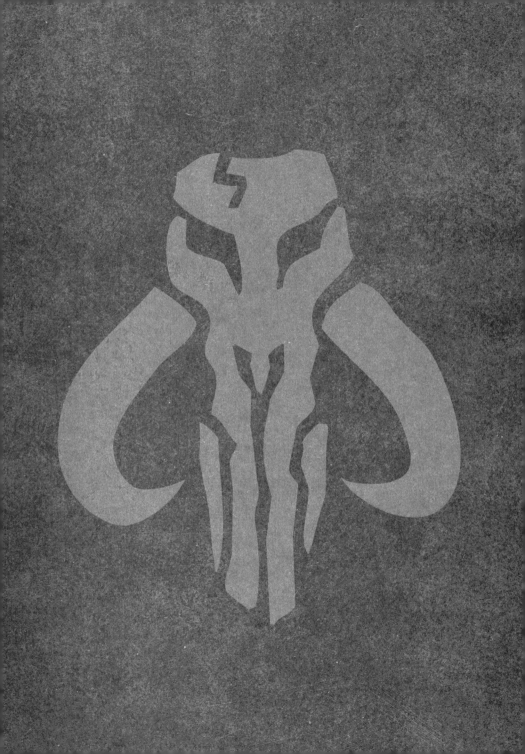

STAR WARS
THE
MANDALORIAN
THE MANGA

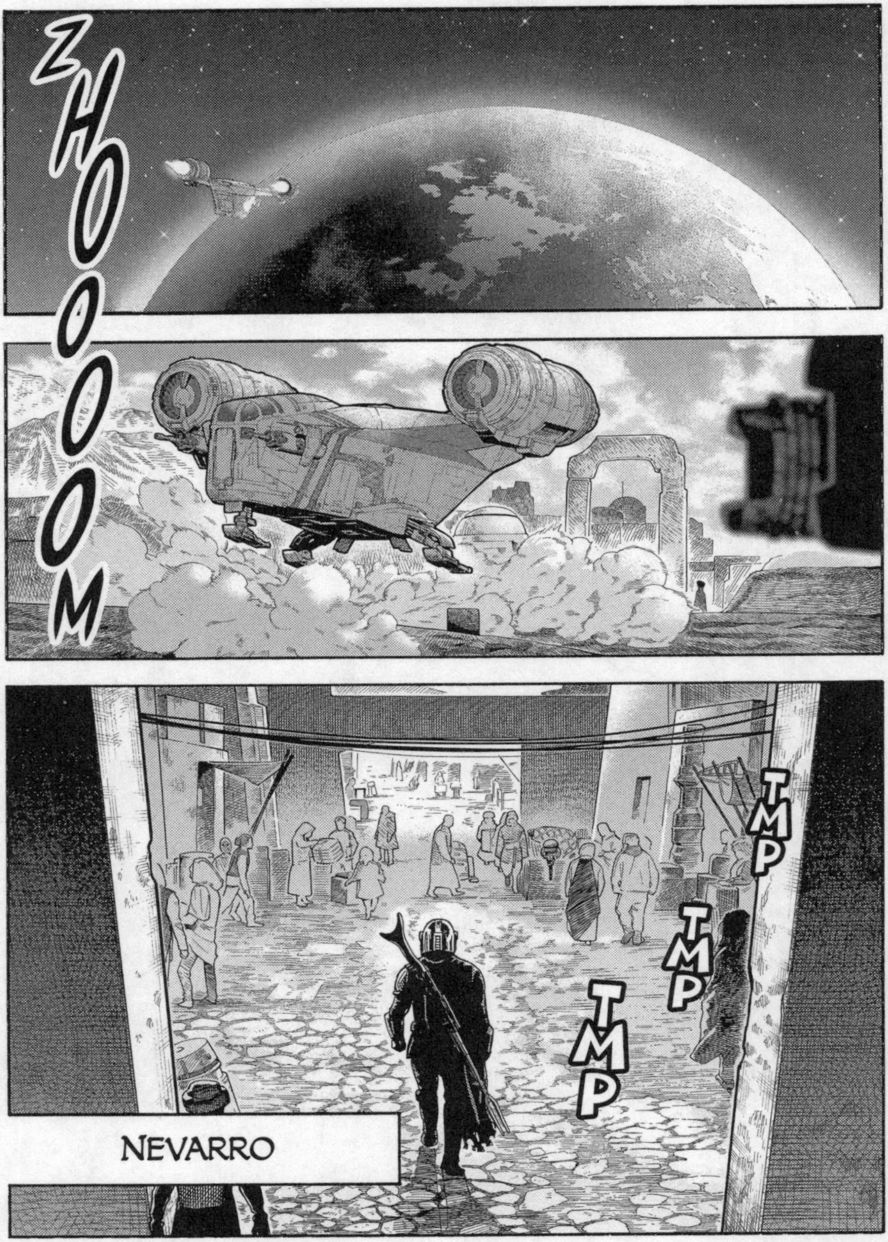
ZHOOOOM
NEVARRO
TMP
TMP
TMP

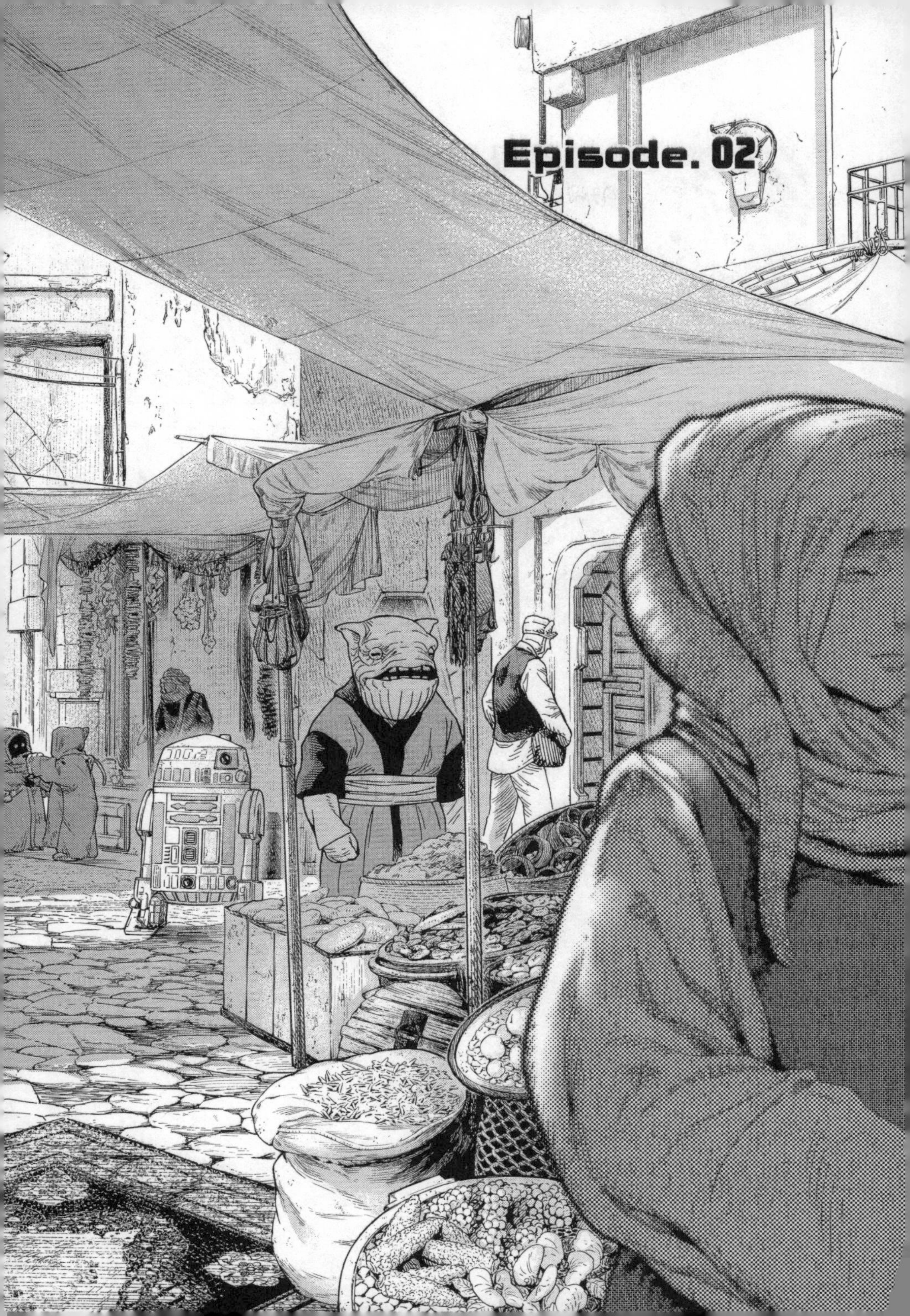
Episode. 02

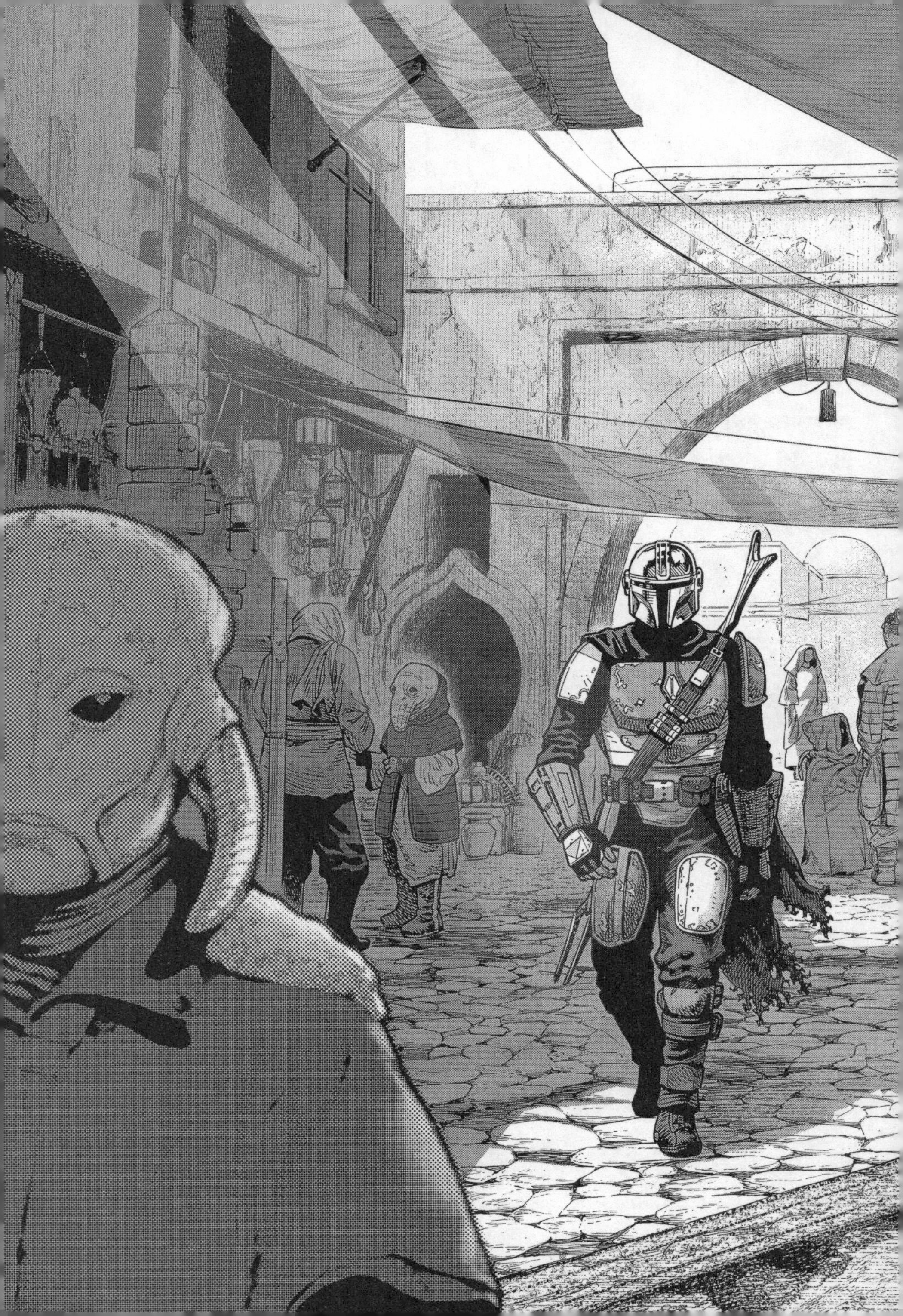

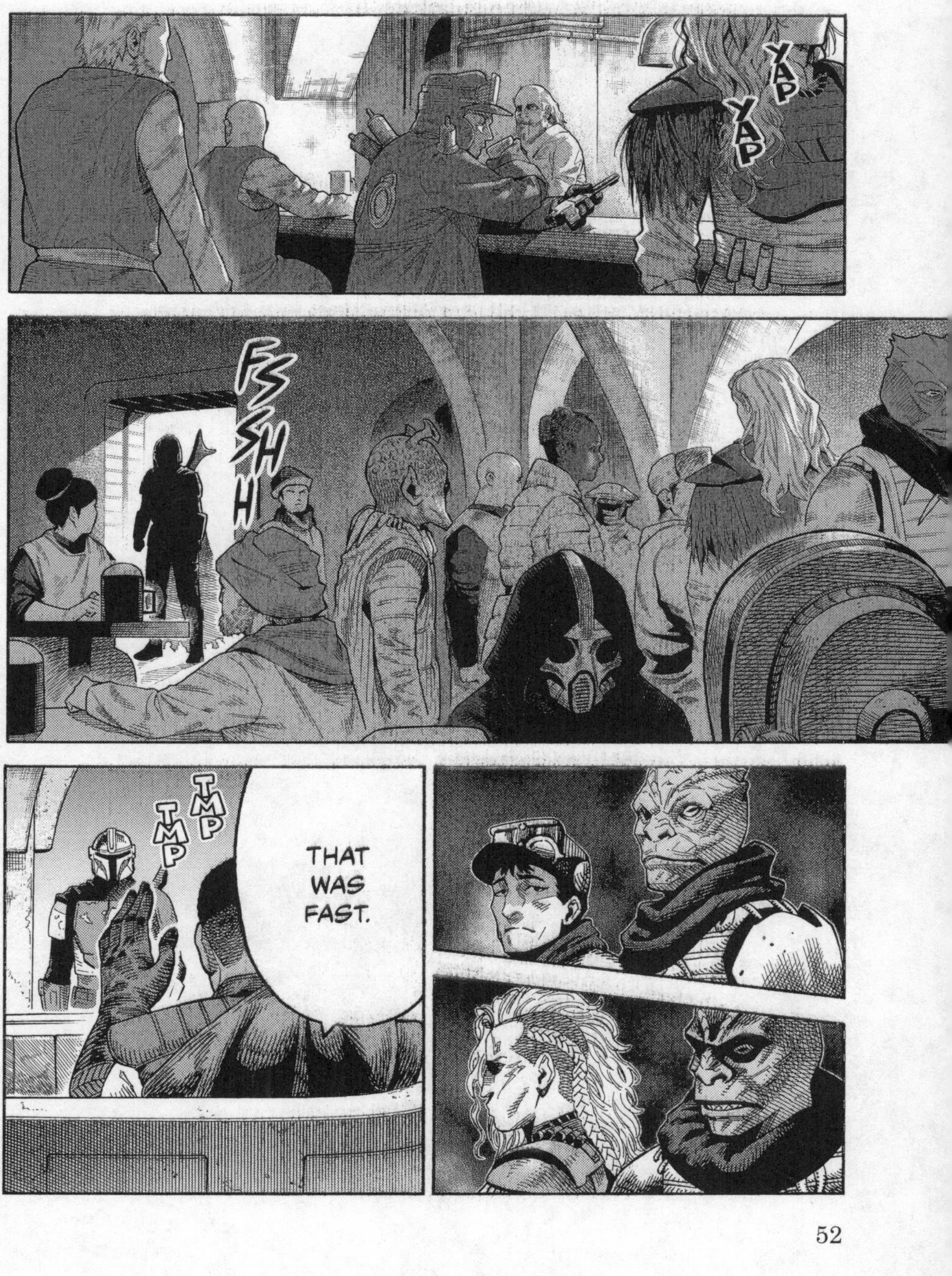
YAP
YAP
YAP
FSSHH
TMP
TMP
THAT WAS FAST.

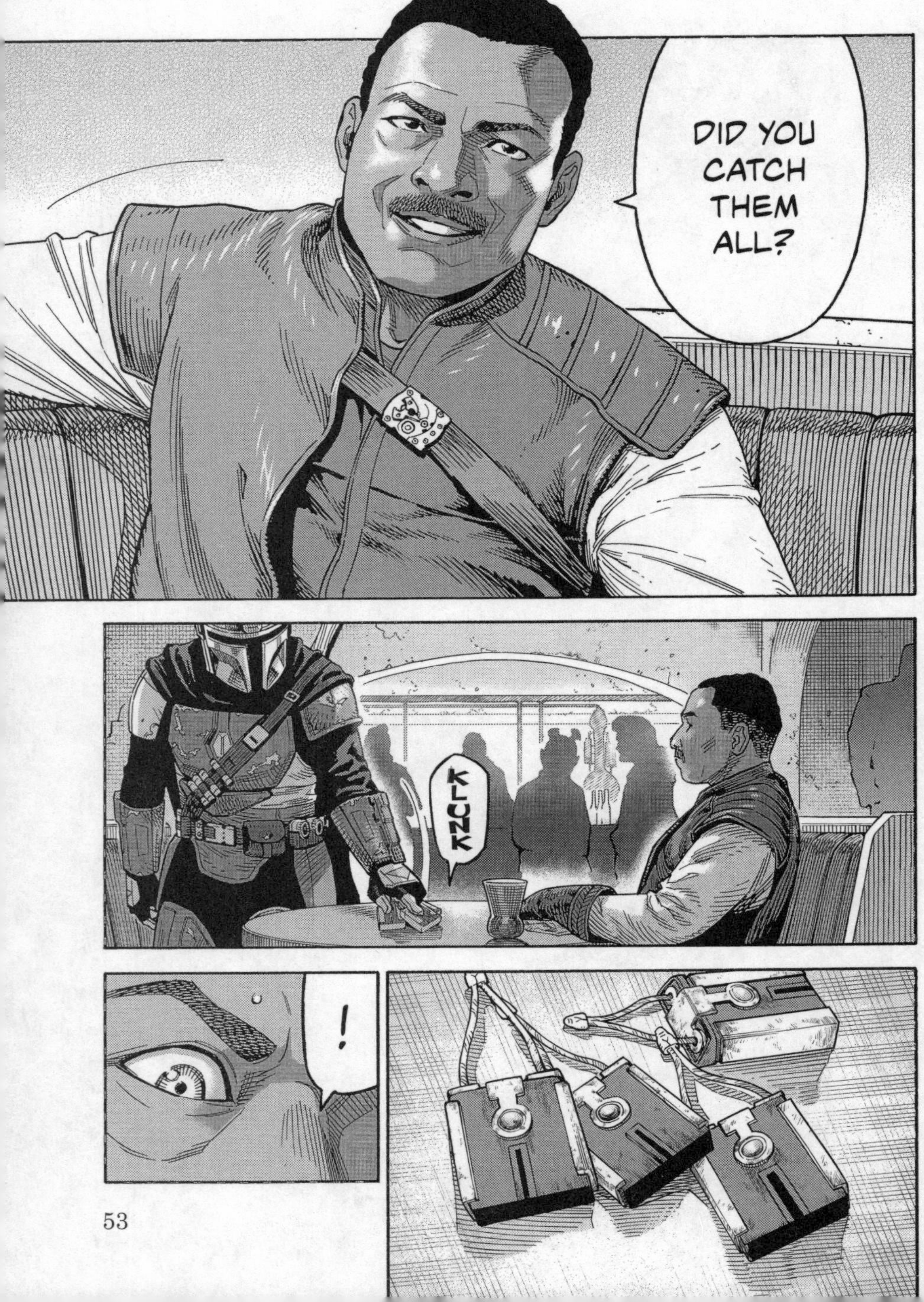
DID YOU CATCH THEM ALL?
KLUNK
!

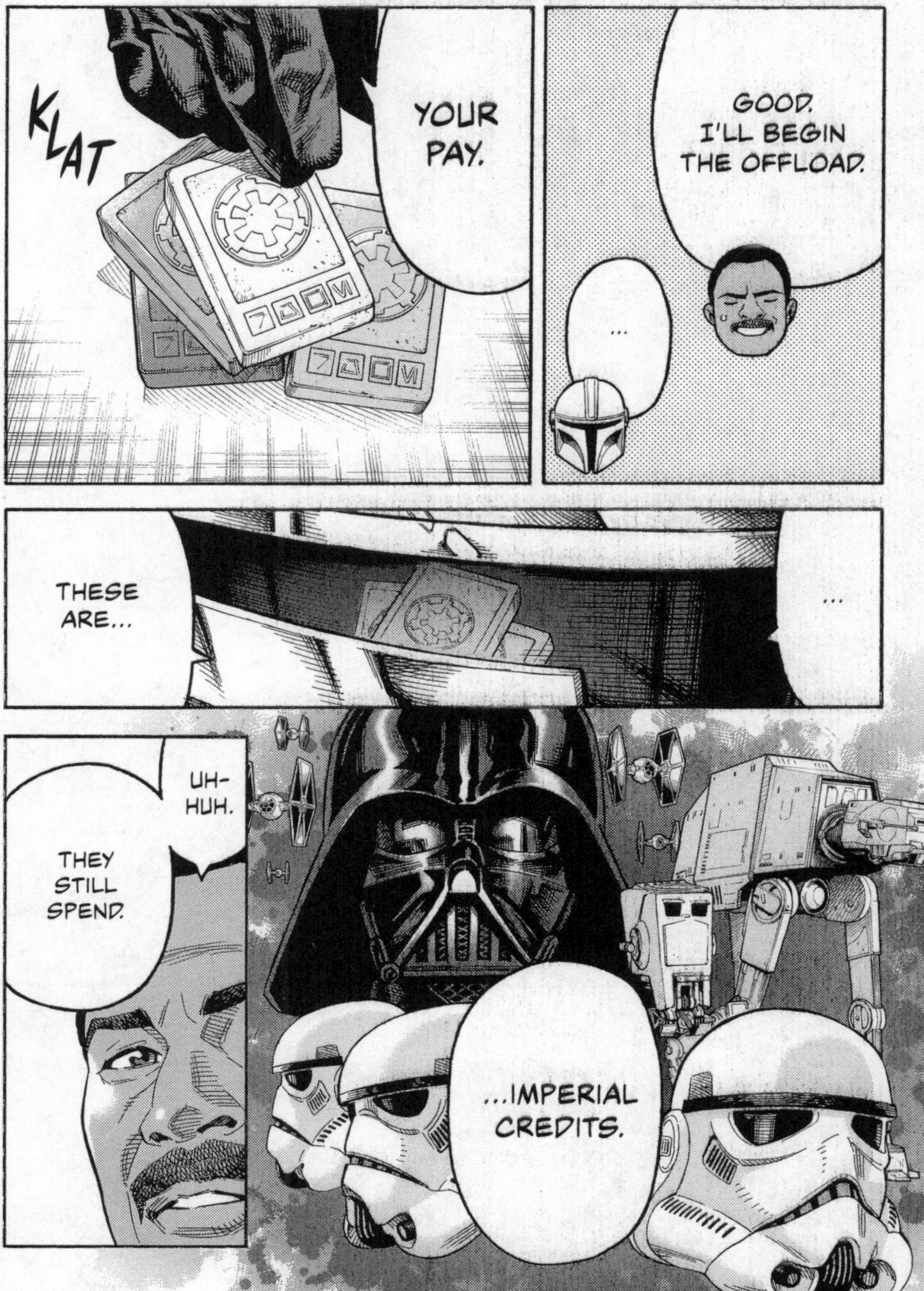
GOOD. I'LL BEGIN THE OFFLOAD.
...
YOUR PAY.
KLAT
...
THESE ARE...
...IMPERIAL CREDITS.
UH-HUH.
THEY STILL SPEND.

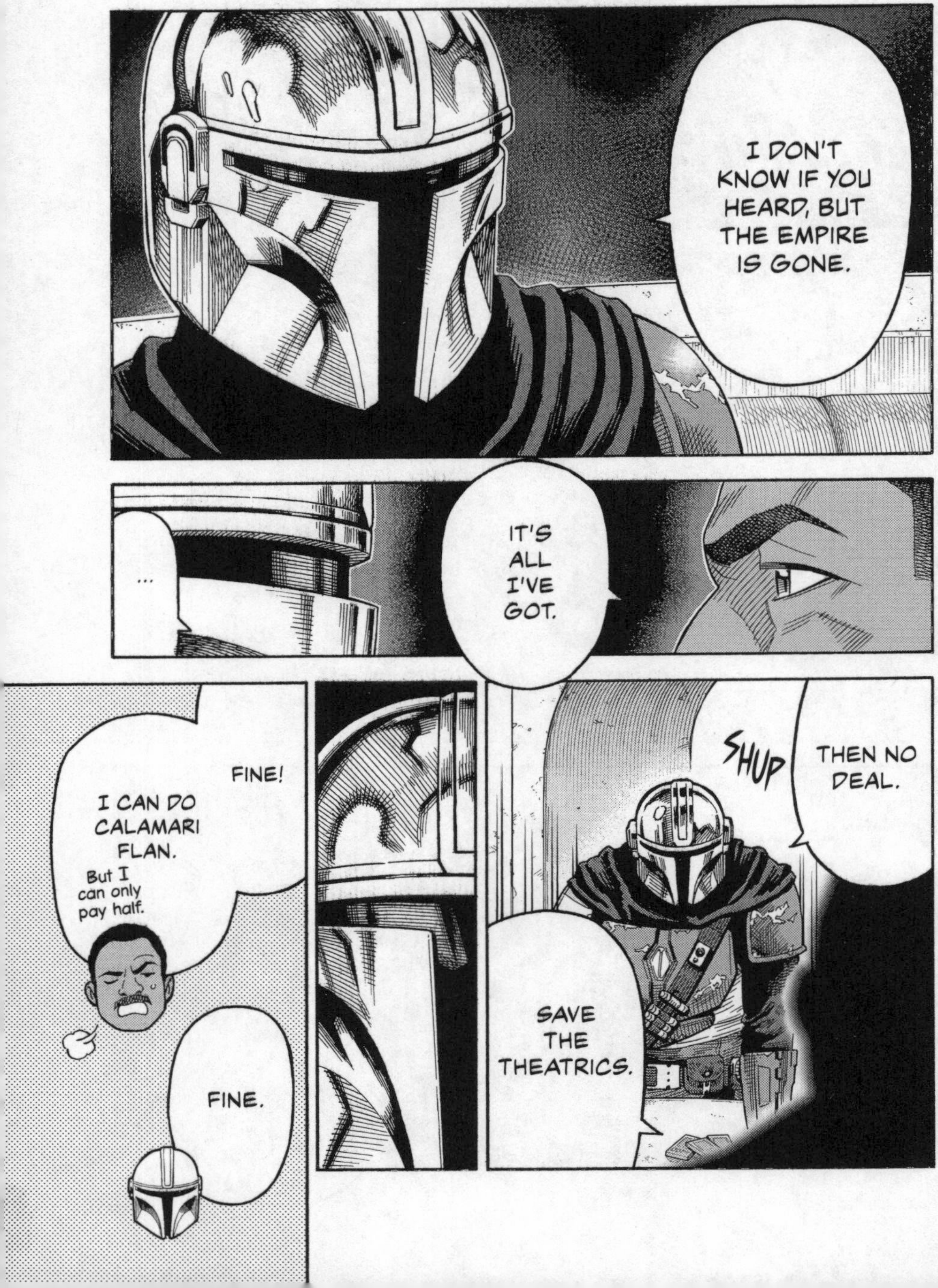
I DON'T KNOW IF YOU HEARD, BUT THE EMPIRE IS GONE.
IT'S ALL I'VE GOT.
...
THEN NO DEAL.
SHUP
SAVE THE THEATRICS.
FINE!
I CAN DO CALAMARI FLAN.
But I can only pay half.
FINE.

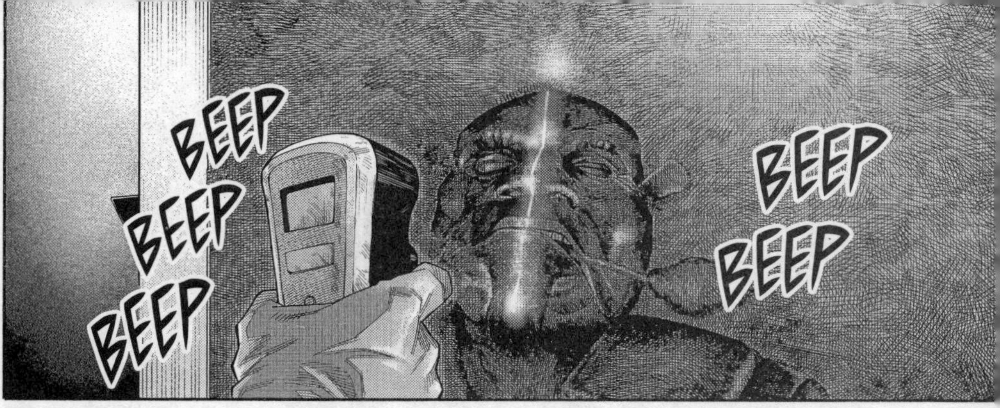
BEEP
BEEP
BEEP
BEEP
BEEP

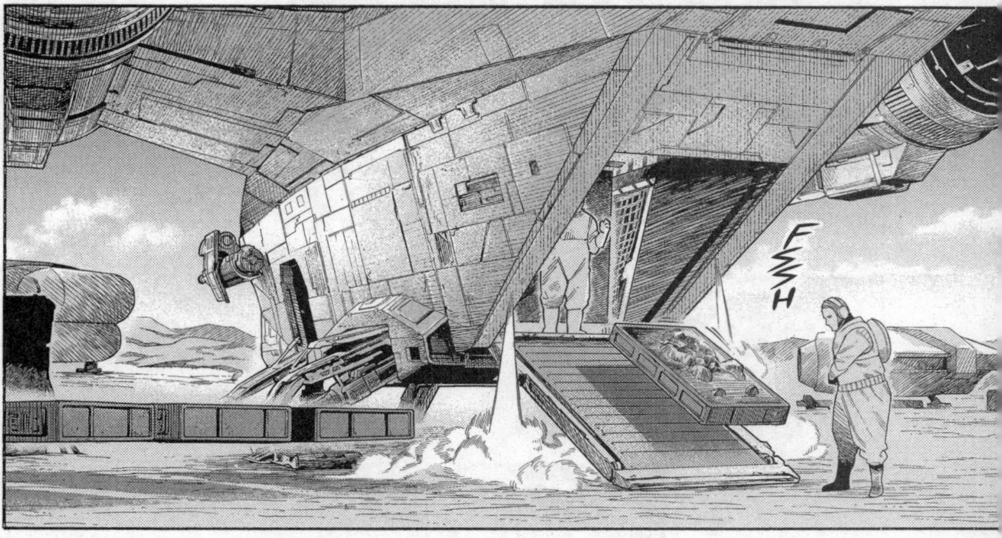
FSSH

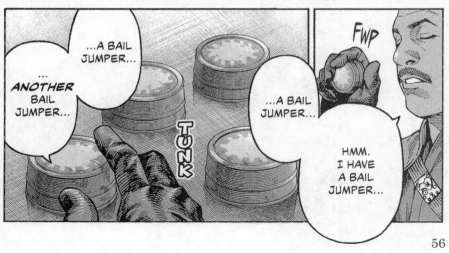

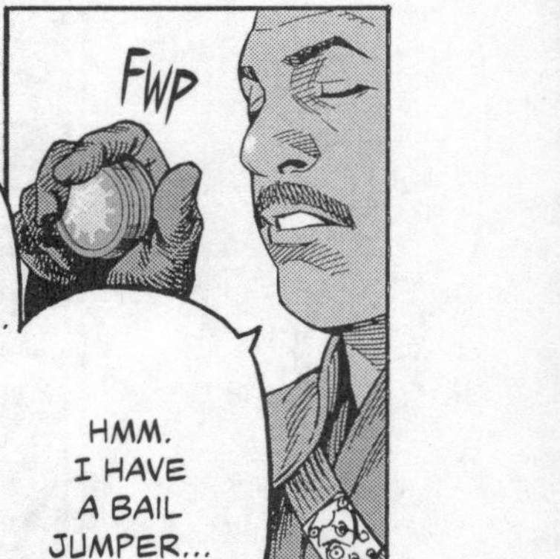
FWP
HMM. I HAVE A BAIL JUMPER...
...A BAIL JUMPER...

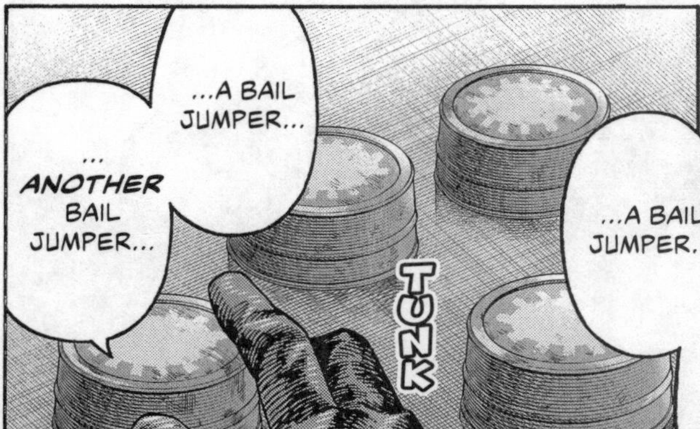
...A BAIL JUMPER...
... *ANOTHER* BAIL JUMPER...
TUNK

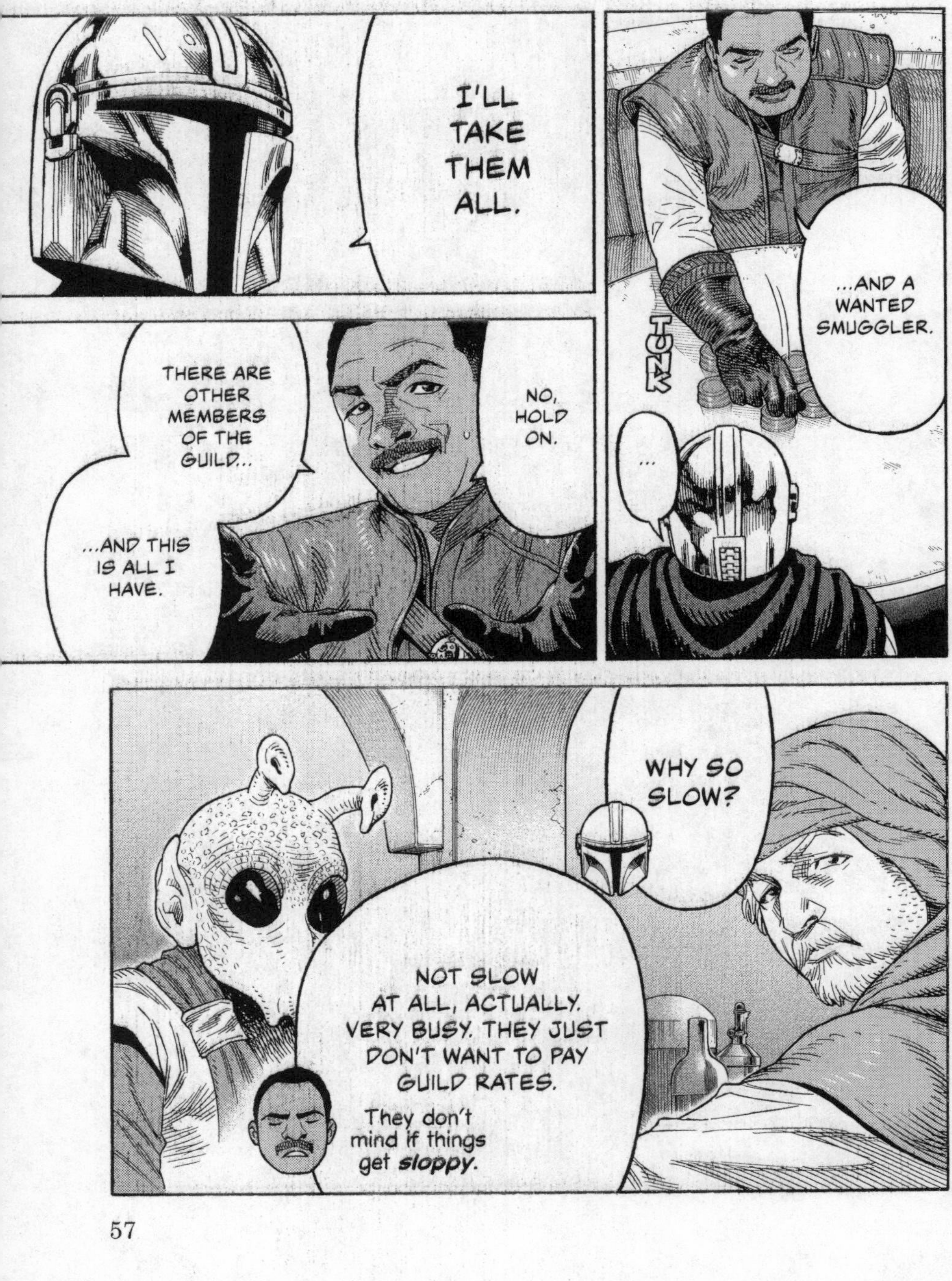
...AND A WANTED SMUGGLER.
TUNK
...
I'LL TAKE THEM ALL.
NO, HOLD ON.
THERE ARE OTHER MEMBERS OF THE GUILD...
...AND THIS IS ALL I HAVE.
WHY SO SLOW?
NOT SLOW AT ALL, ACTUALLY. VERY BUSY. THEY JUST DON'T WANT TO PAY GUILD RATES.
They don't mind if things get *sloppy*.

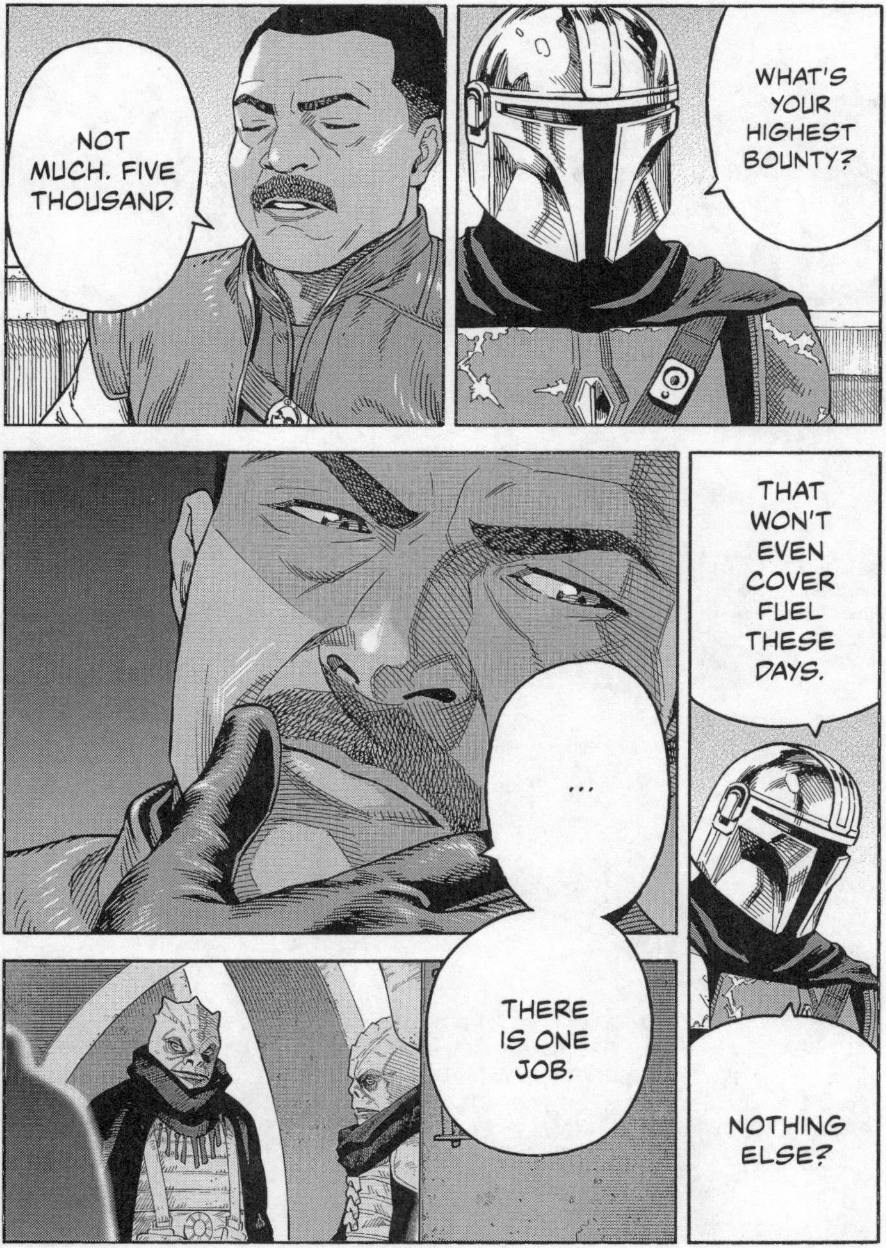
WHAT'S YOUR HIGHEST BOUNTY?
NOT MUCH. FIVE THOUSAND.
THAT WON'T EVEN COVER FUEL THESE DAYS.
NOTHING ELSE?
...
THERE IS ONE JOB.

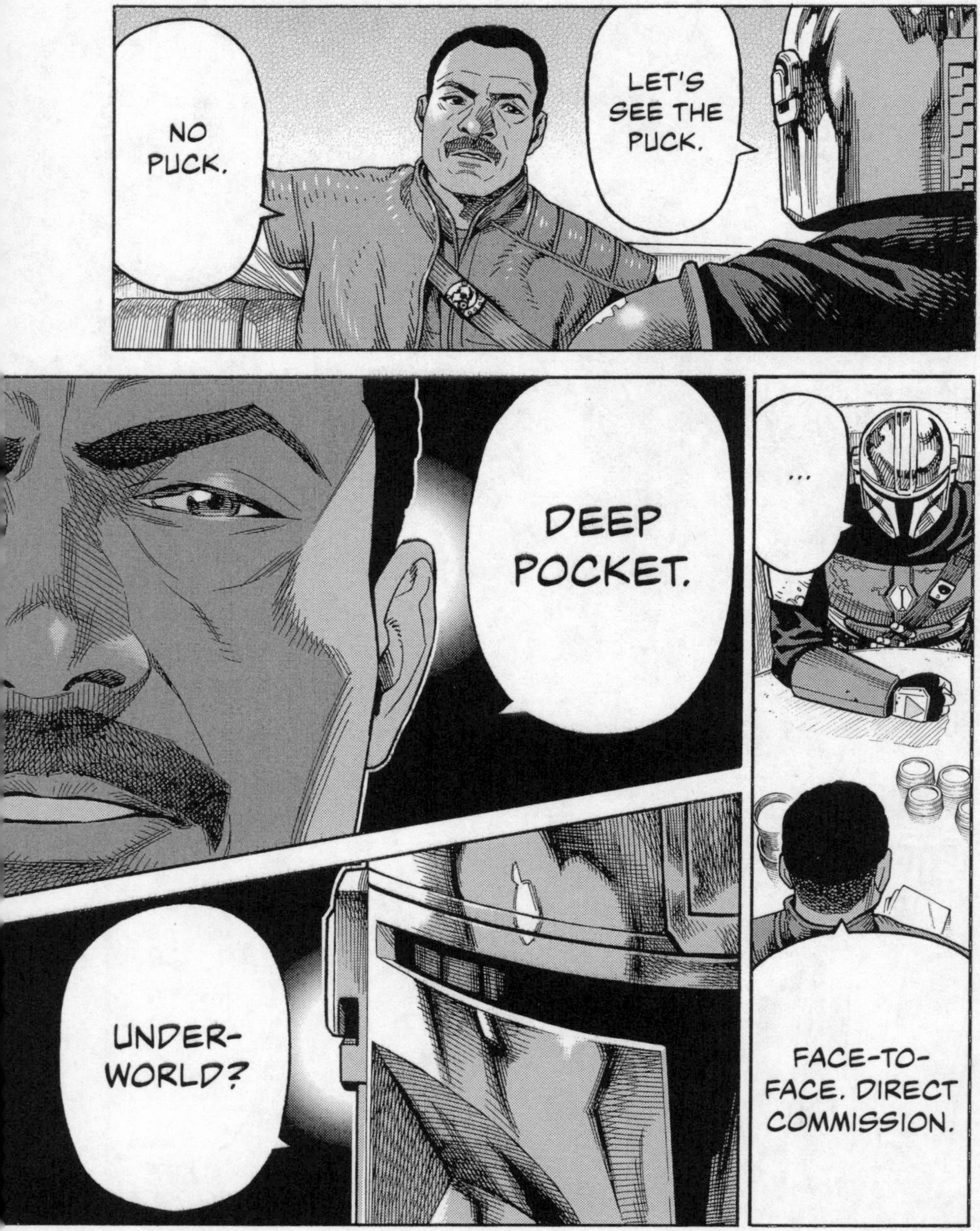
LET'S SEE THE PUCK.
NO PUCK.
...
FACE-TO-FACE. DIRECT COMMISSION.
DEEP POCKET.
UNDER-WORLD?

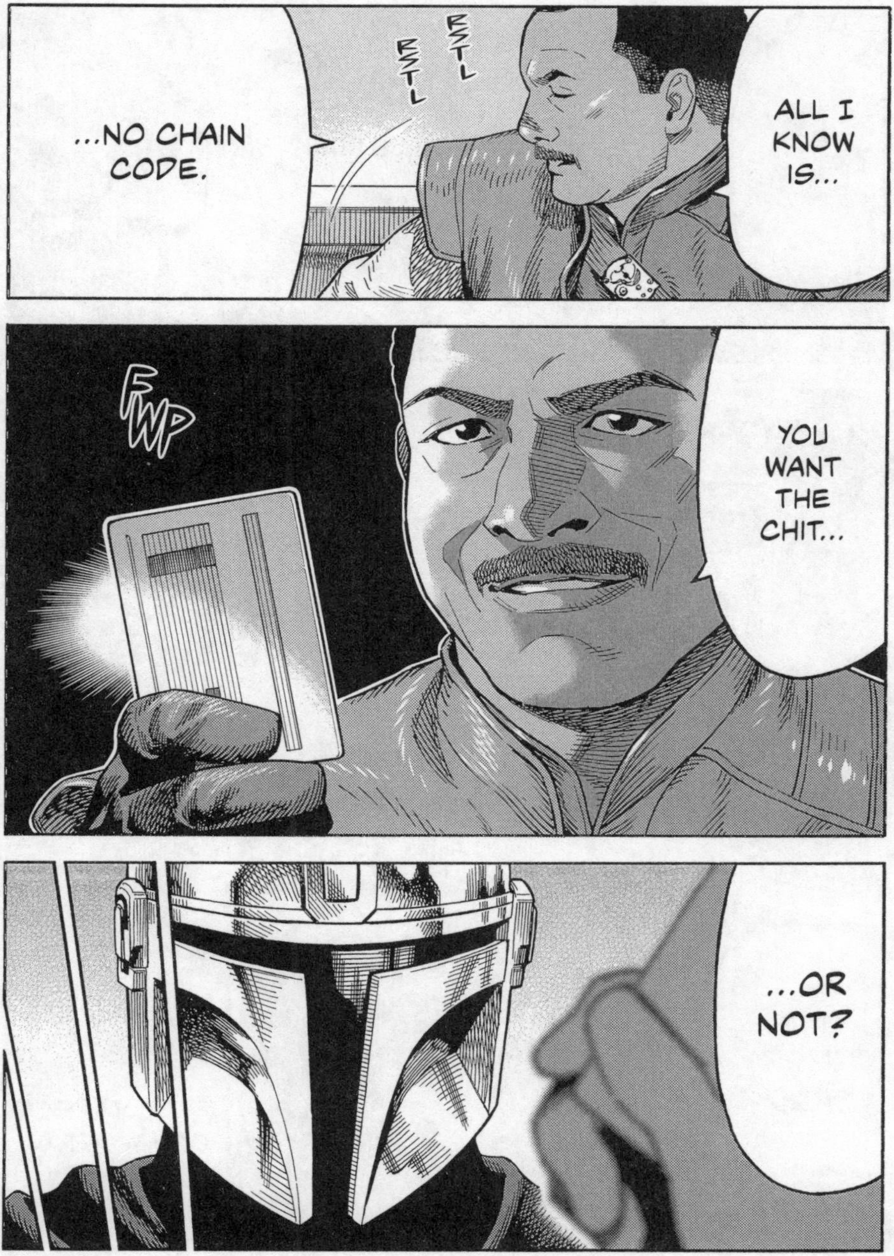
ALL I KNOW IS...
RSTL RSTL
...NO CHAIN CODE.
YOU WANT THE CHIT...
FWP
...OR NOT?

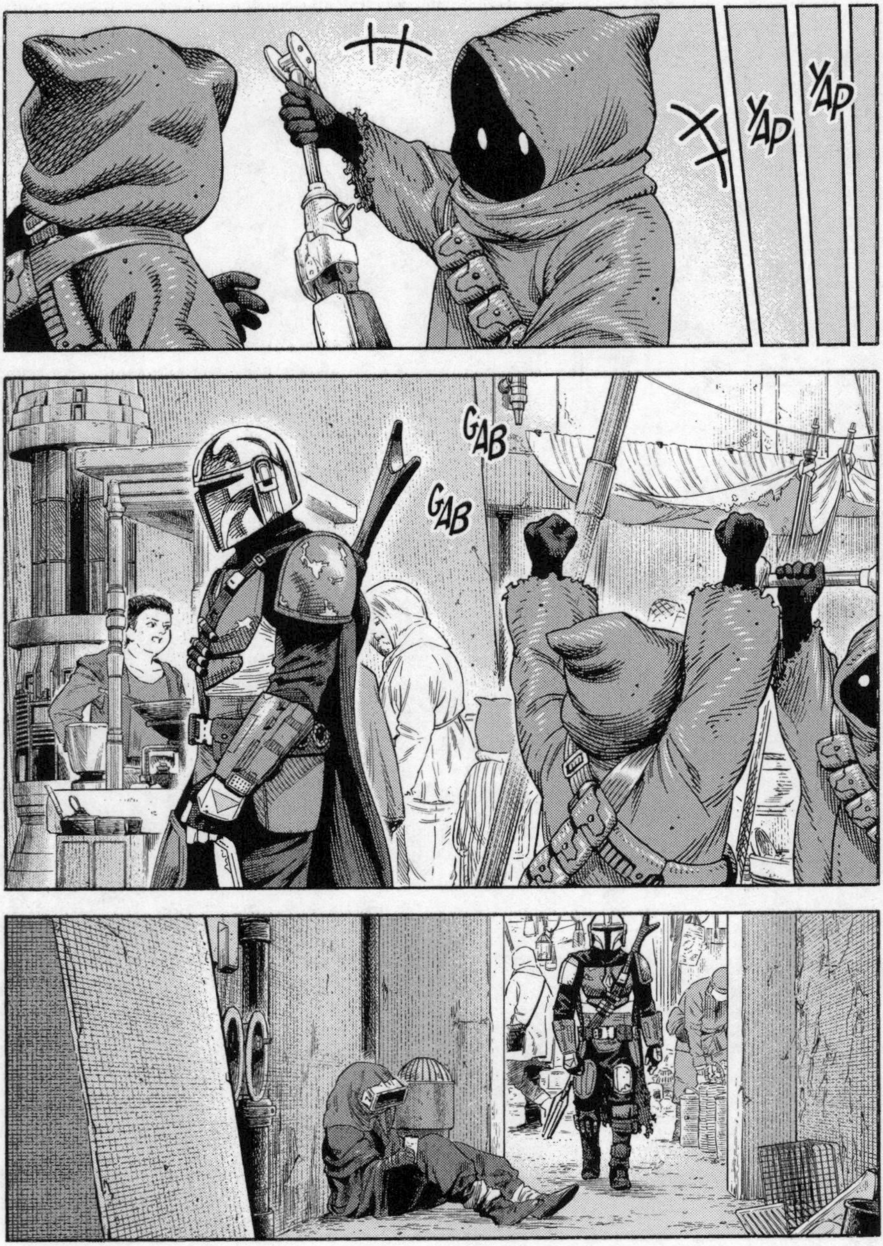
YAP
YAP
GAB
GAB

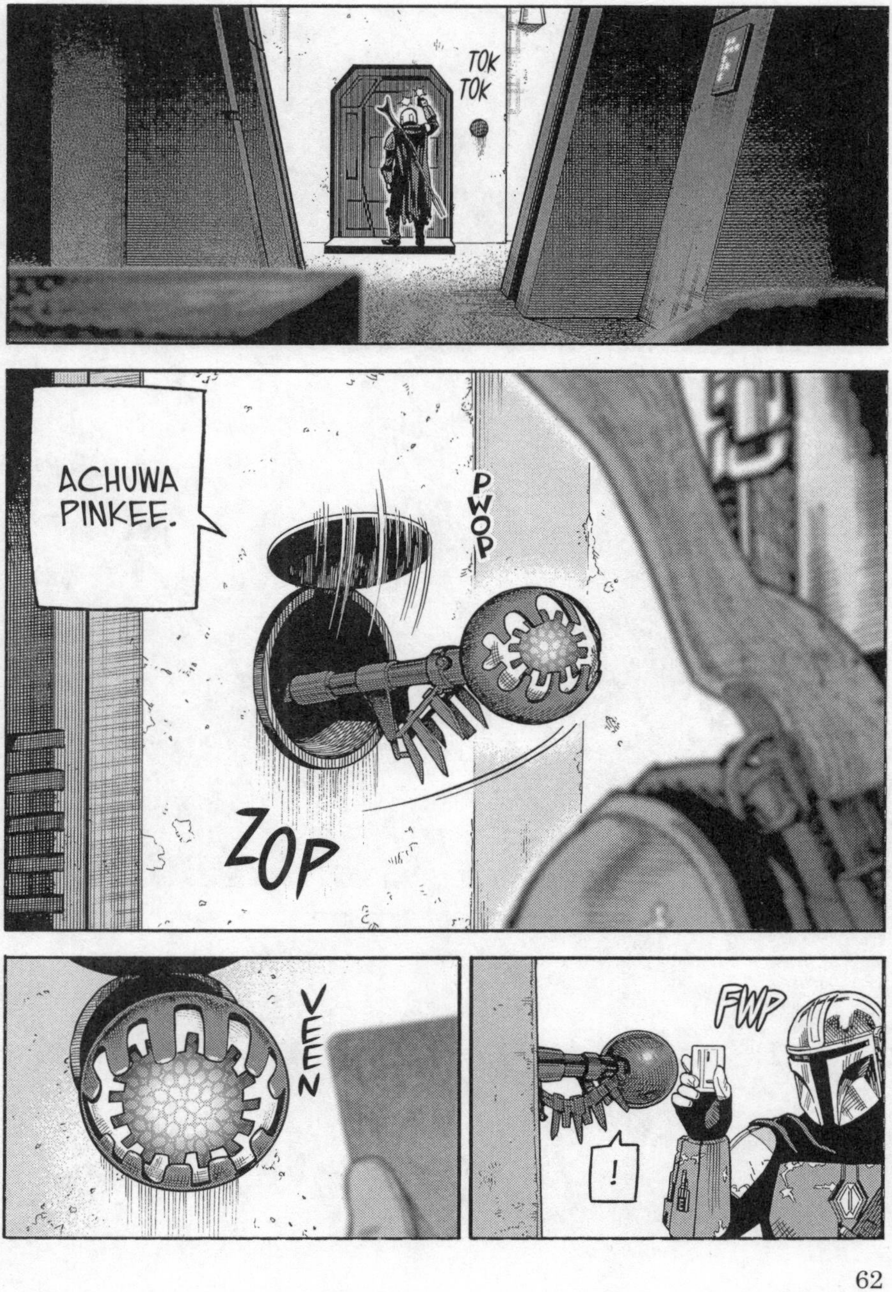
TOK
TOK
ACHUWA PINKEE.
PWOP
ZOP
FWP
!
VEEN

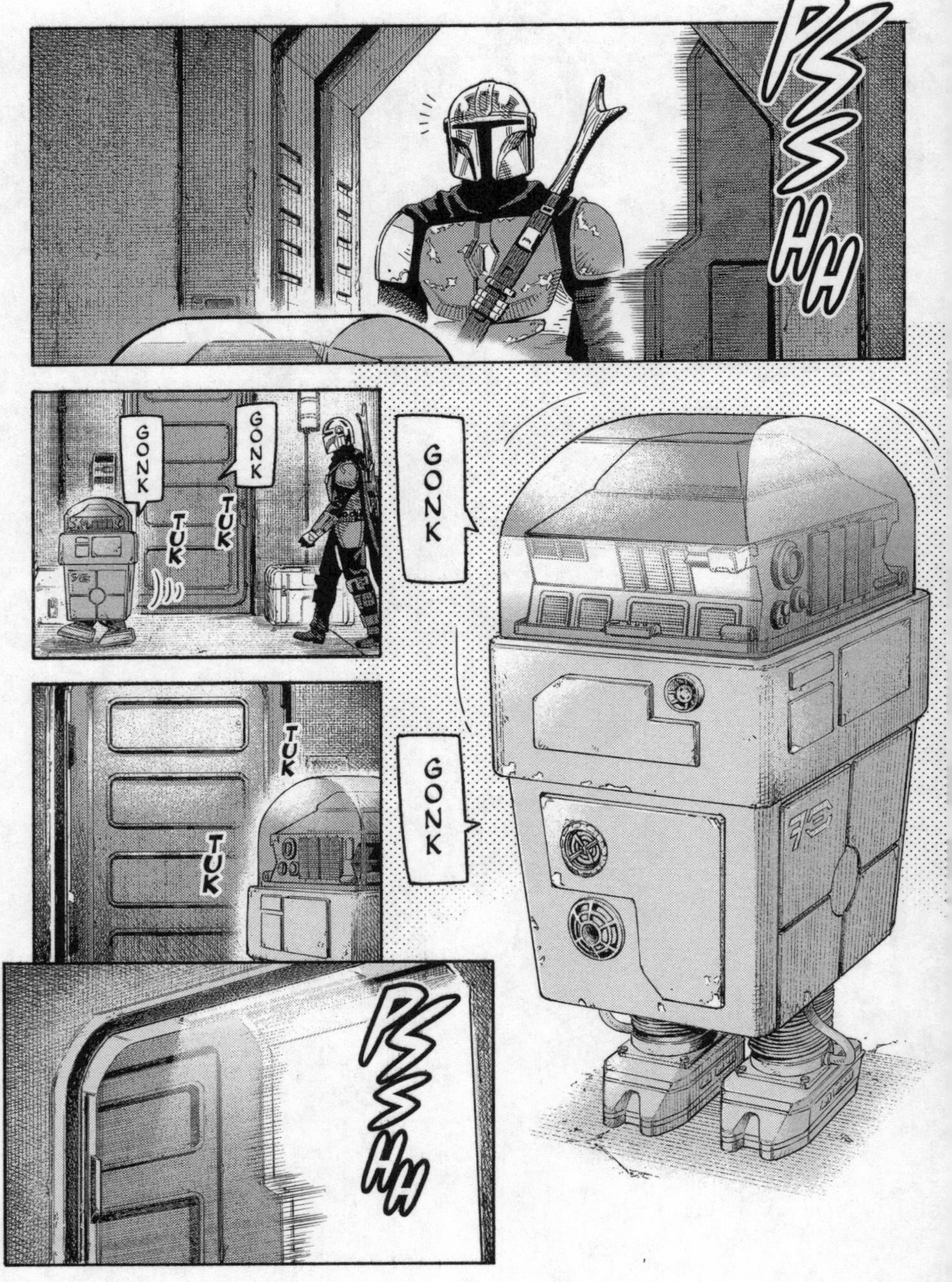
PSSHH
GONK
GONK
GONK
TUK
GONK
TUK
TUK
TUK
PSSHH

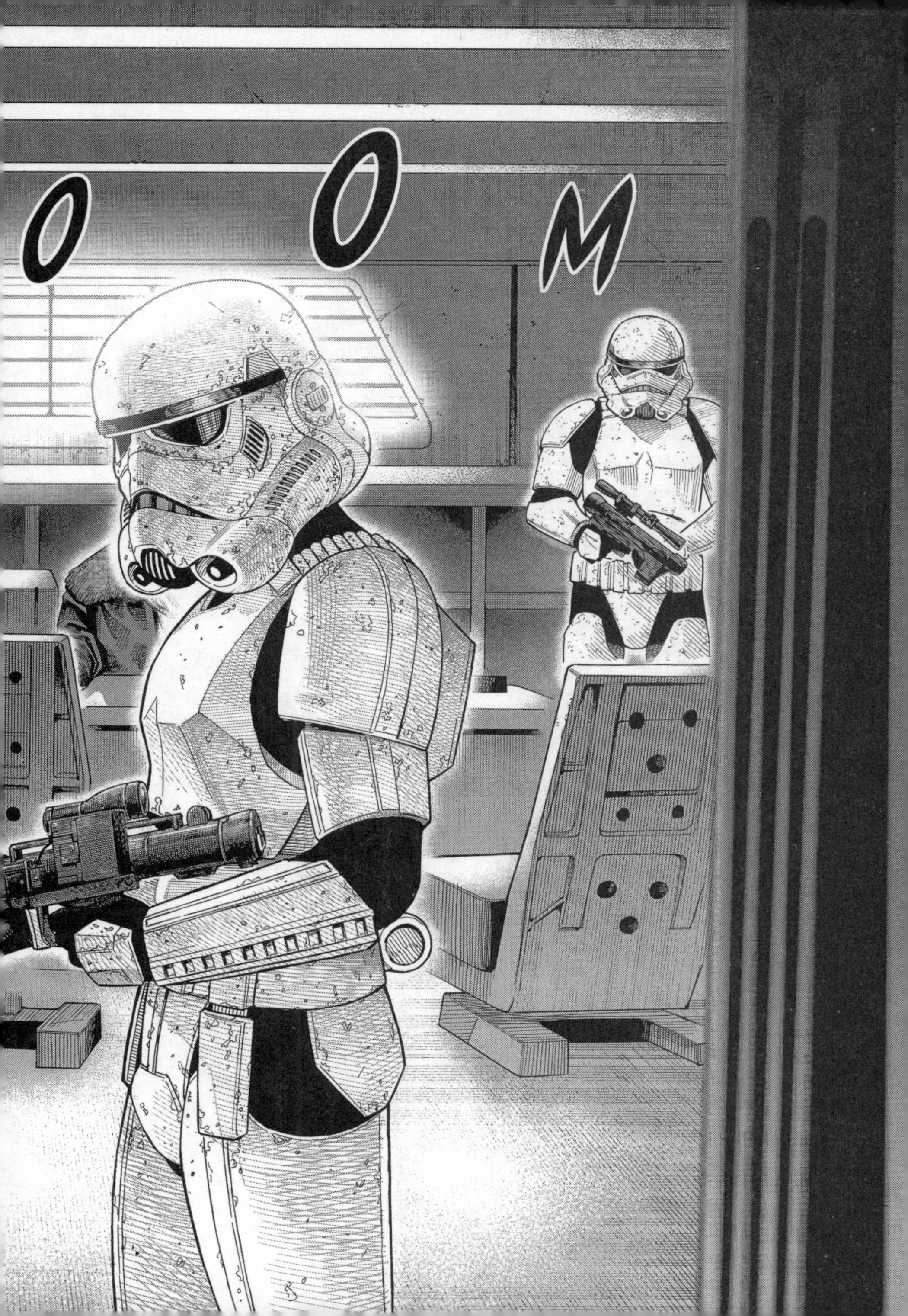
OOM

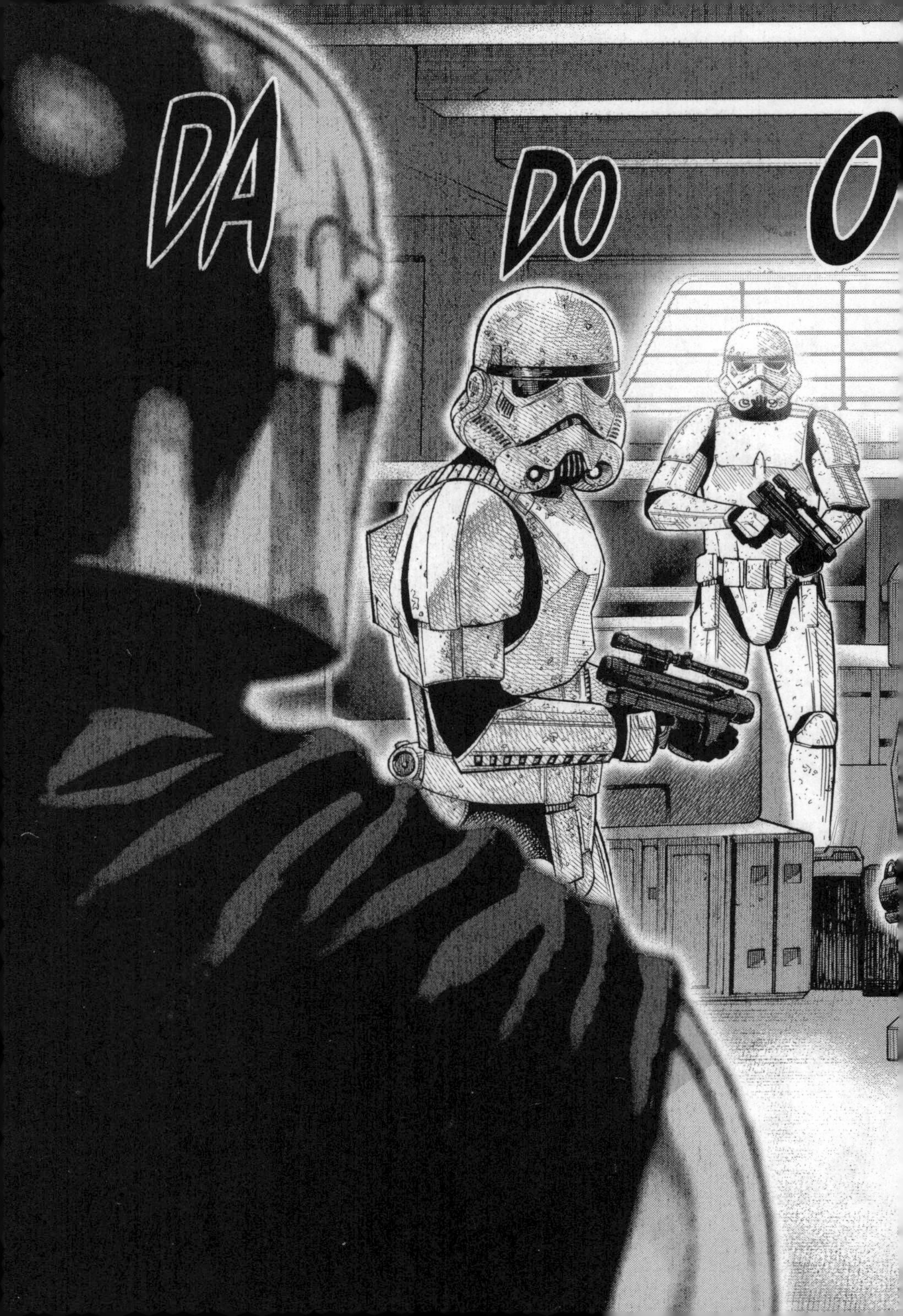
O
DO
DA

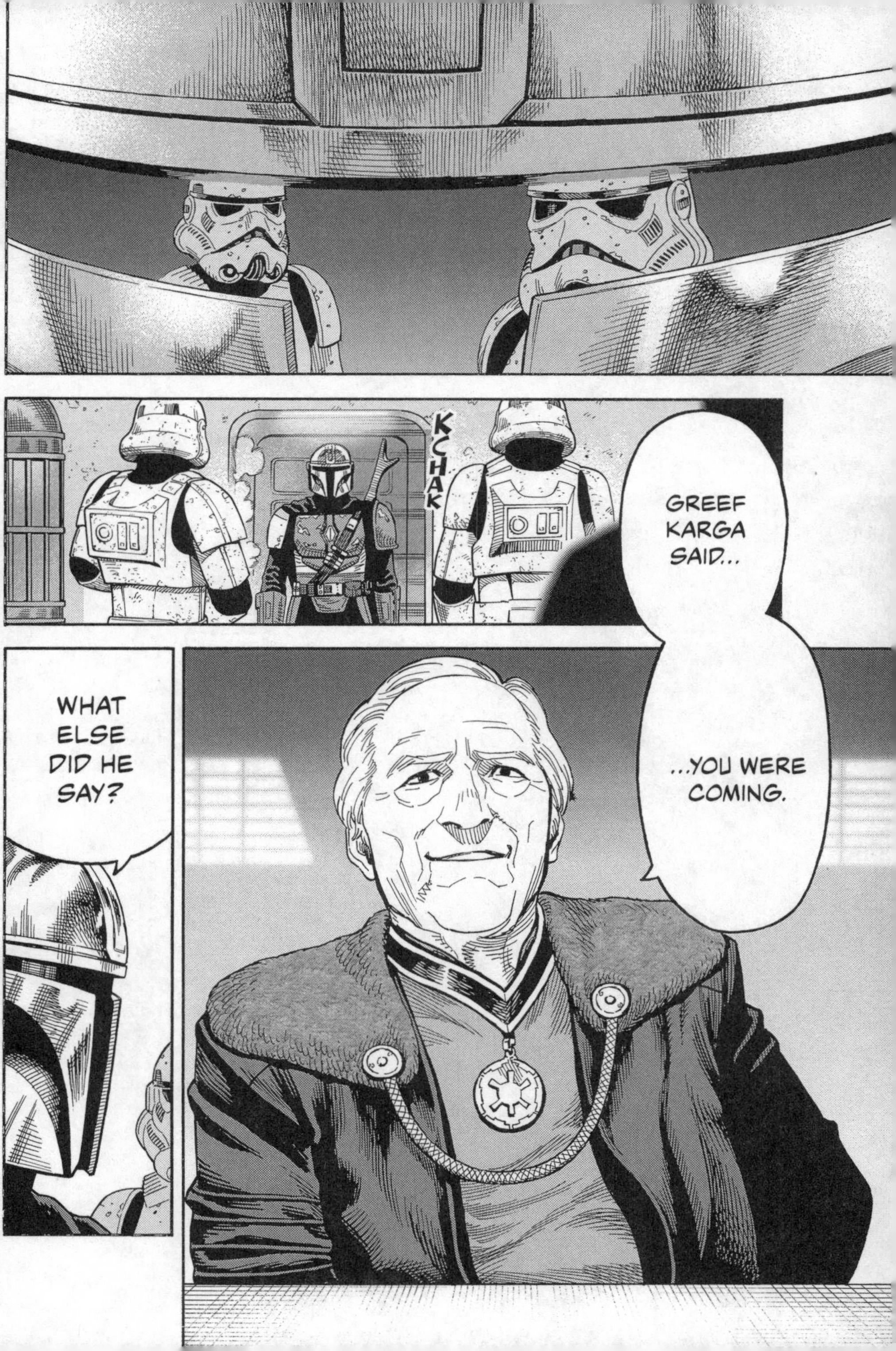
KCHAK
GREEF KARGA SAID...
...YOU WERE COMING.
WHAT ELSE DID HE SAY?

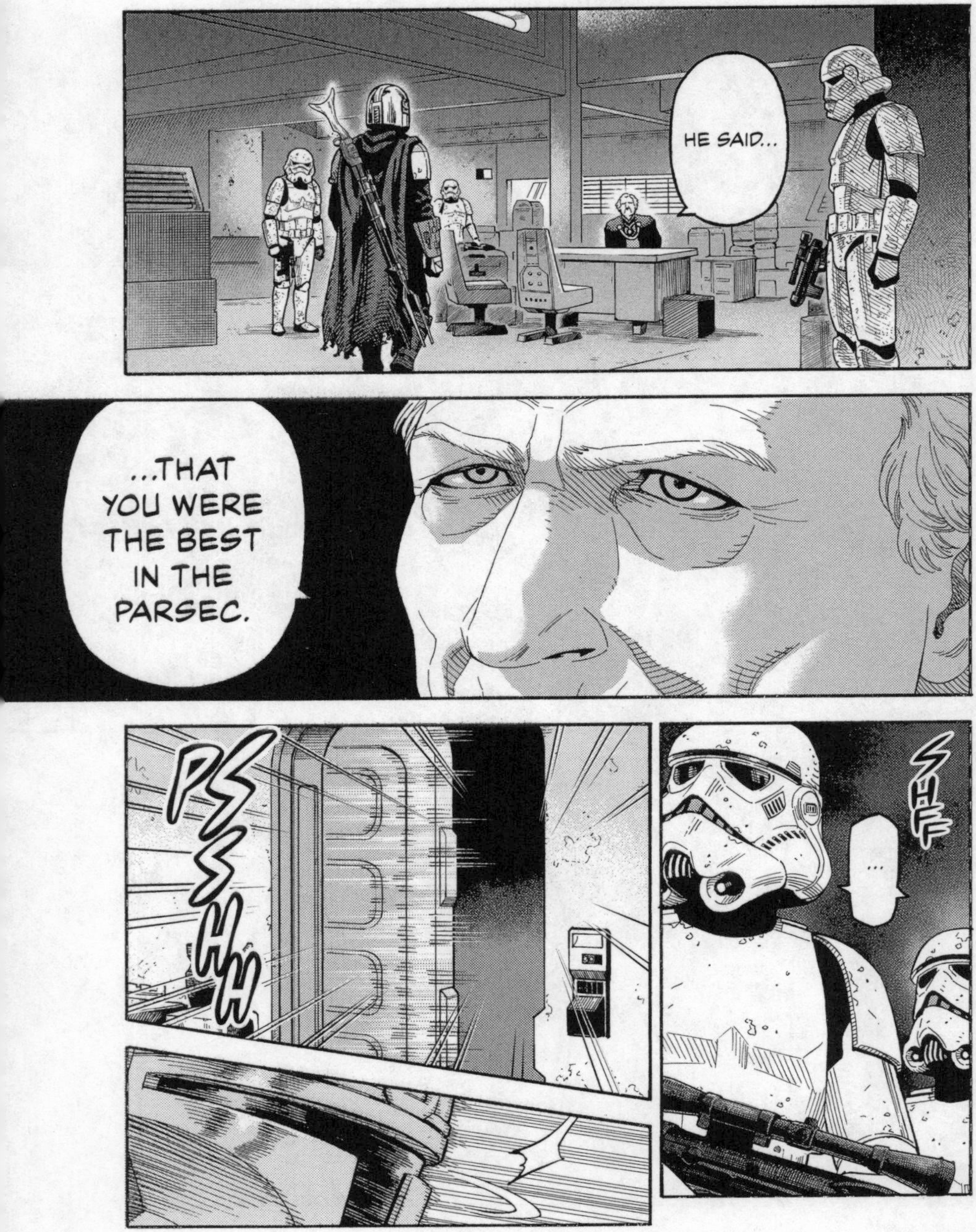
HE SAID...
...THAT YOU WERE THE BEST IN THE PARSEC.
SHFF
...
PSSHHH

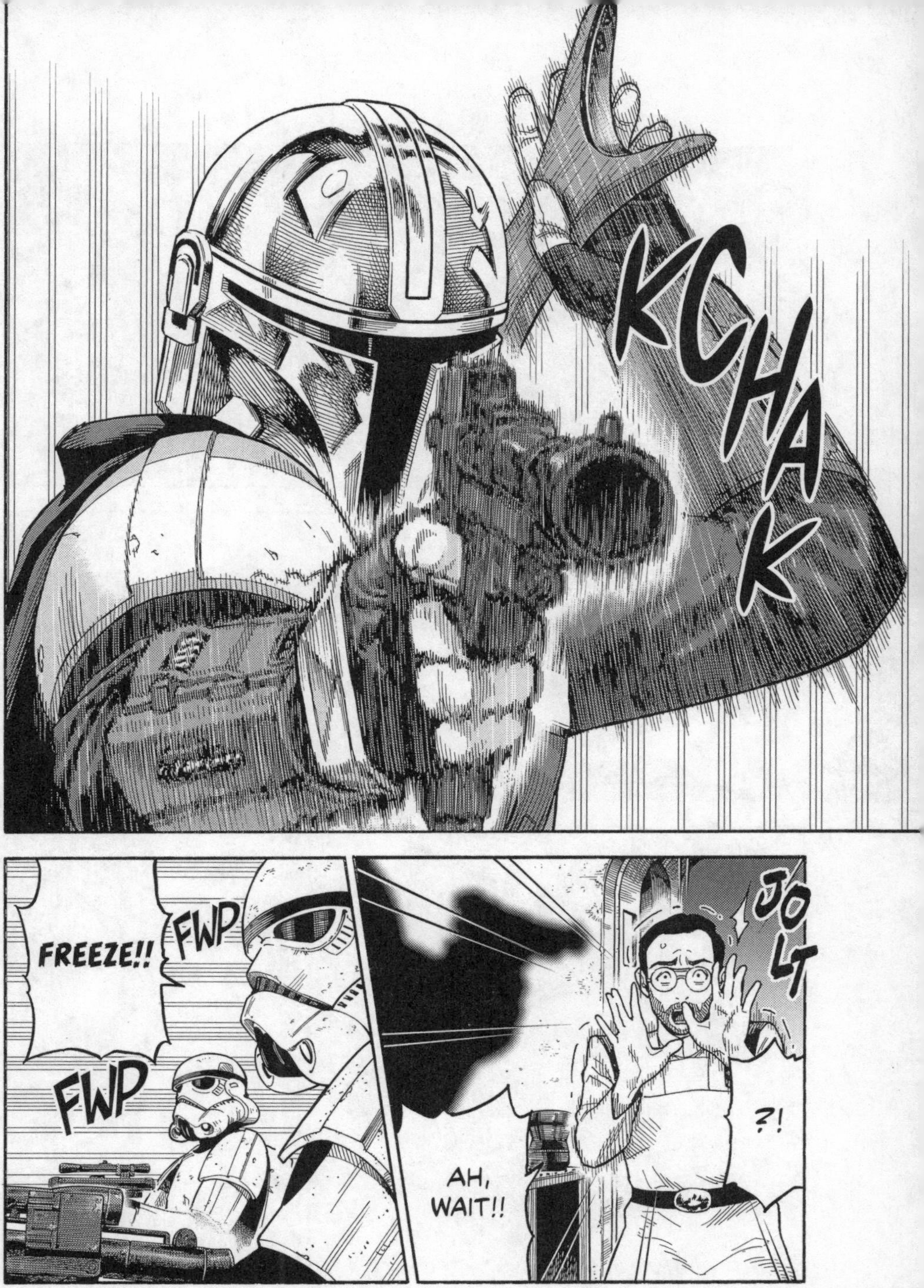
KCHAK
JOLT
?!
AH, WAIT!!
FREEZE!!
FWP
FWP

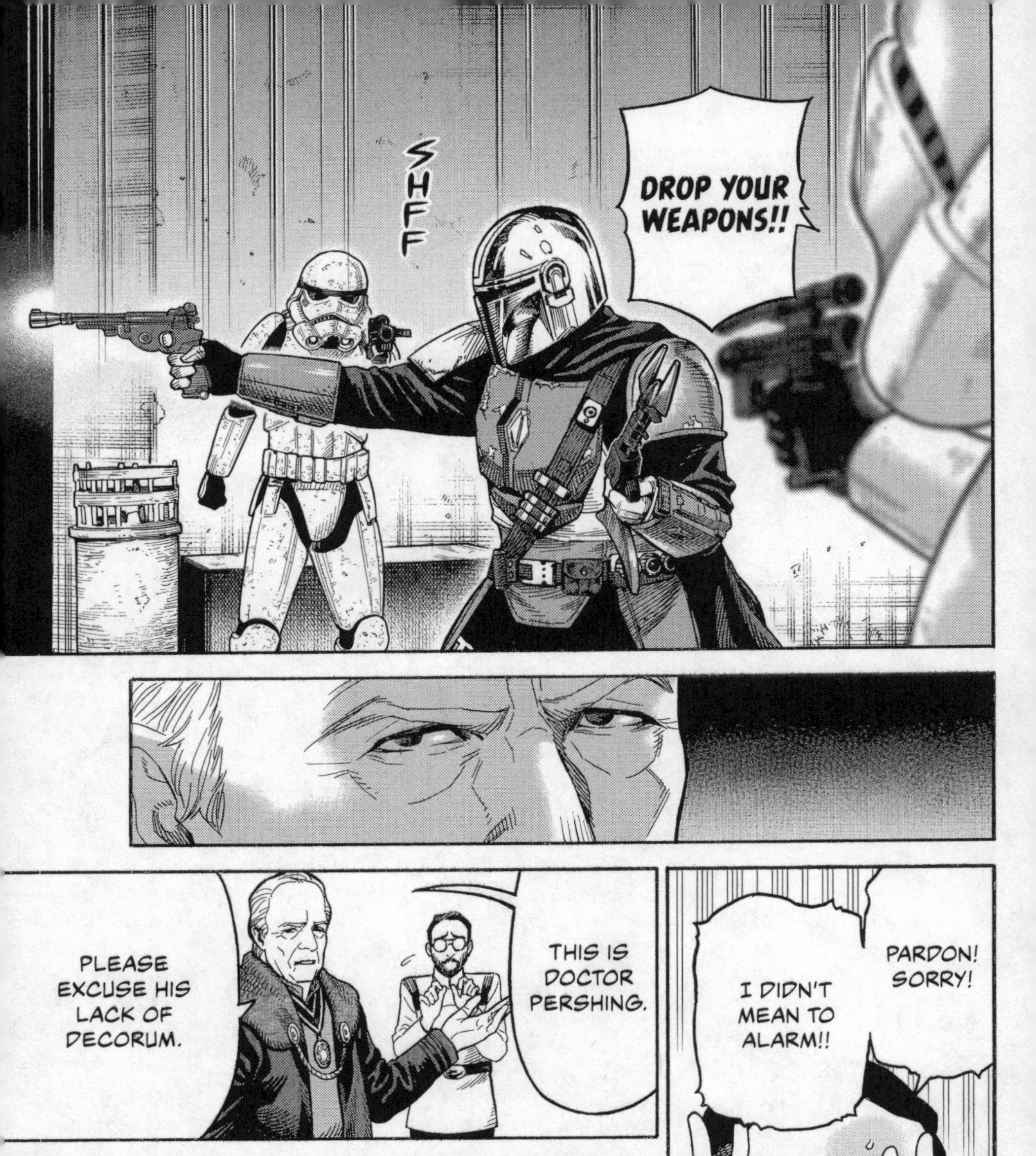
DROP YOUR WEAPONS!!
SHFF
PARDON! SORRY!
I DIDN'T MEAN TO ALARM!!
THIS IS DOCTOR PERSHING.
PLEASE EXCUSE HIS LACK OF DECORUM.
HIS ENTHUSIASM OUTWEIGHS HIS DISCRETION.
...

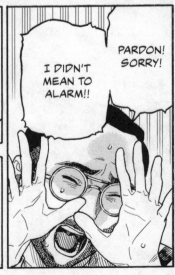

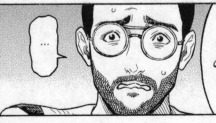

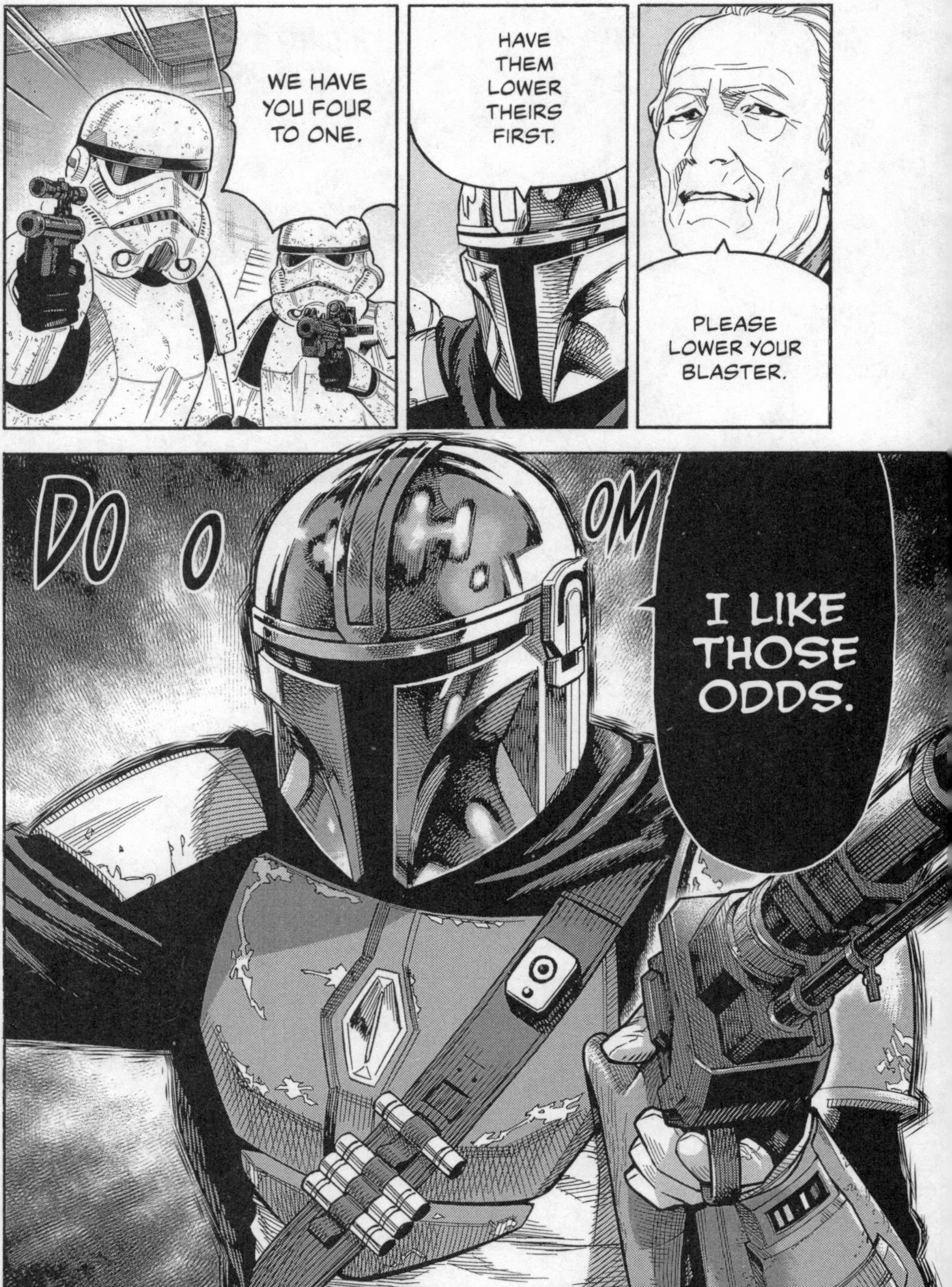
PLEASE LOWER YOUR BLASTER.
HAVE THEM LOWER THEIRS FIRST.
WE HAVE YOU FOUR TO ONE.
I LIKE THOSE ODDS.
DO O OM

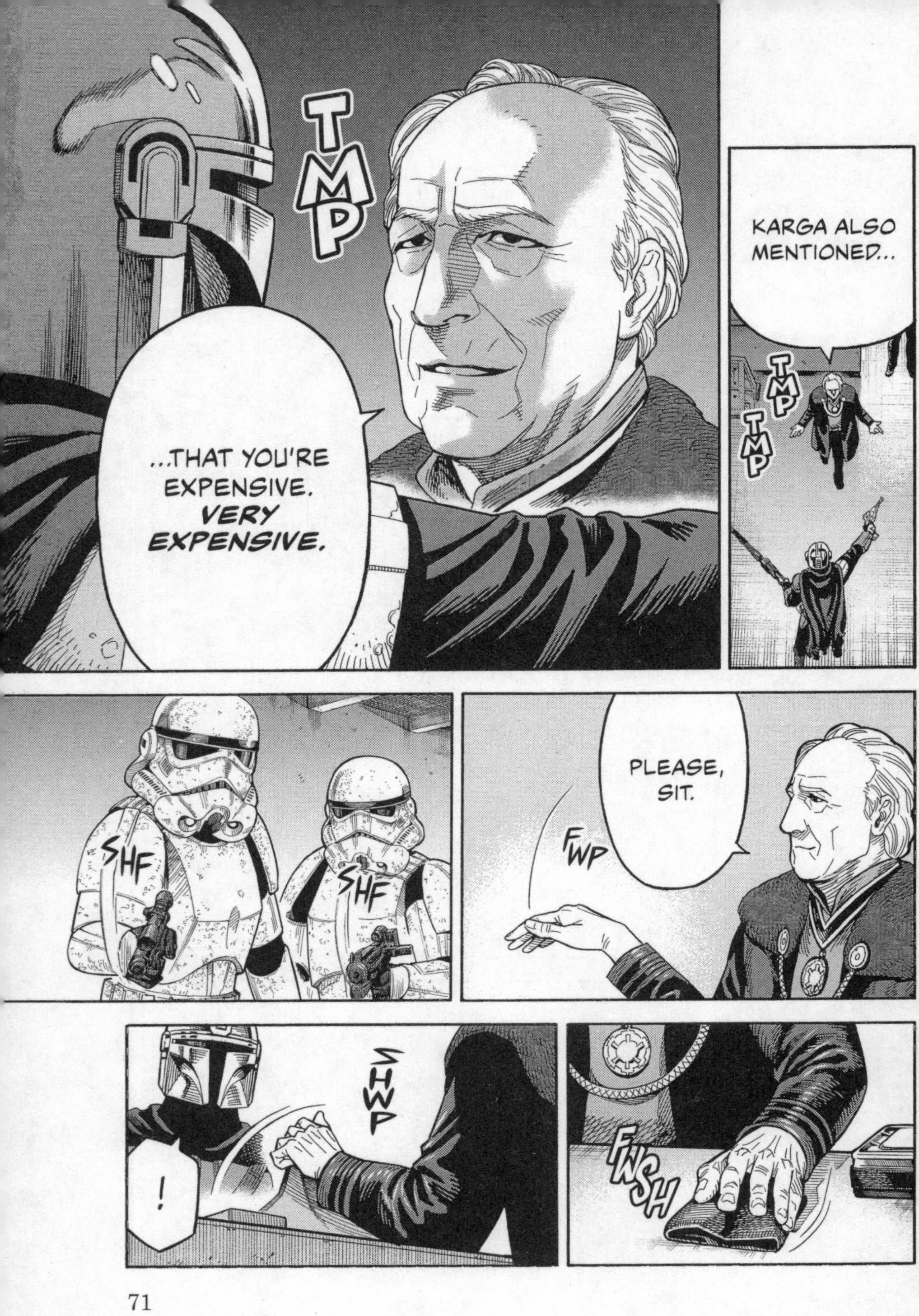
KARGA ALSO MENTIONED...
TMP
TMP
TMP
...THAT YOU'RE EXPENSIVE. VERY EXPENSIVE.
PLEASE, SIT.
FWP
SHF
SHF
FWSH
SHWP
!

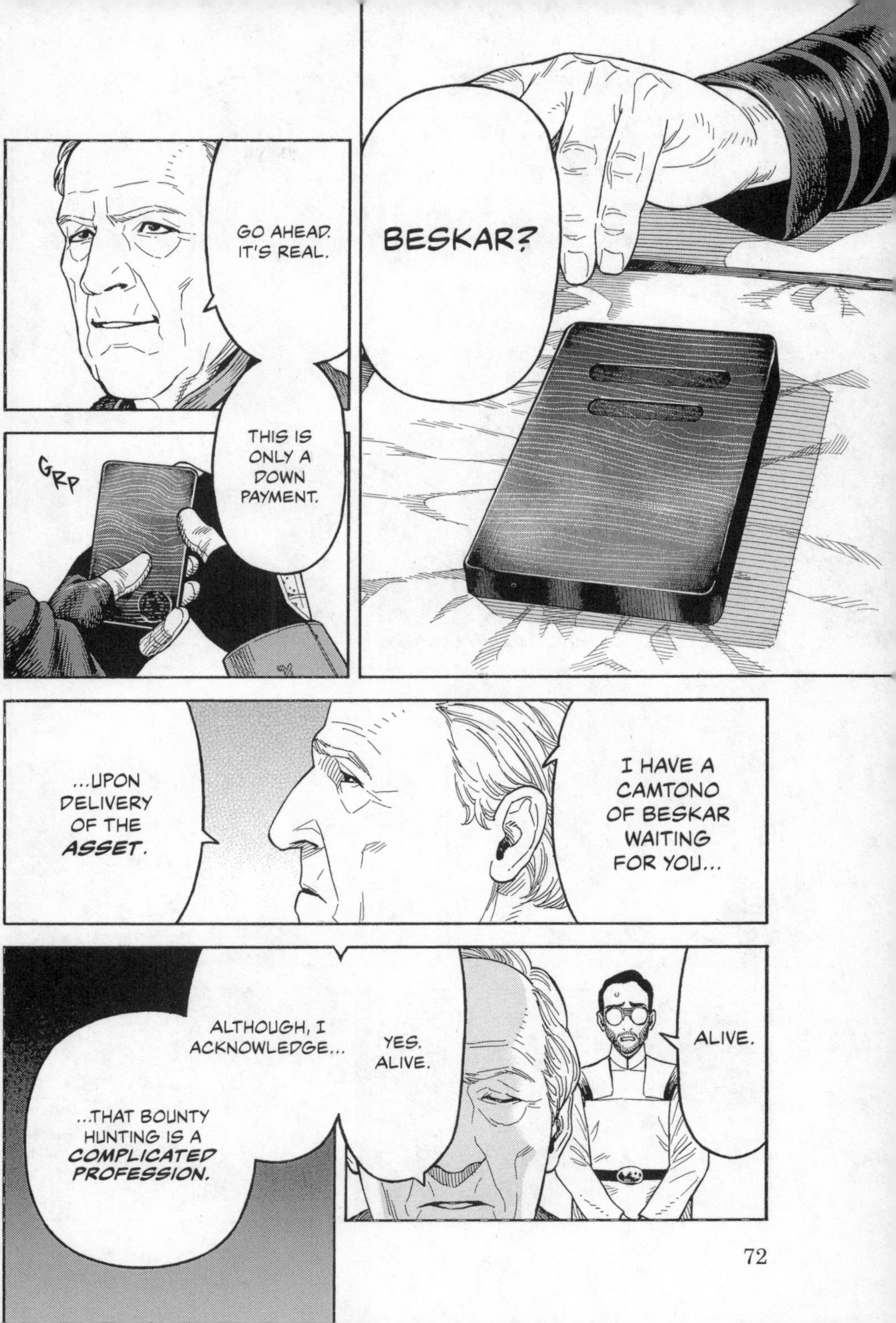
BESKAR?
GO AHEAD. IT'S REAL.
GRP
THIS IS ONLY A DOWN PAYMENT.
I HAVE A CAMTONO OF BESKAR WAITING FOR YOU...
...UPON DELIVERY OF THE ASSET.
ALIVE.
YES. ALIVE.
ALTHOUGH, I ACKNOWLEDGE...
...THAT BOUNTY HUNTING IS A COMPLICATED PROFESSION.

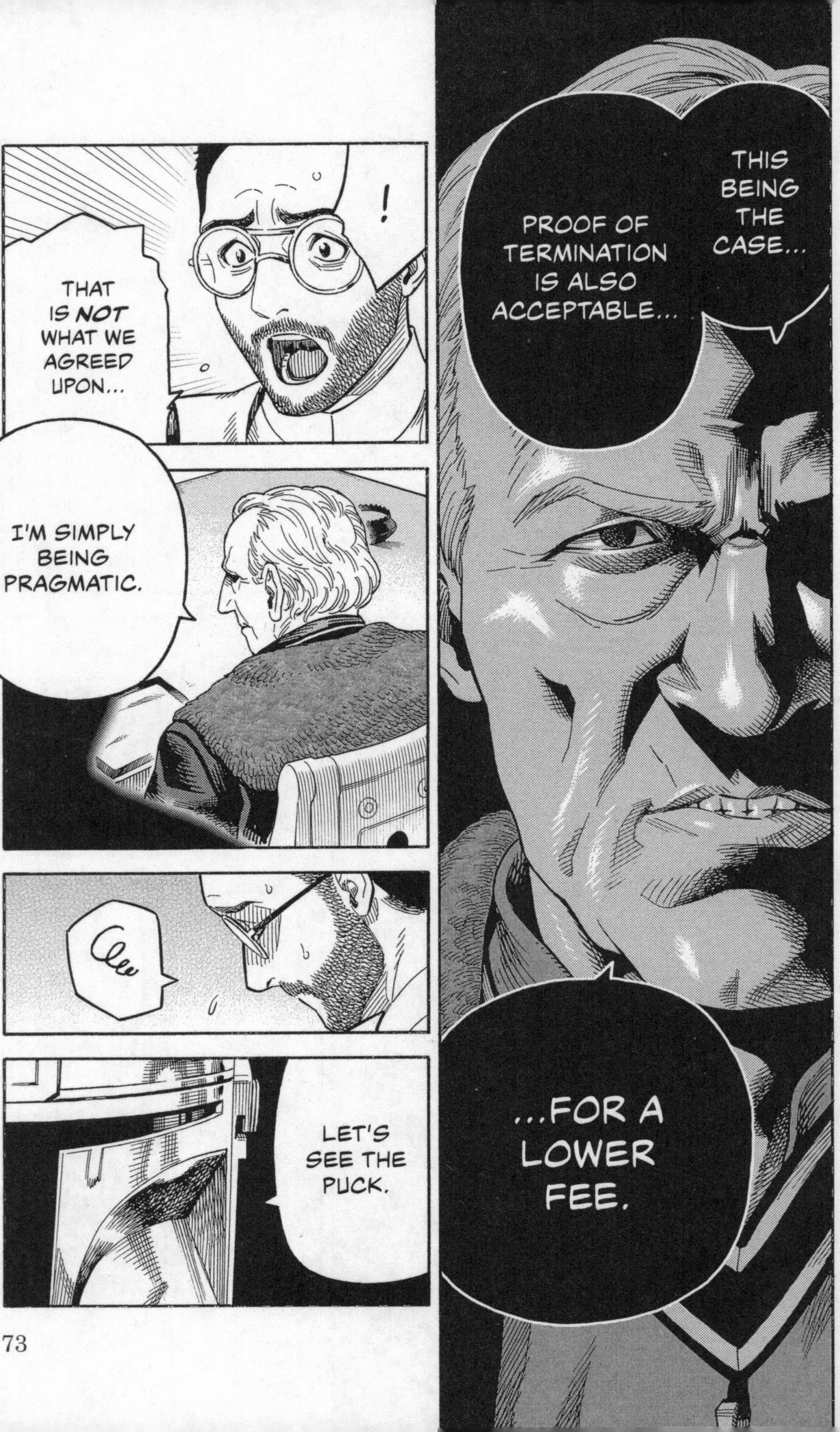
THIS BEING THE CASE...
PROOF OF TERMINATION IS ALSO ACCEPTABLE...
...FOR A LOWER FEE.
THAT IS **NOT** WHAT WE AGREED UPON...
I'M SIMPLY BEING PRAGMATIC.
LET'S SEE THE PUCK.

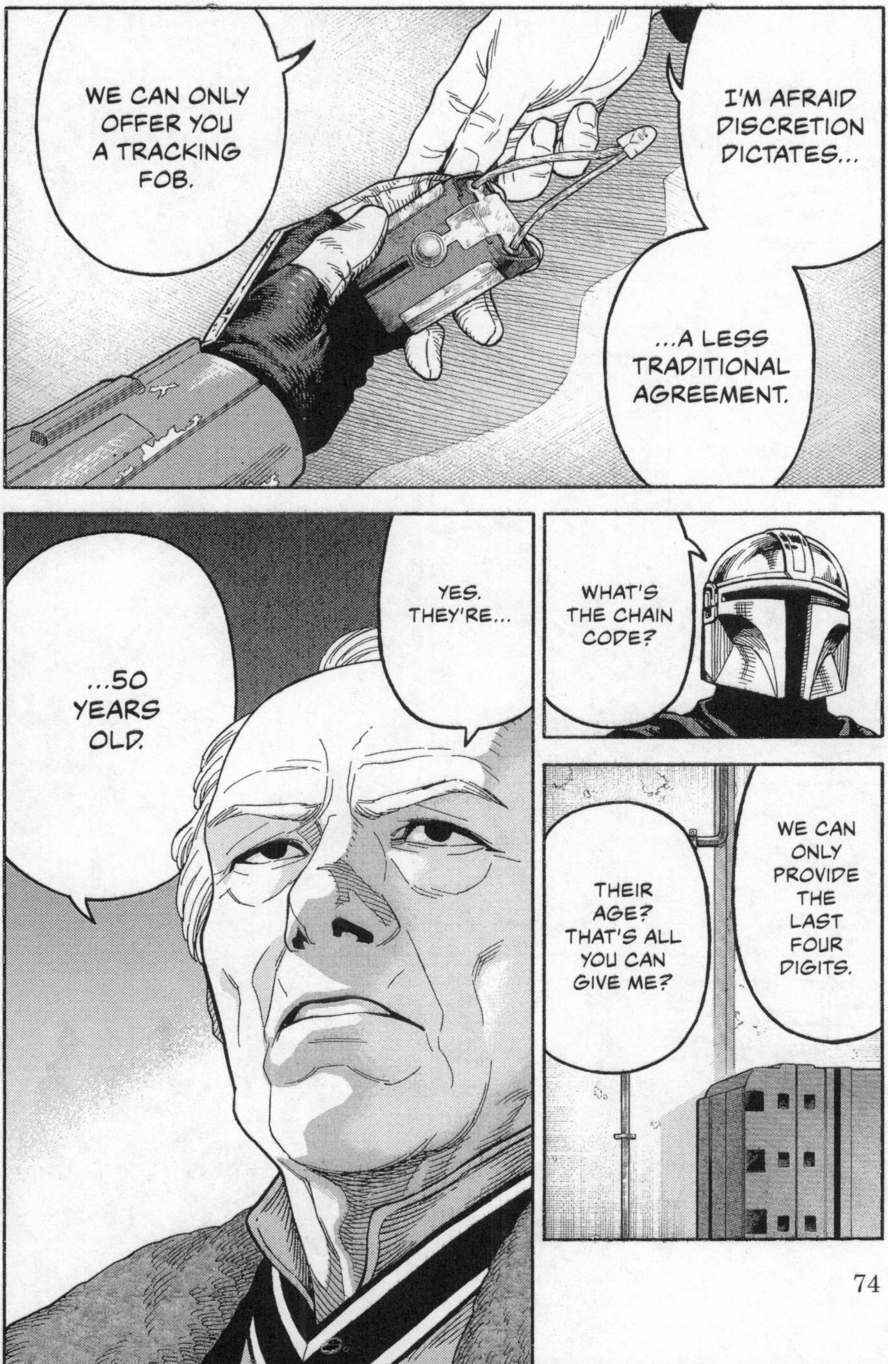
I'M AFRAID DISCRETION DICTATES...
...A LESS TRADITIONAL AGREEMENT.
WE CAN ONLY OFFER YOU A TRACKING FOB.
WHAT'S THE CHAIN CODE?
WE CAN ONLY PROVIDE THE LAST FOUR DIGITS.
THEIR AGE? THAT'S ALL YOU CAN GIVE ME?
YES. THEY'RE...
...50 YEARS OLD.

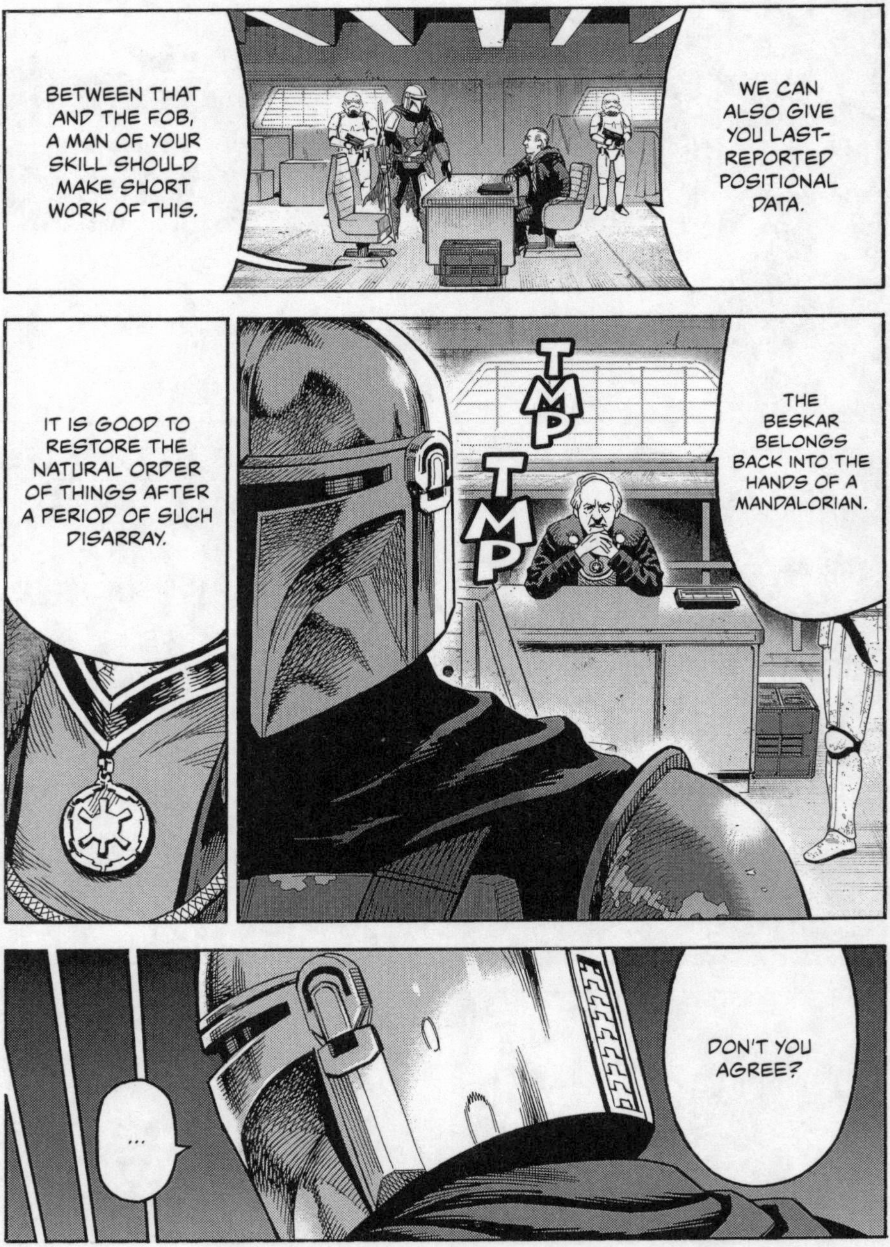
WE CAN ALSO GIVE YOU LAST-REPORTED POSITIONAL DATA.
BETWEEN THAT AND THE FOB, A MAN OF YOUR SKILL SHOULD MAKE SHORT WORK OF THIS.
THE BESKAR BELONGS BACK INTO THE HANDS OF A MANDALORIAN.
TMP TMP
IT IS GOOD TO RESTORE THE NATURAL ORDER OF THINGS AFTER A PERIOD OF SUCH DISARRAY.
DON'T YOU AGREE?
...

SZZZZL
MRAWR!
MRAWR!
TMP
TMP
PEEK
PEEK
TMP

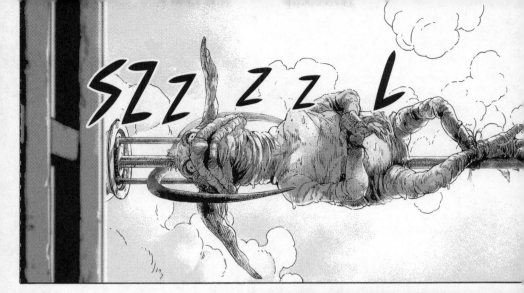

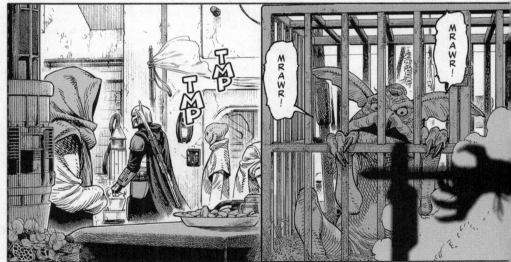

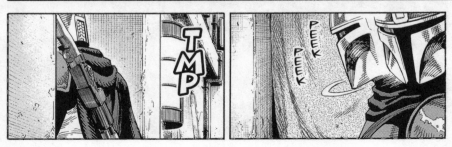

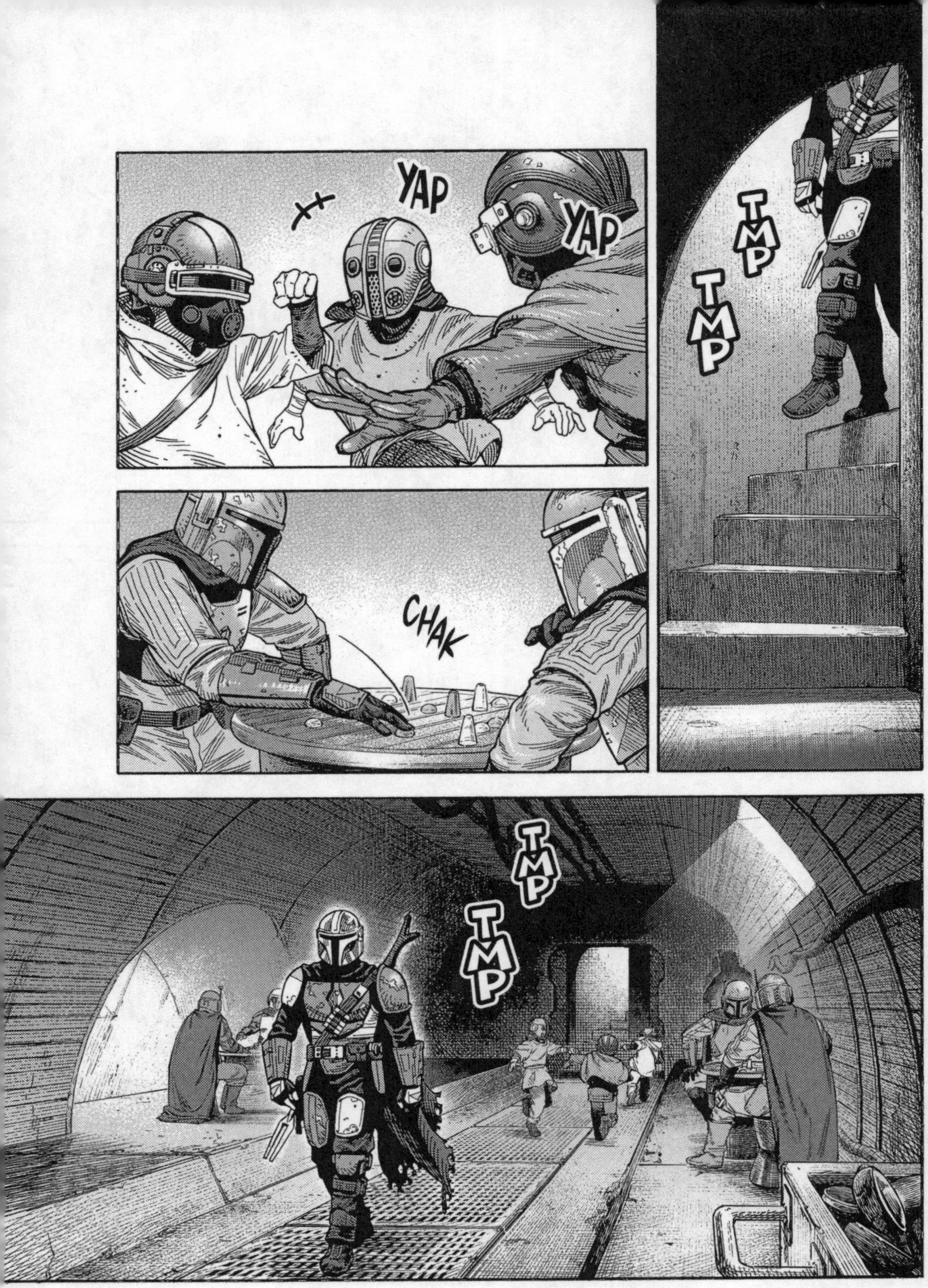
TMP
TMP
YAP
YAP
CHAK
TMP
TMP

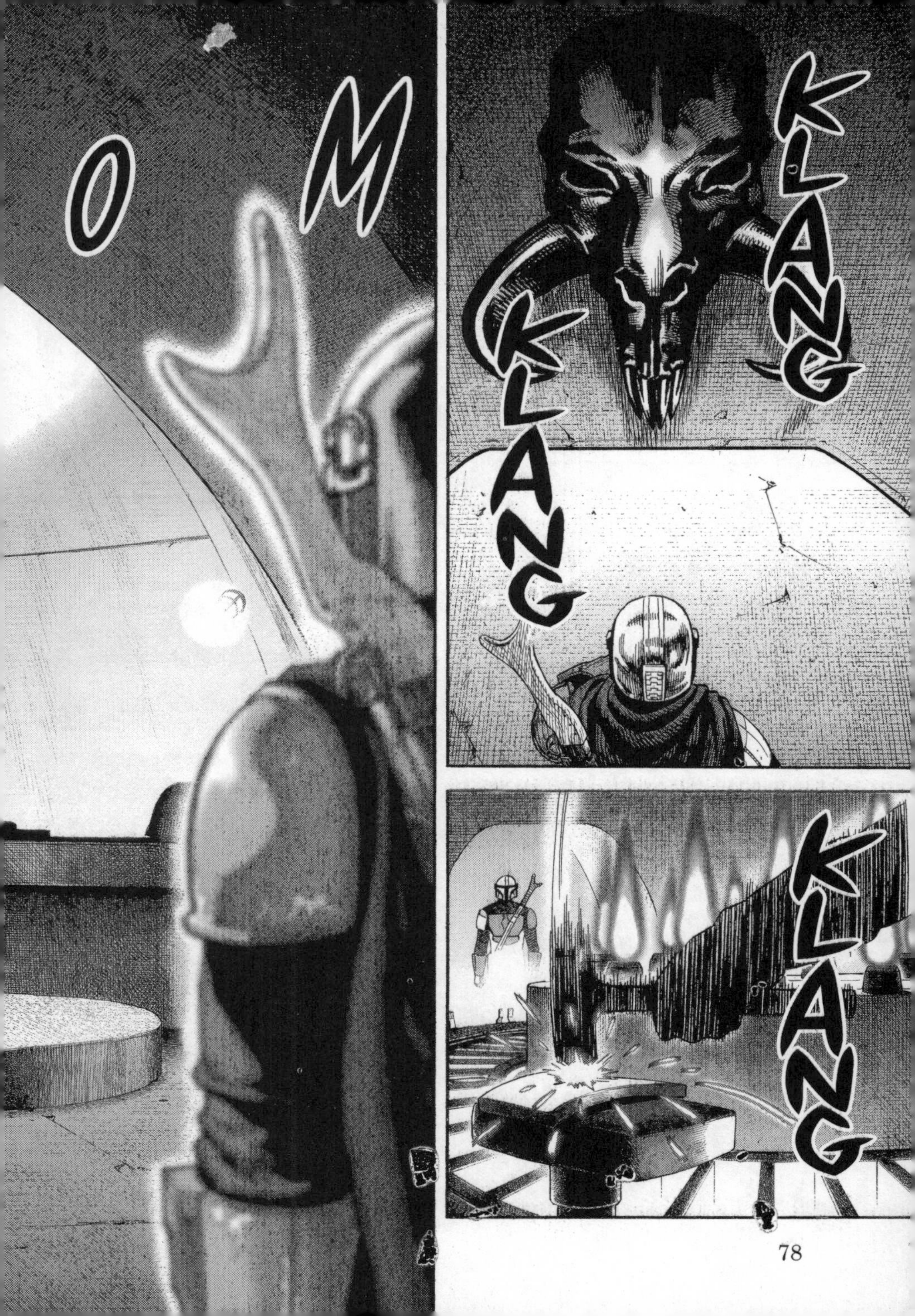
KLANG
KLANG
KLANG
O M

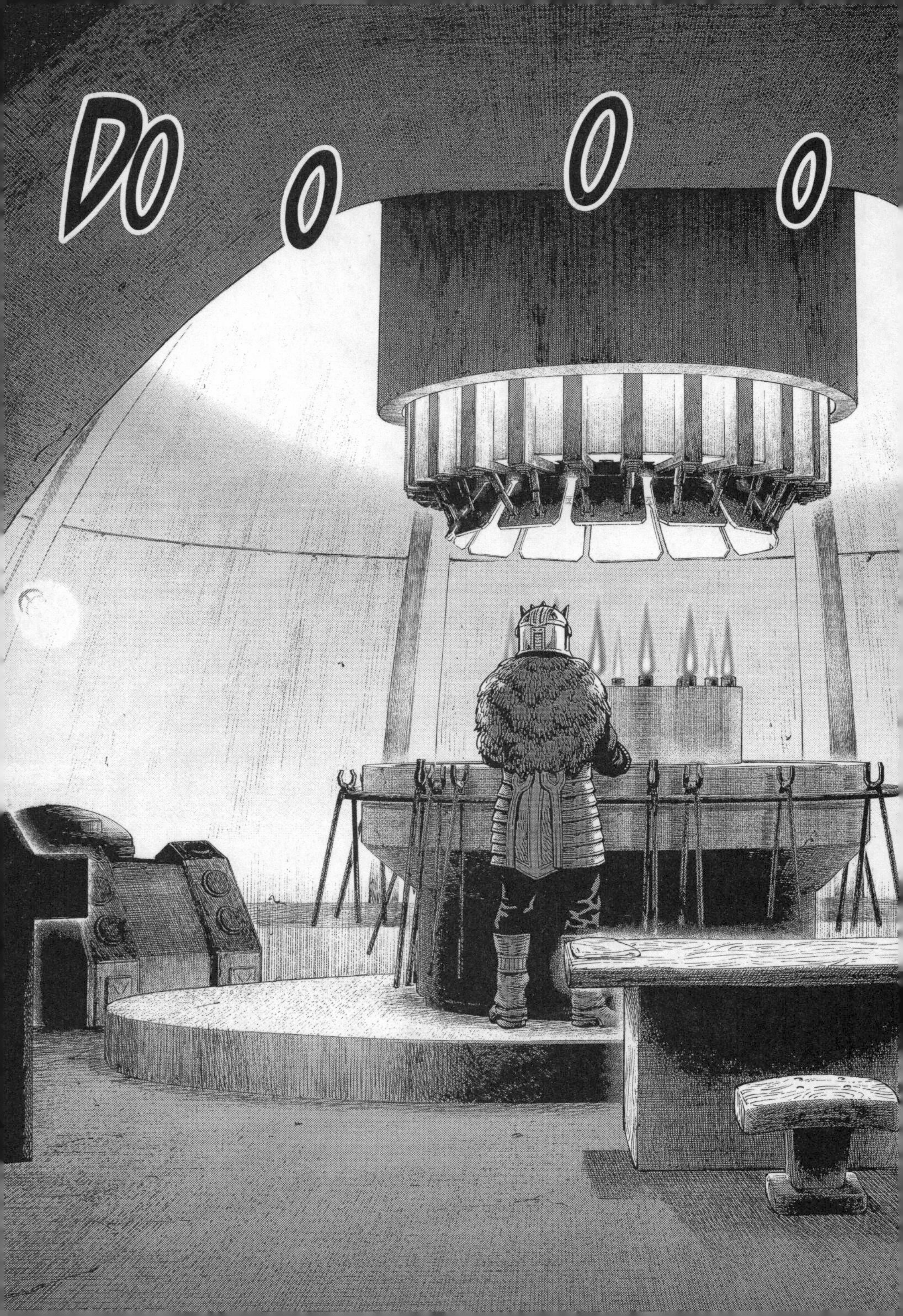
DO O O O

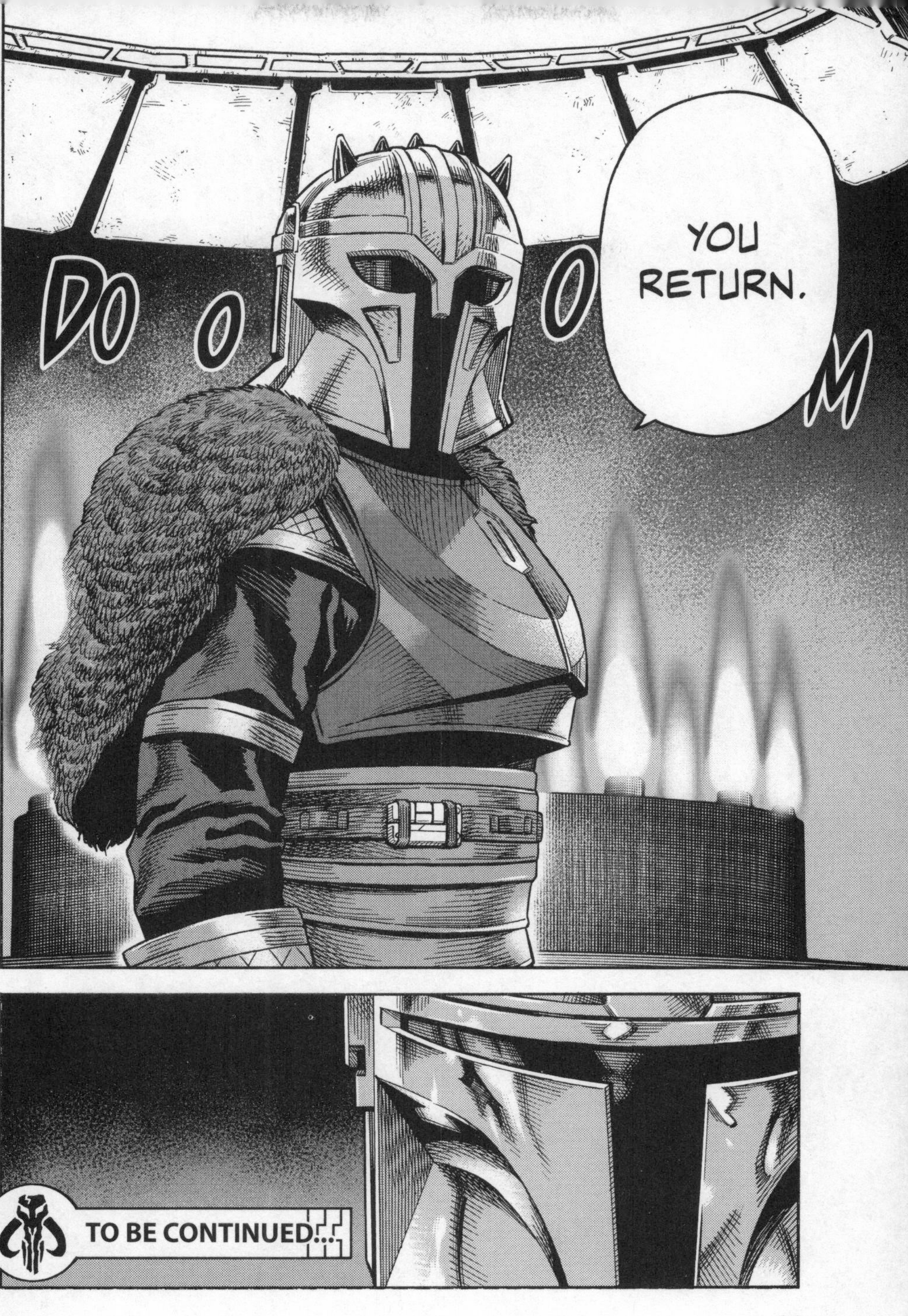
YOU RETURN.
DOOOOM
TO BE CONTINUED...

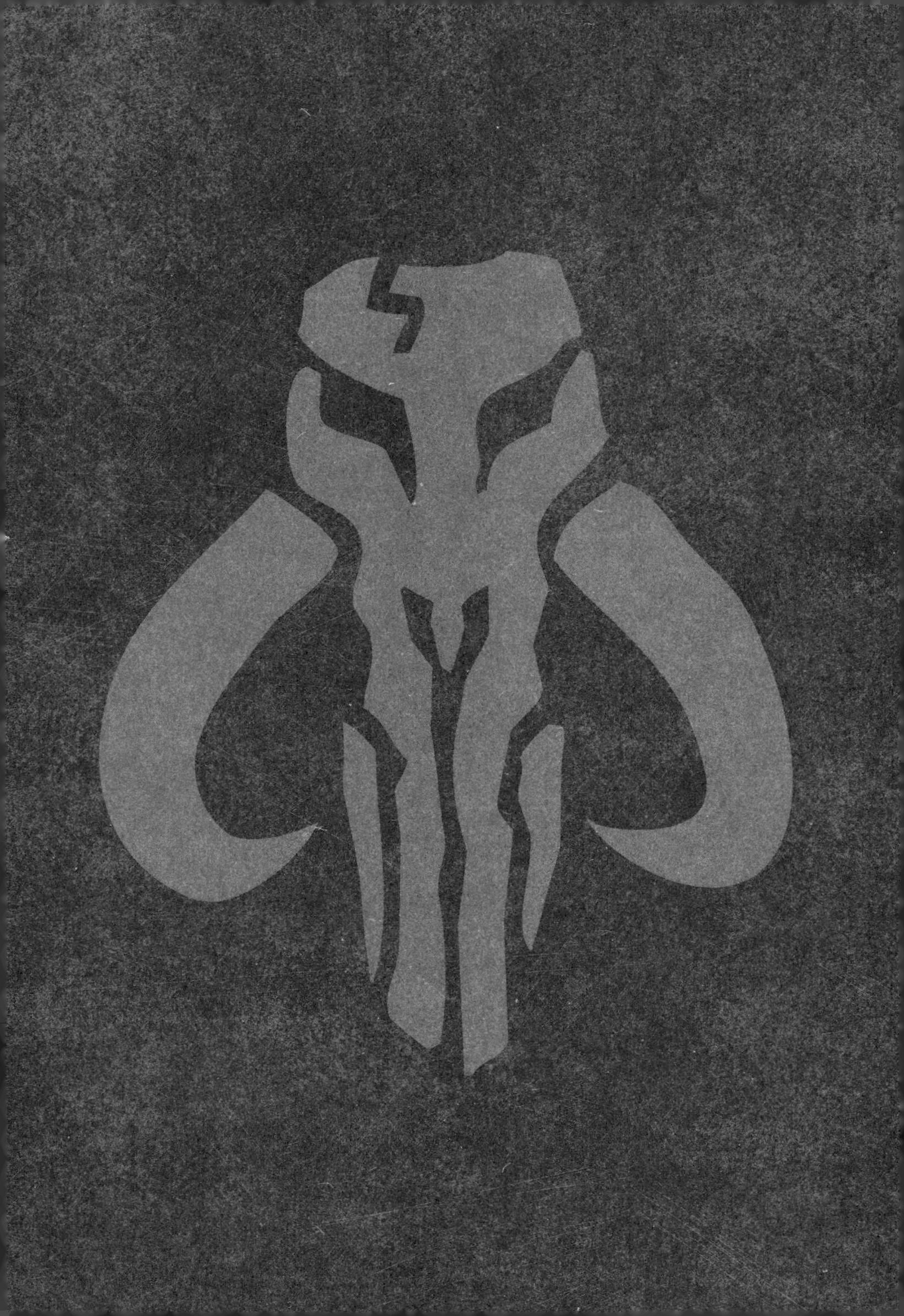

STAR·WARS

THE

MANDALORIAN

THE MANGA

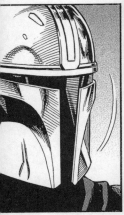

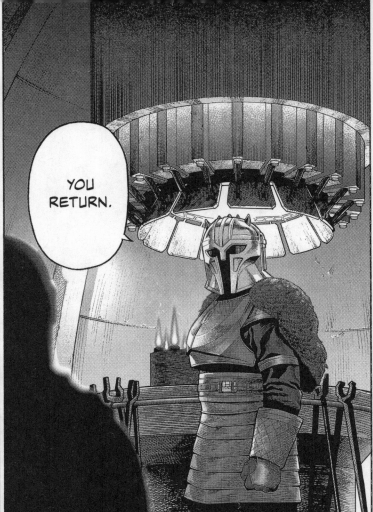

YOU RETURN.

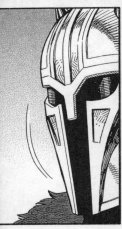

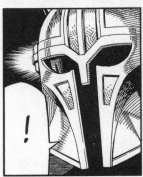

!

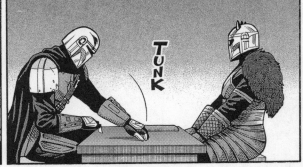

TUNK

Episode. 03

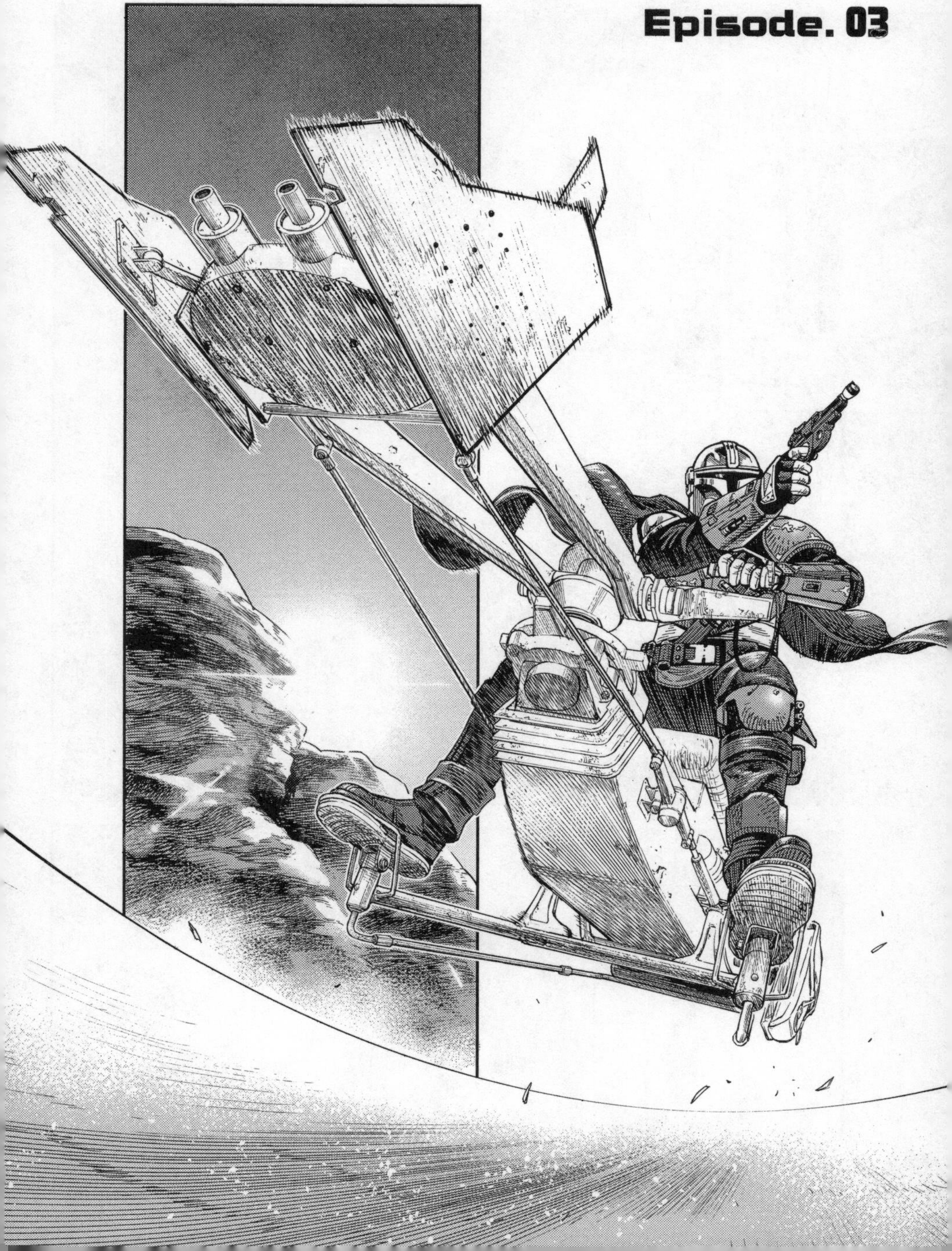

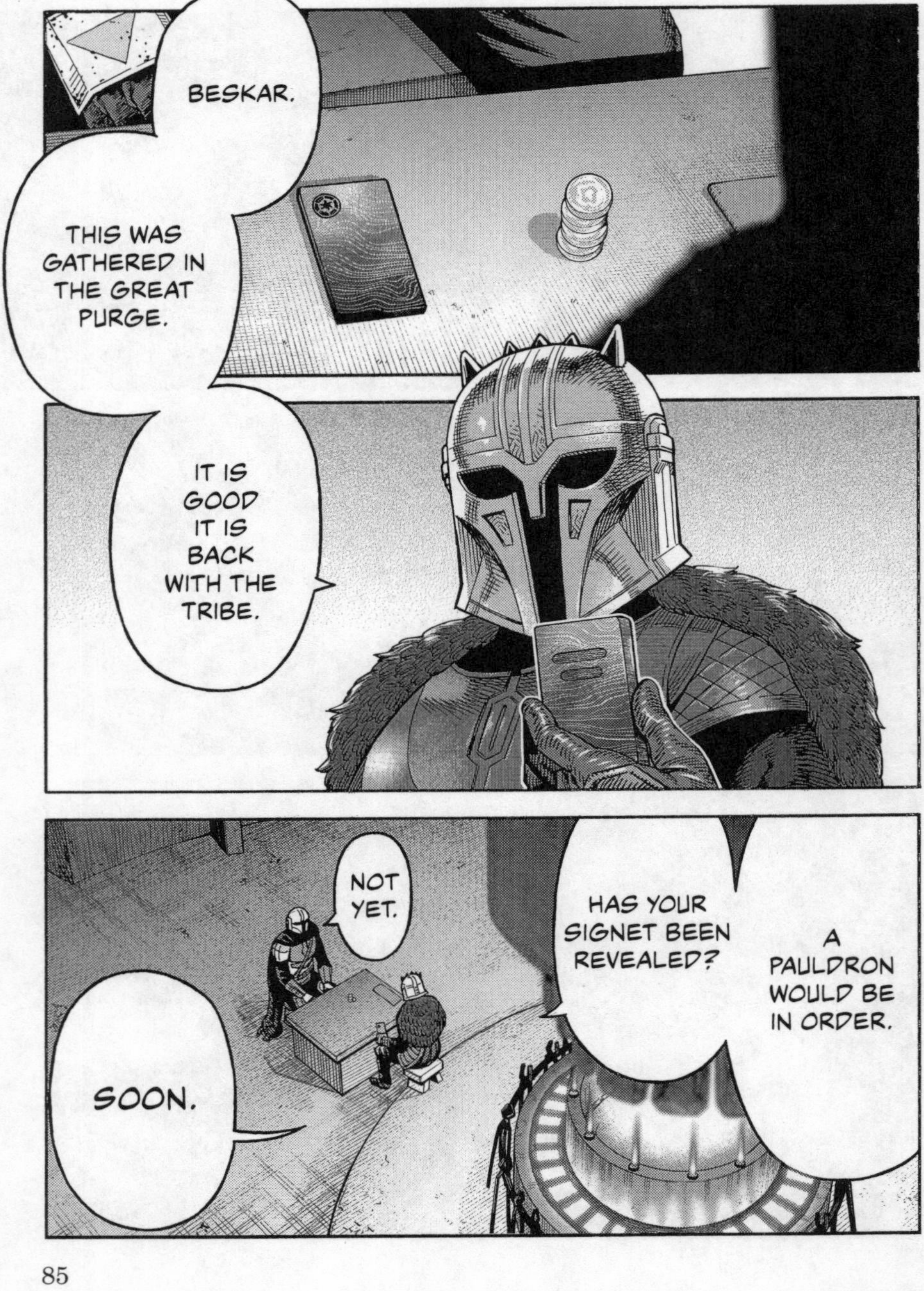
BESKAR.
THIS WAS GATHERED IN THE GREAT PURGE.
IT IS GOOD IT IS BACK WITH THE TRIBE.
A PAULDRON WOULD BE IN ORDER.
HAS YOUR SIGNET BEEN REVEALED?
NOT YET.
SOON.

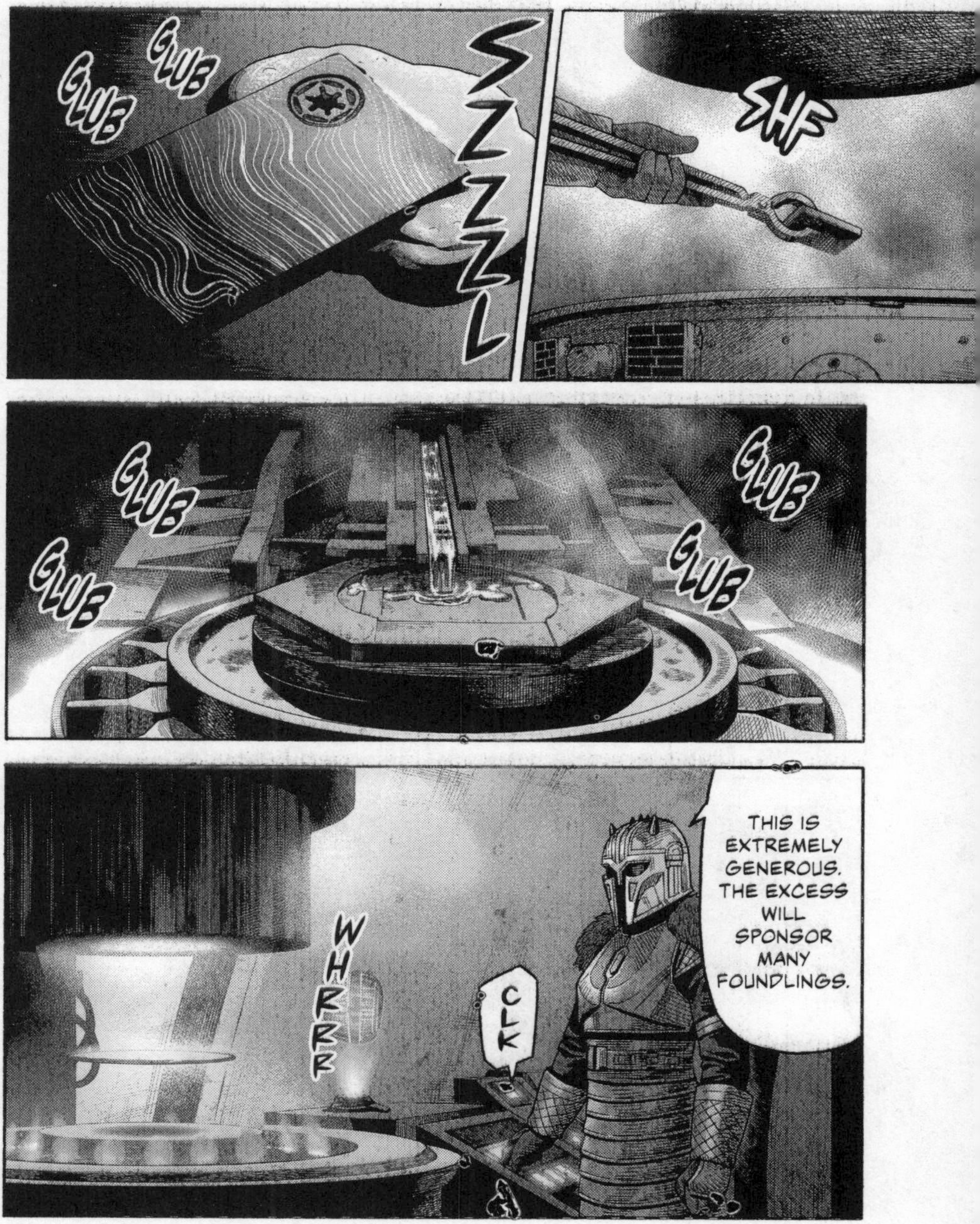
SHF
SZZZL
GLUB
GLUB
GLUB
GLUB
GLUB
GLUB
THIS IS EXTREMELY GENEROUS. THE EXCESS WILL SPONSOR MANY FOUNDLINGS.
CLK
WHRRR

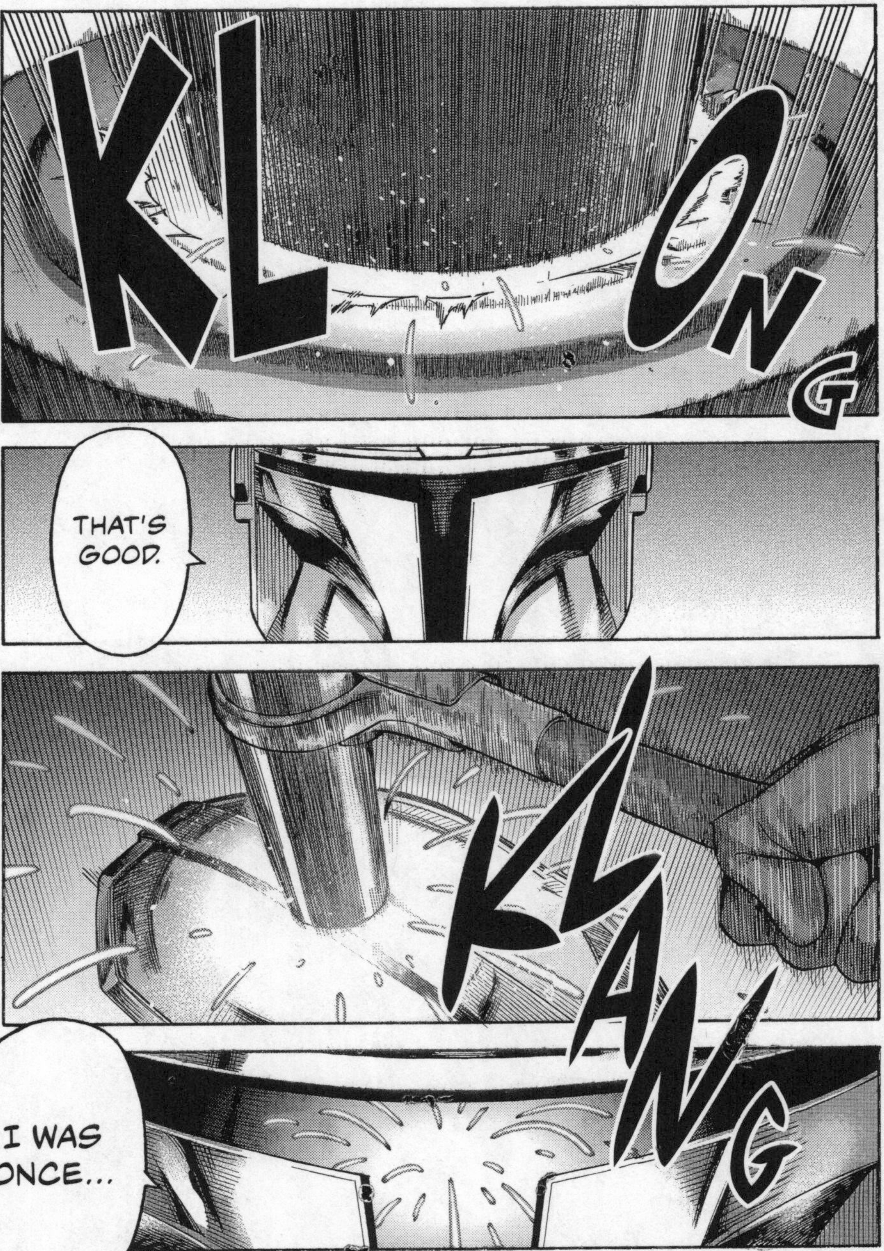
KLONG
THAT'S GOOD.
KLANG
I WAS ONCE...

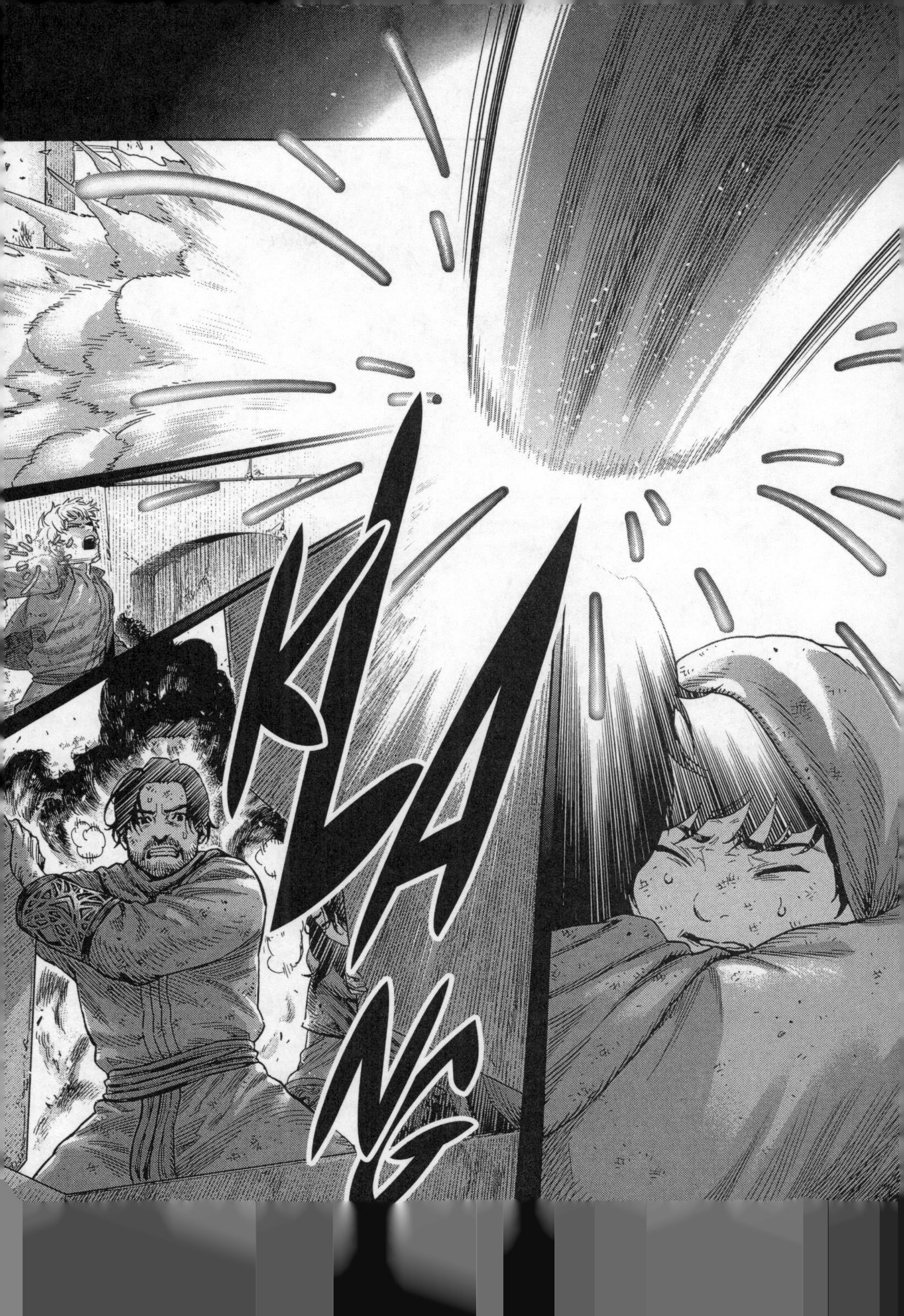
KLANG

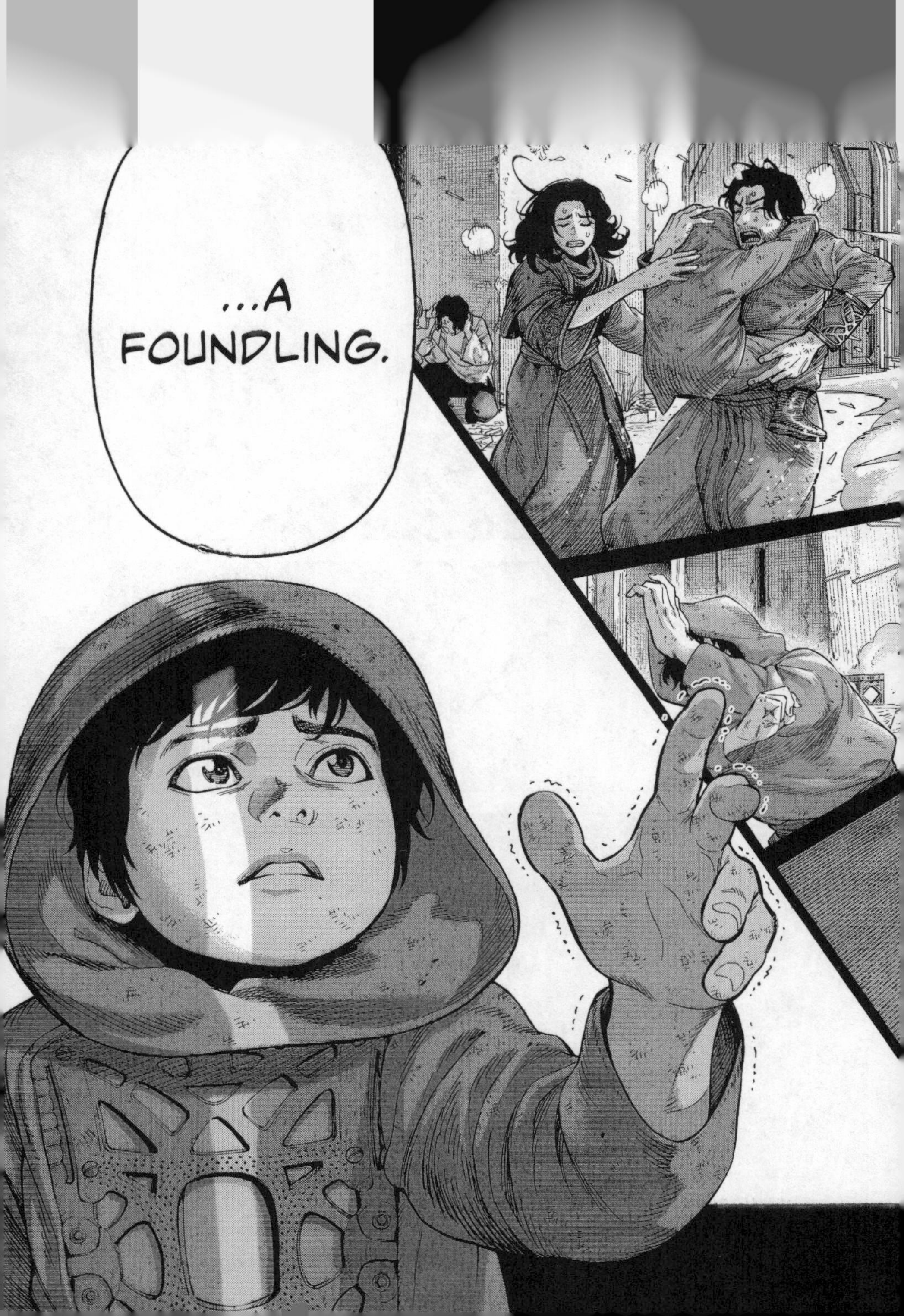
...A FOUNDLING.

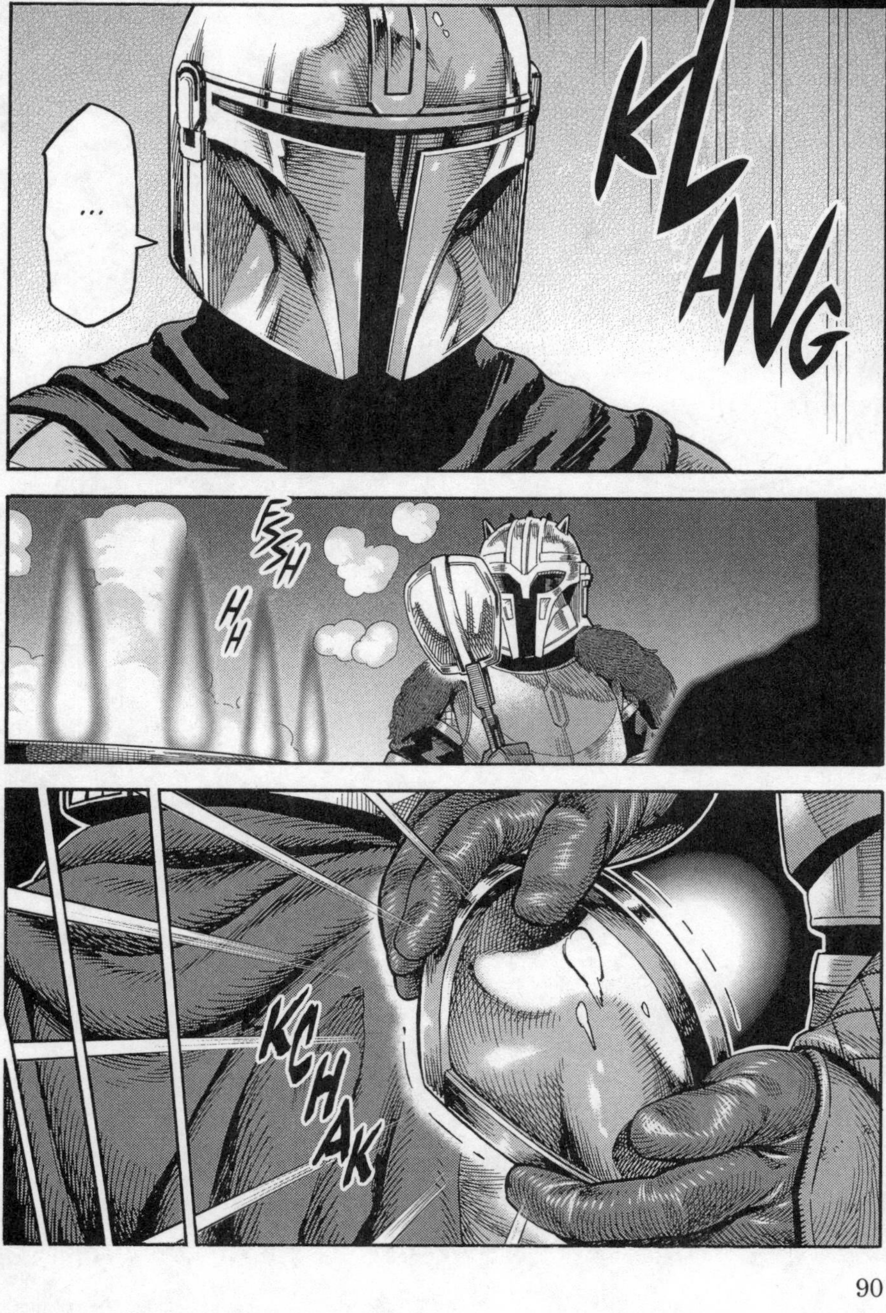
KLANG
...
FSSHHH
KCHAK

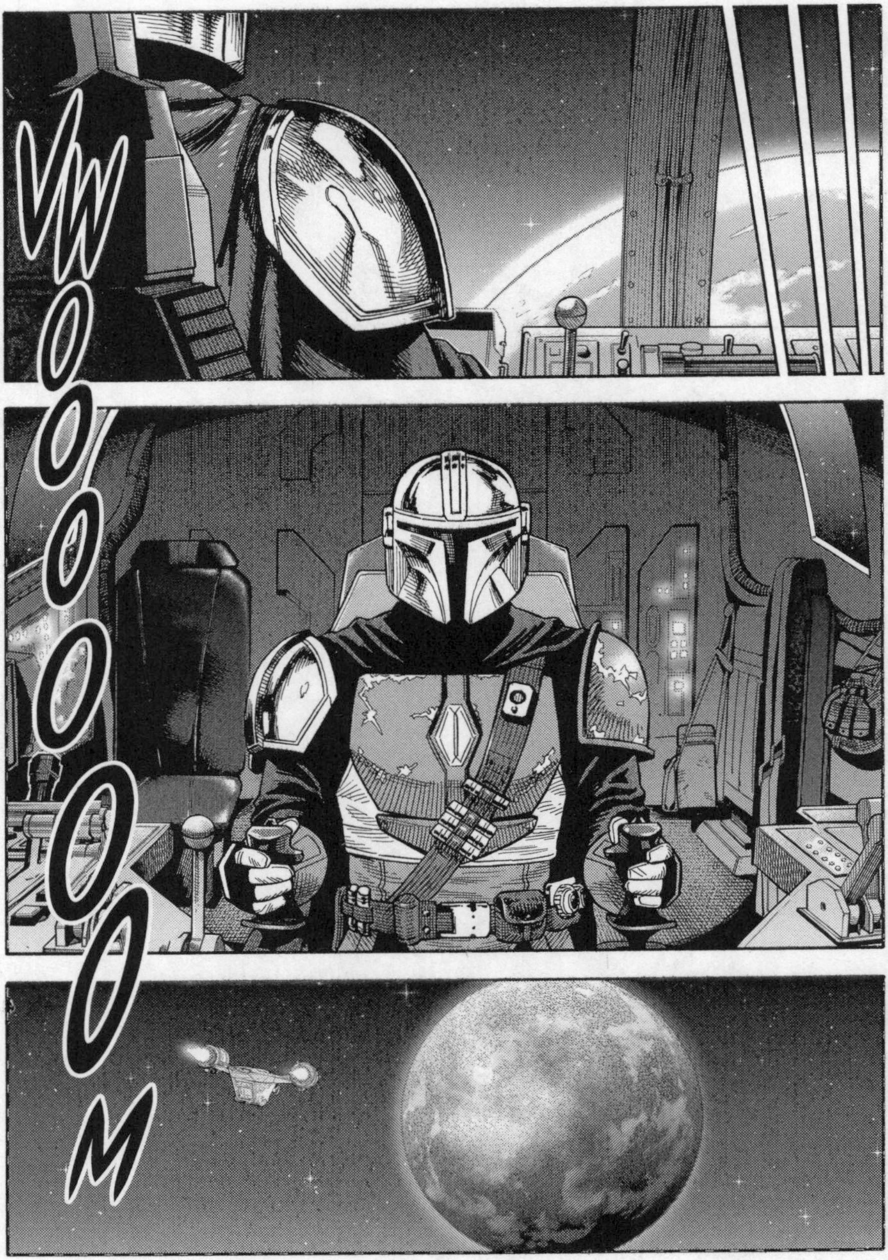
VWOOOOOOOOM

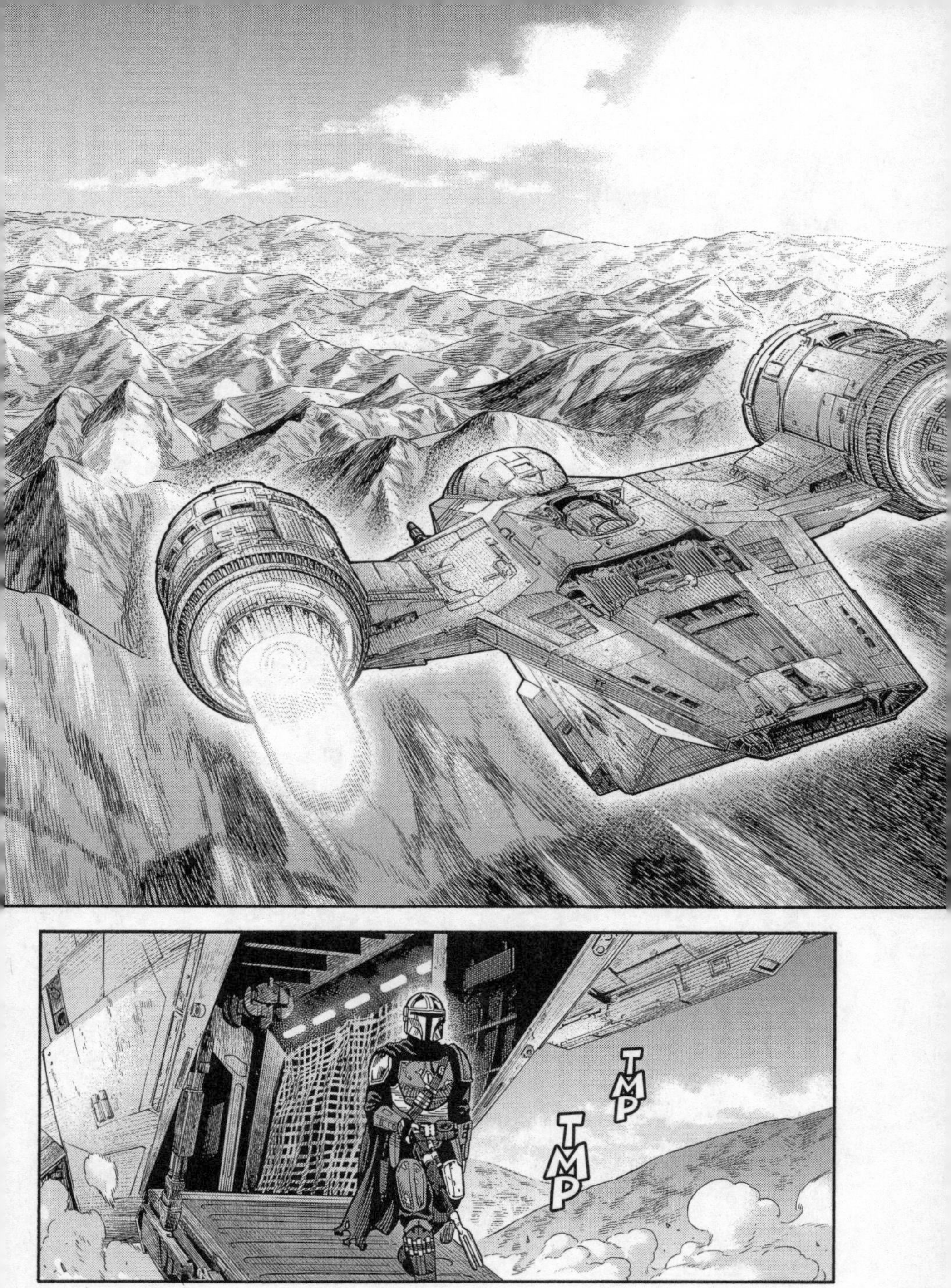
TMP
TMP

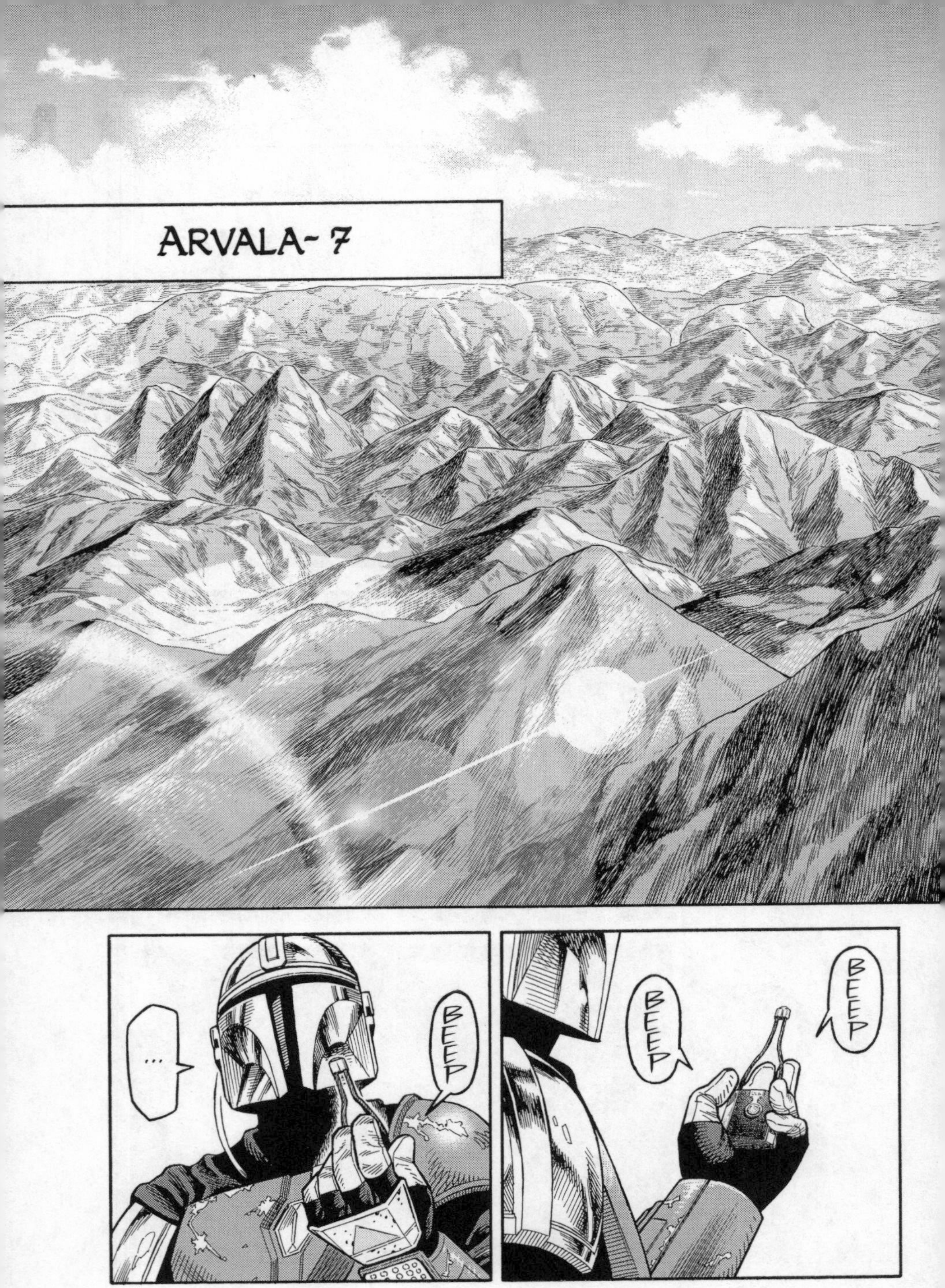
ARVALA- 7
BEEP
BEEP
BEEP
...

CHK
VEEEEEEN
...
FWP

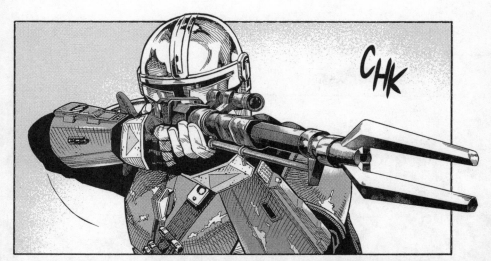

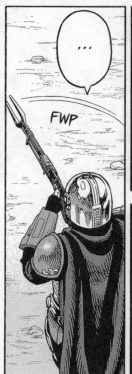

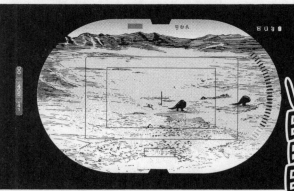

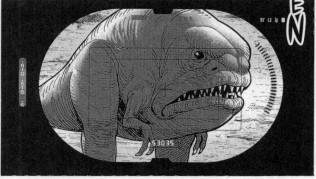

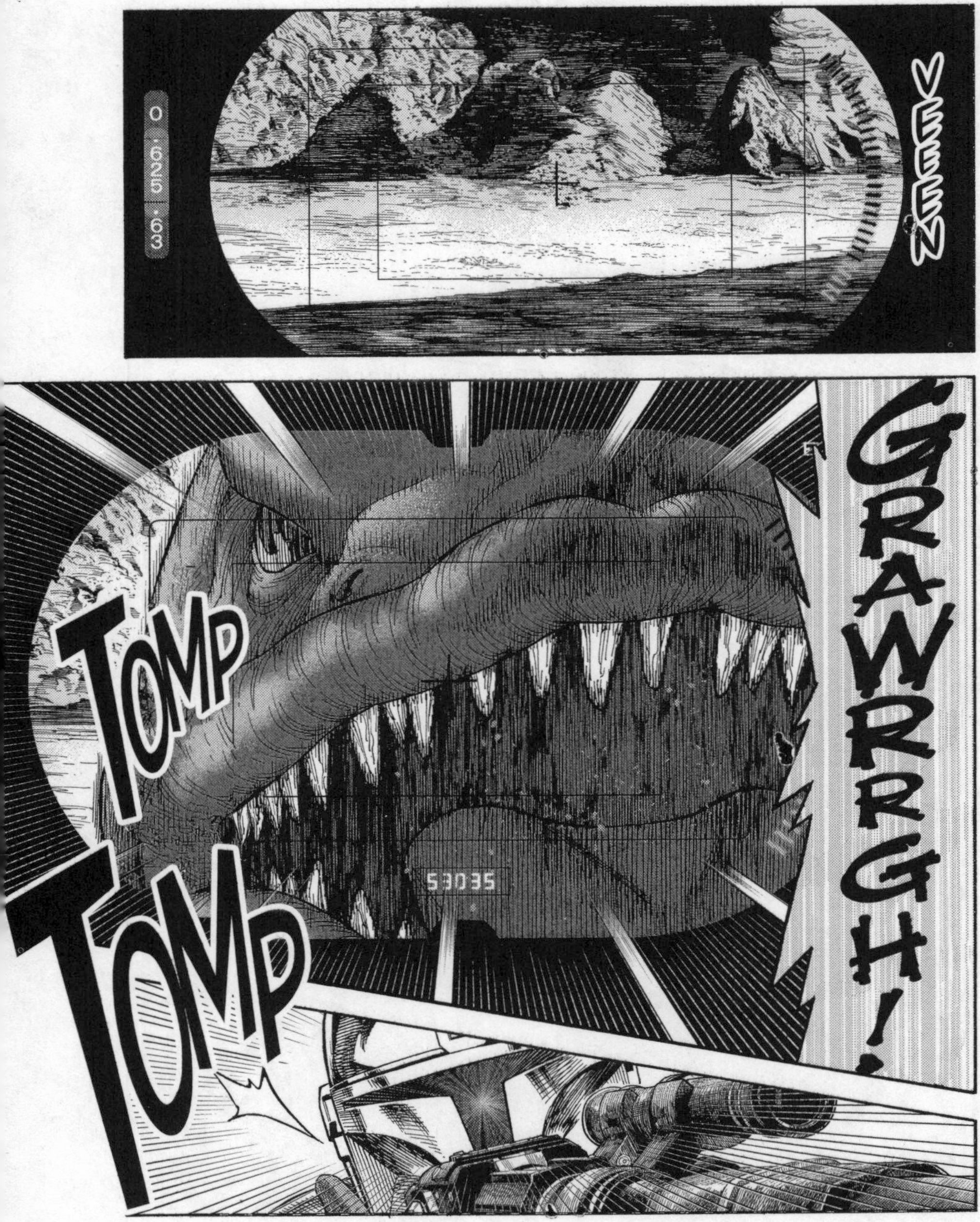
0 · 625 · 63
VEEEN
GRAWRRGH!
53035
TOMP
TOMP

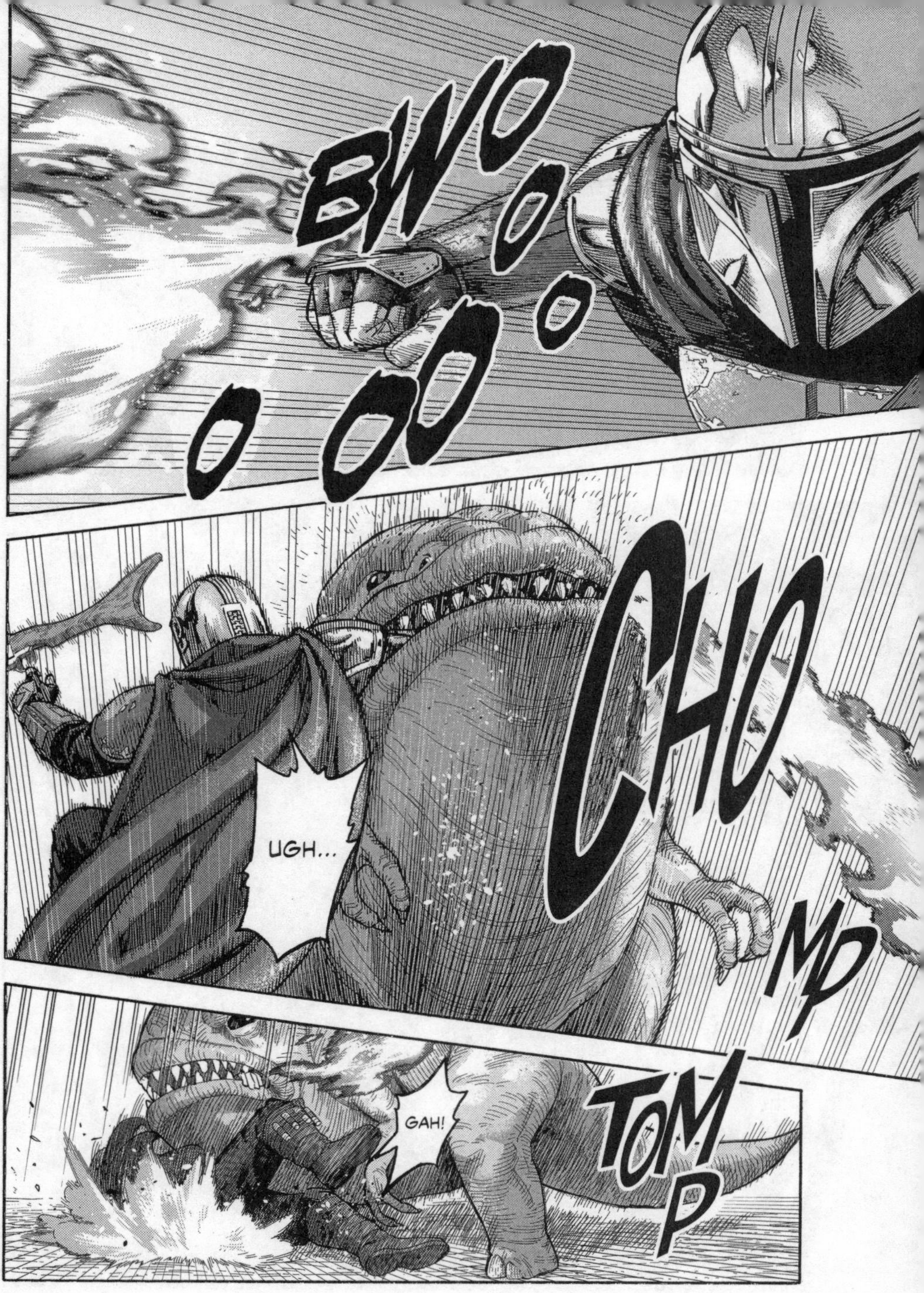
BWOOOOOOO
CHOMP
UGH...
TOMP
GAH!

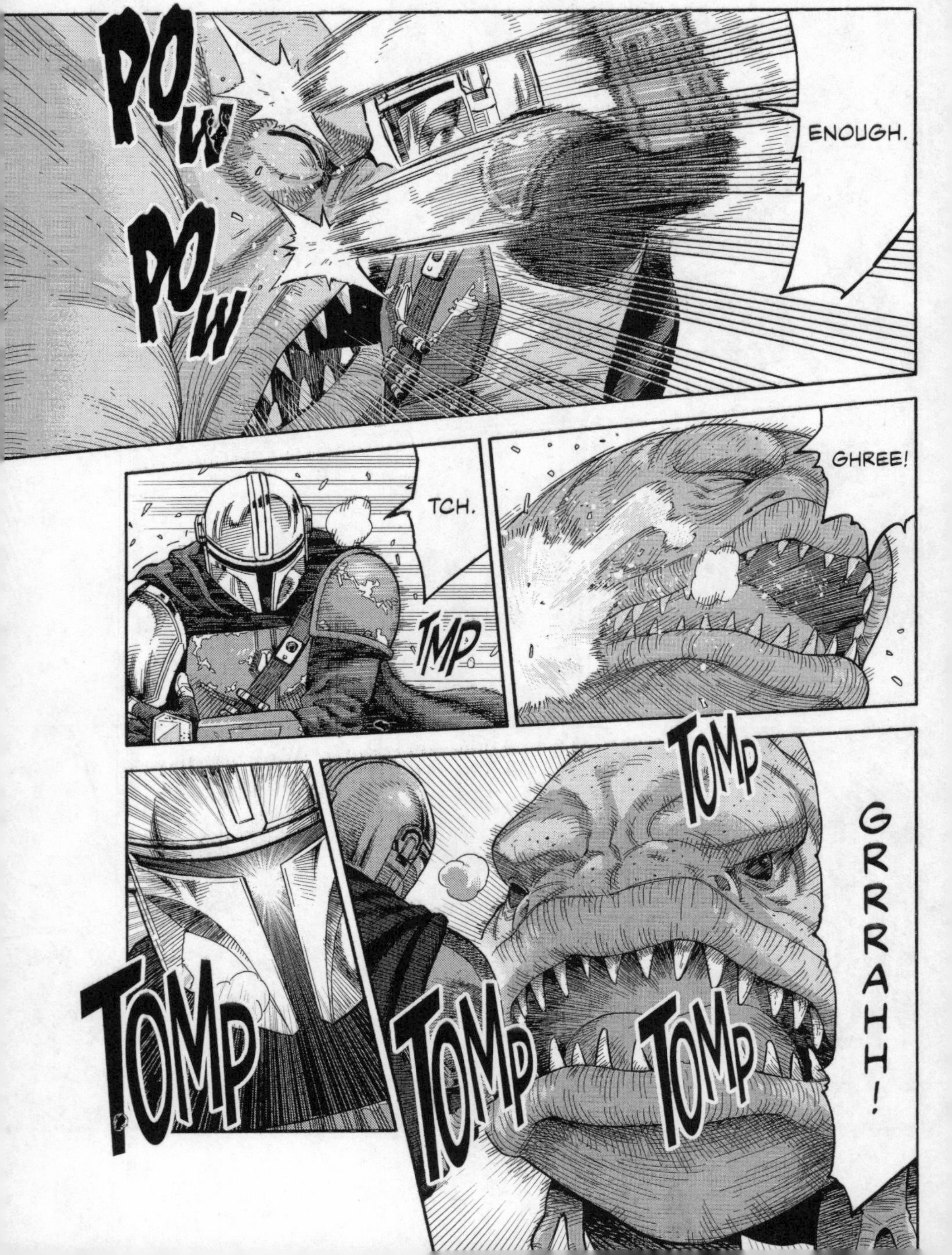
ENOUGH.
POW
POW
GHREE!
TCH.
TMP
GRRRAHH!
TOMP
TOMP
TOMP
TOMP

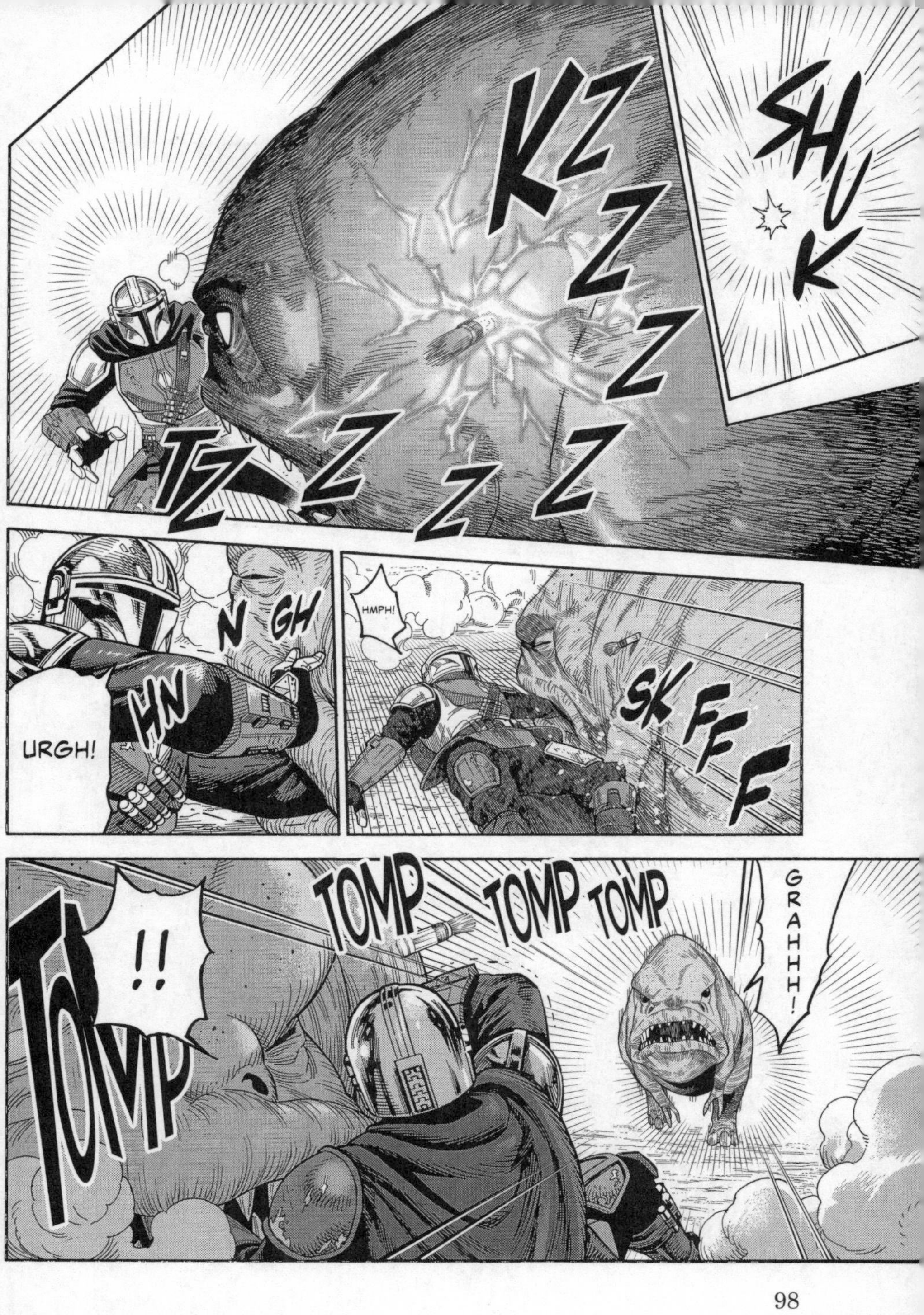
SHUK
KZZZZZ
TZZZZZ
HMPH!
SKFFF
NGH
HN
URGH!
GRAHHH!
TOMP TOMP TOMP
!!
TOMP

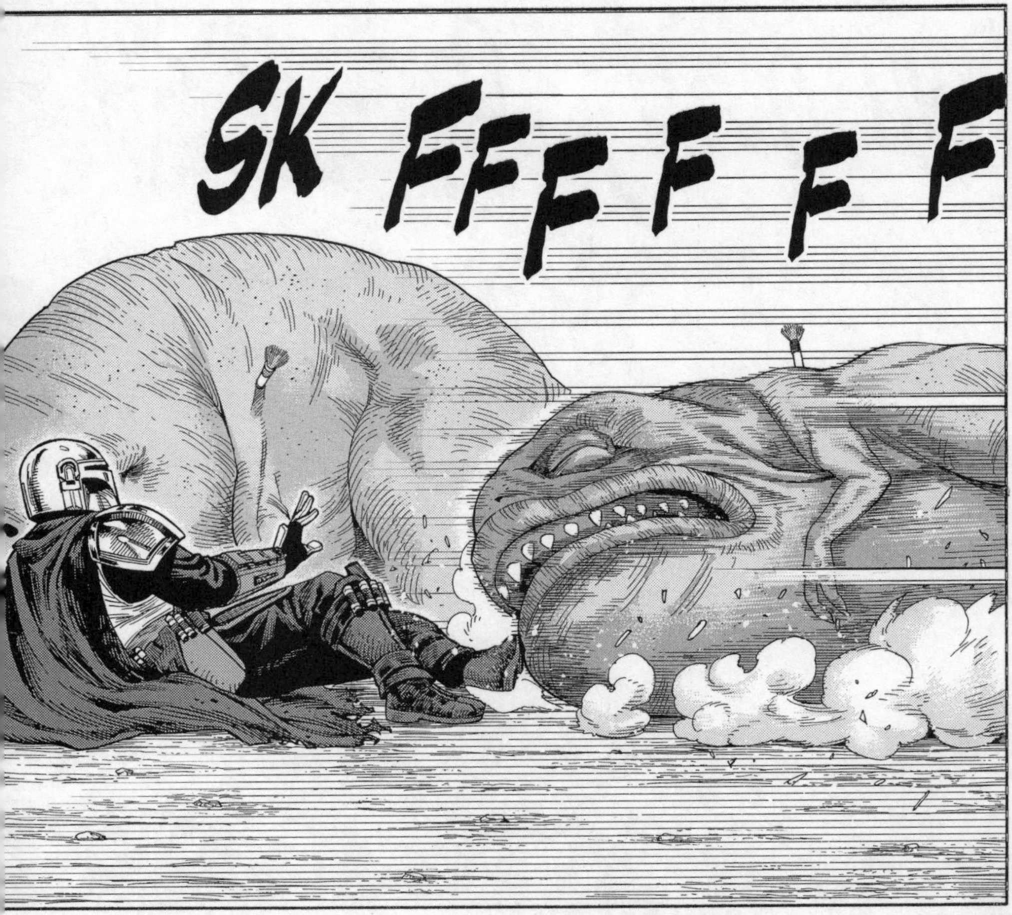
SK FFFF F F F

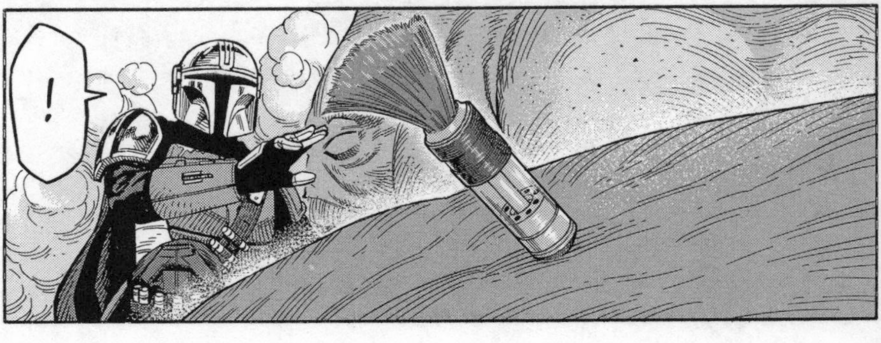
!

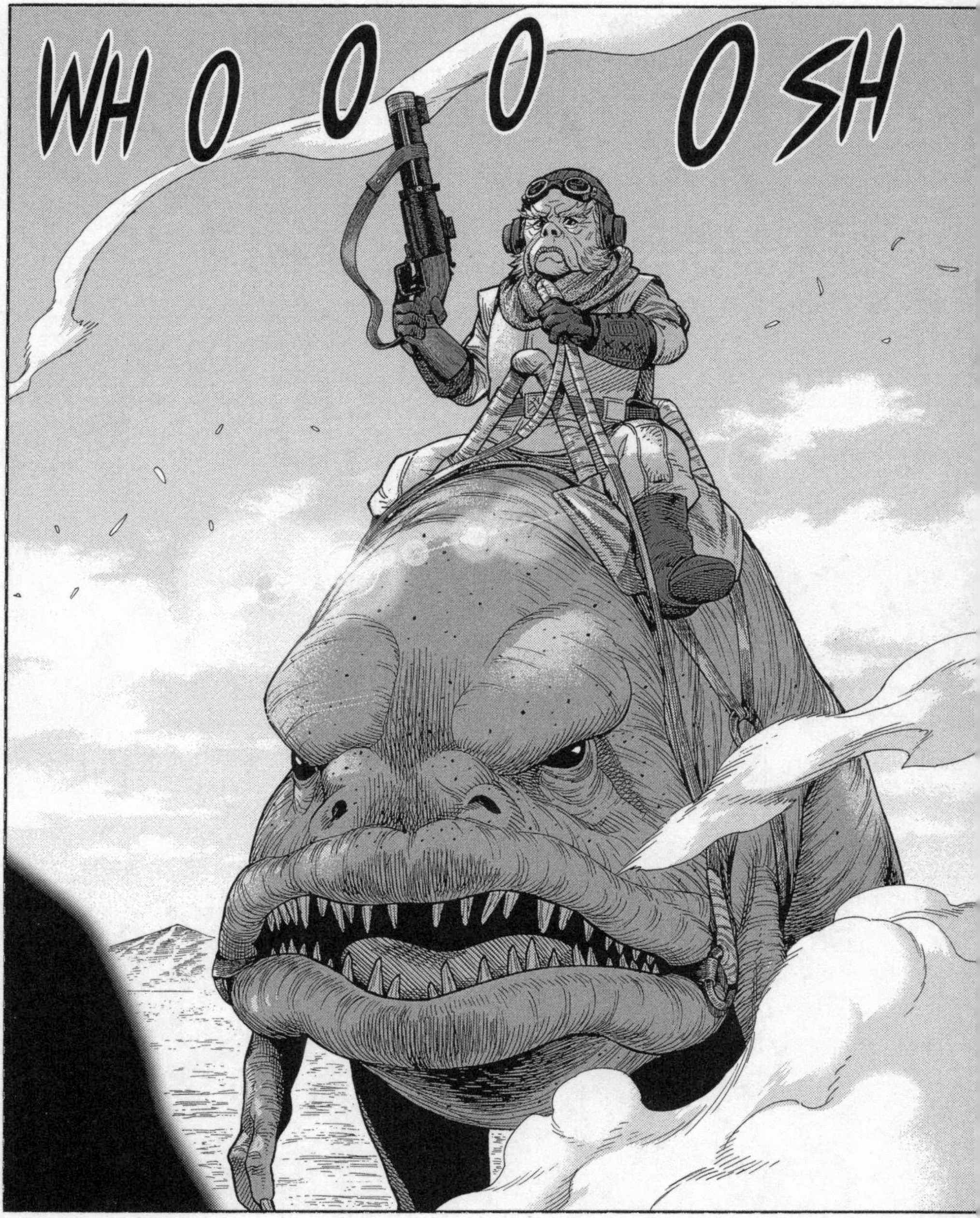
WHOOOOOSH

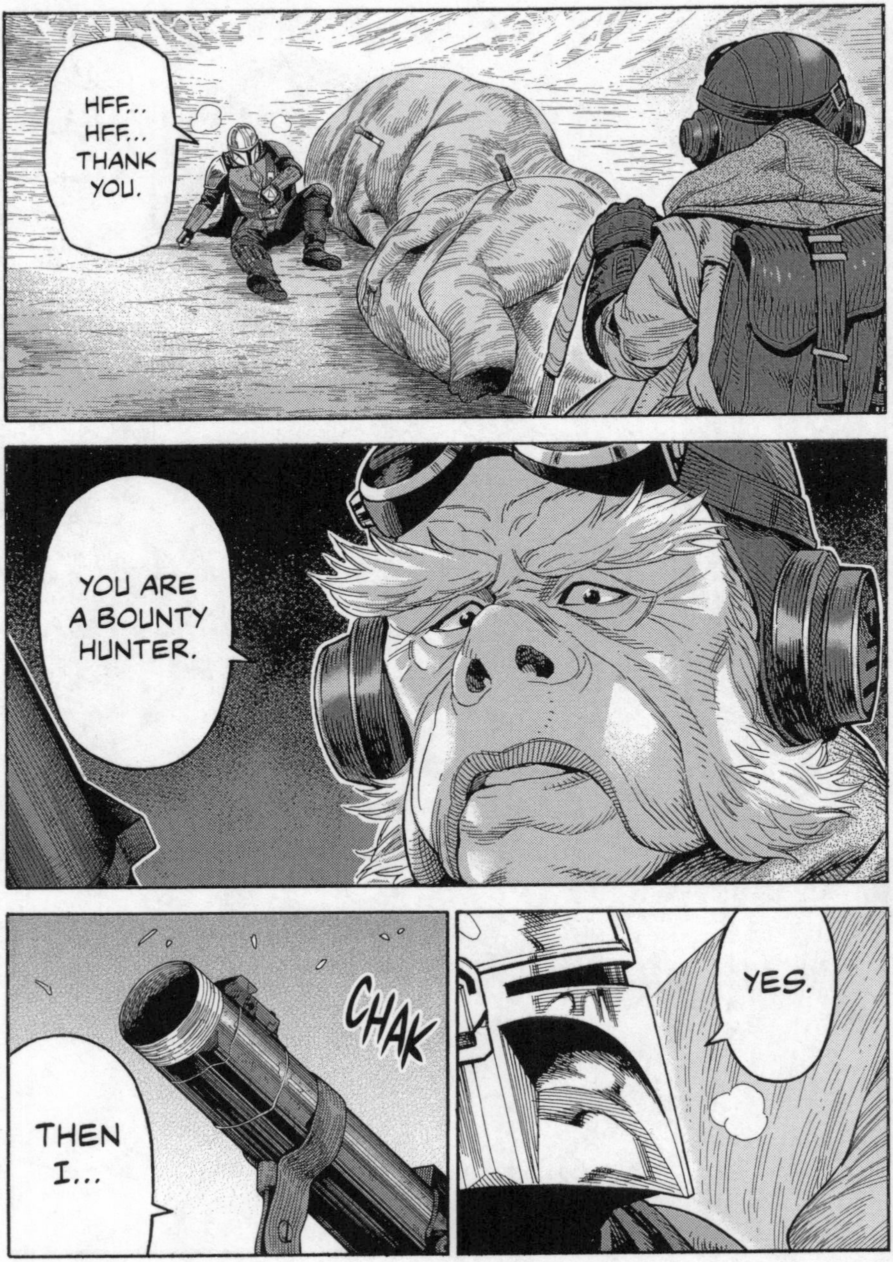
HFF... HFF... THANK YOU.
YOU ARE A BOUNTY HUNTER.
YES.
CHAK
THEN I...

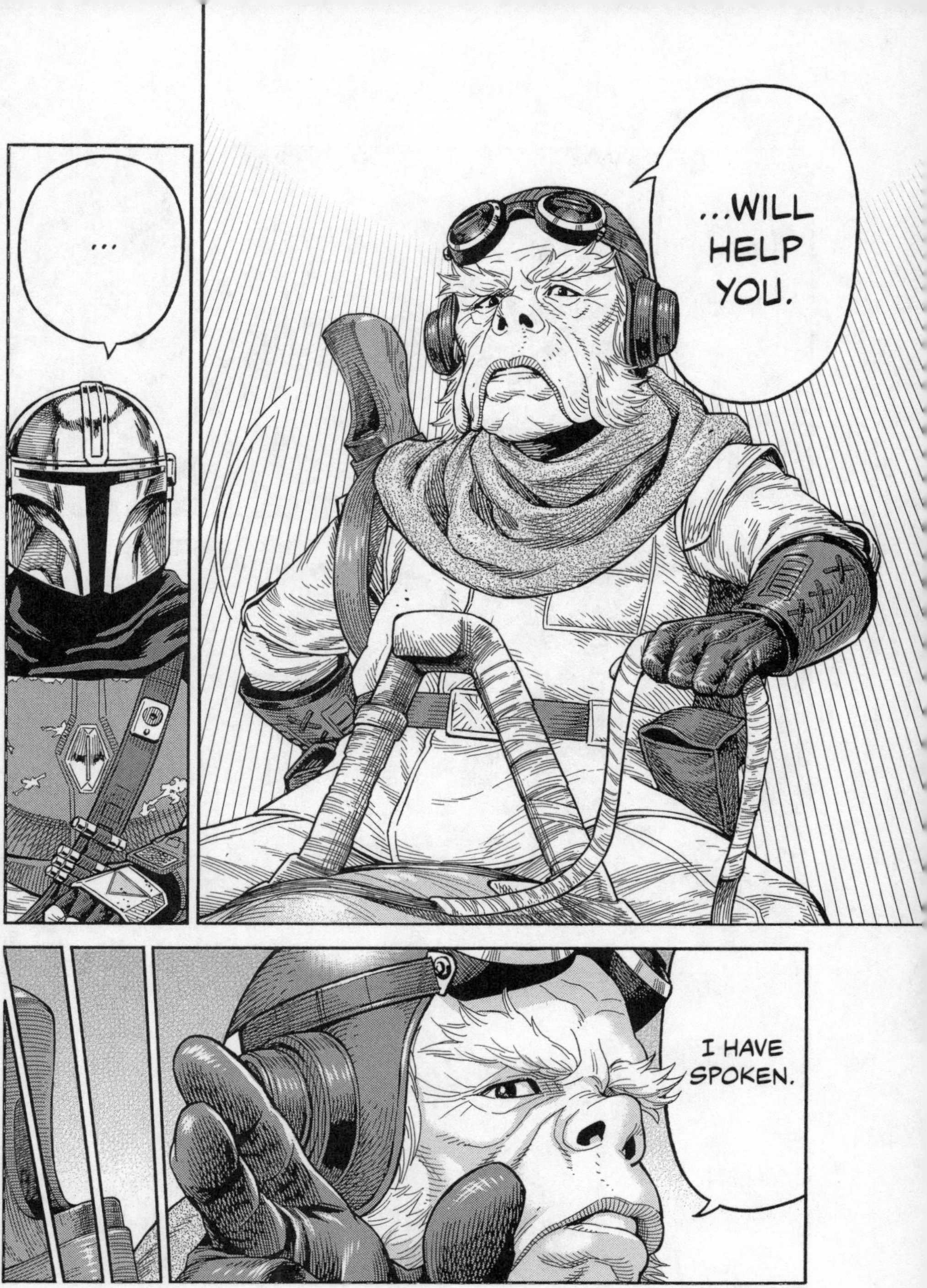
...WILL HELP YOU.
...
I HAVE SPOKEN.

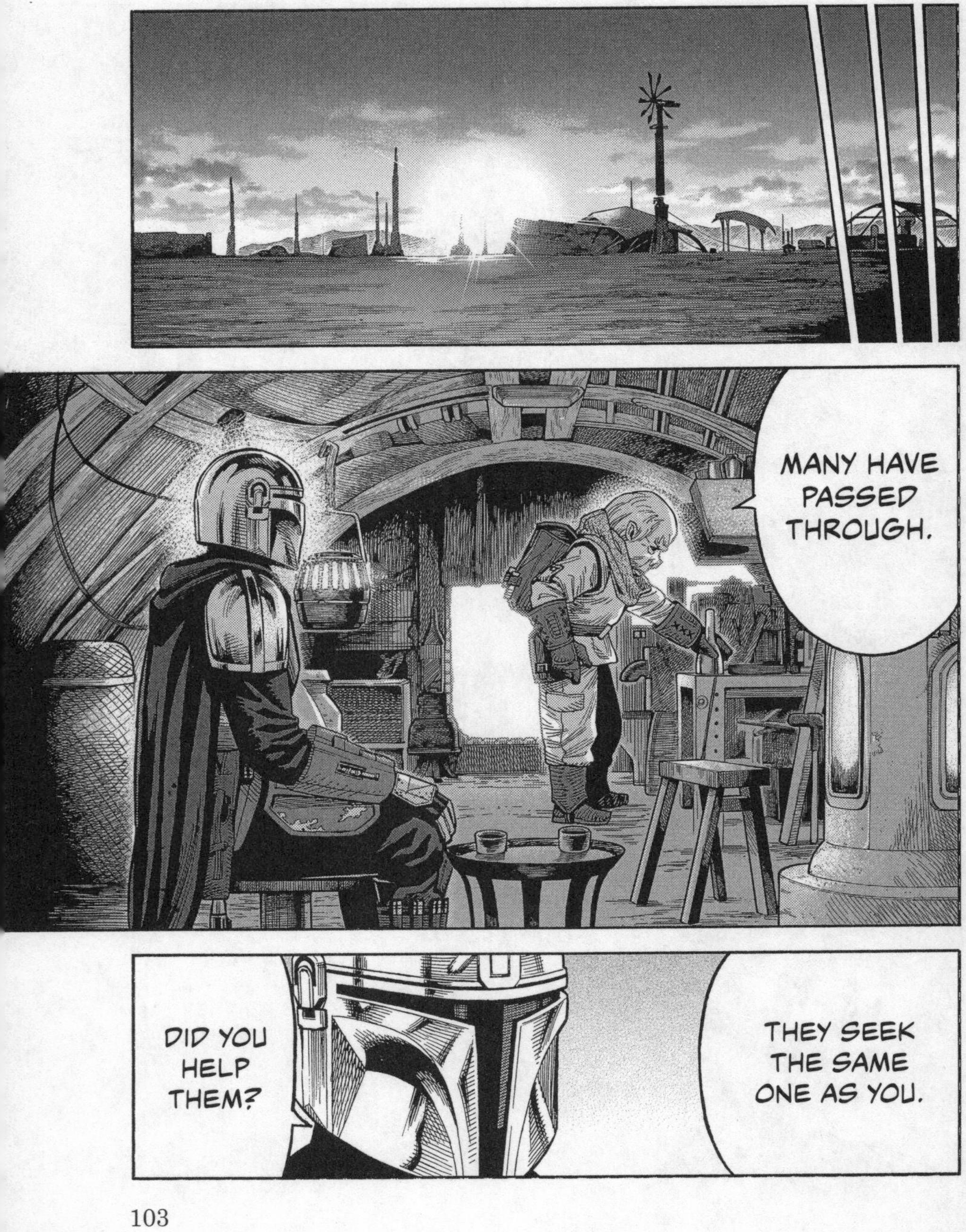
MANY HAVE PASSED THROUGH.
THEY SEEK THE SAME ONE AS YOU.
DID YOU HELP THEM?

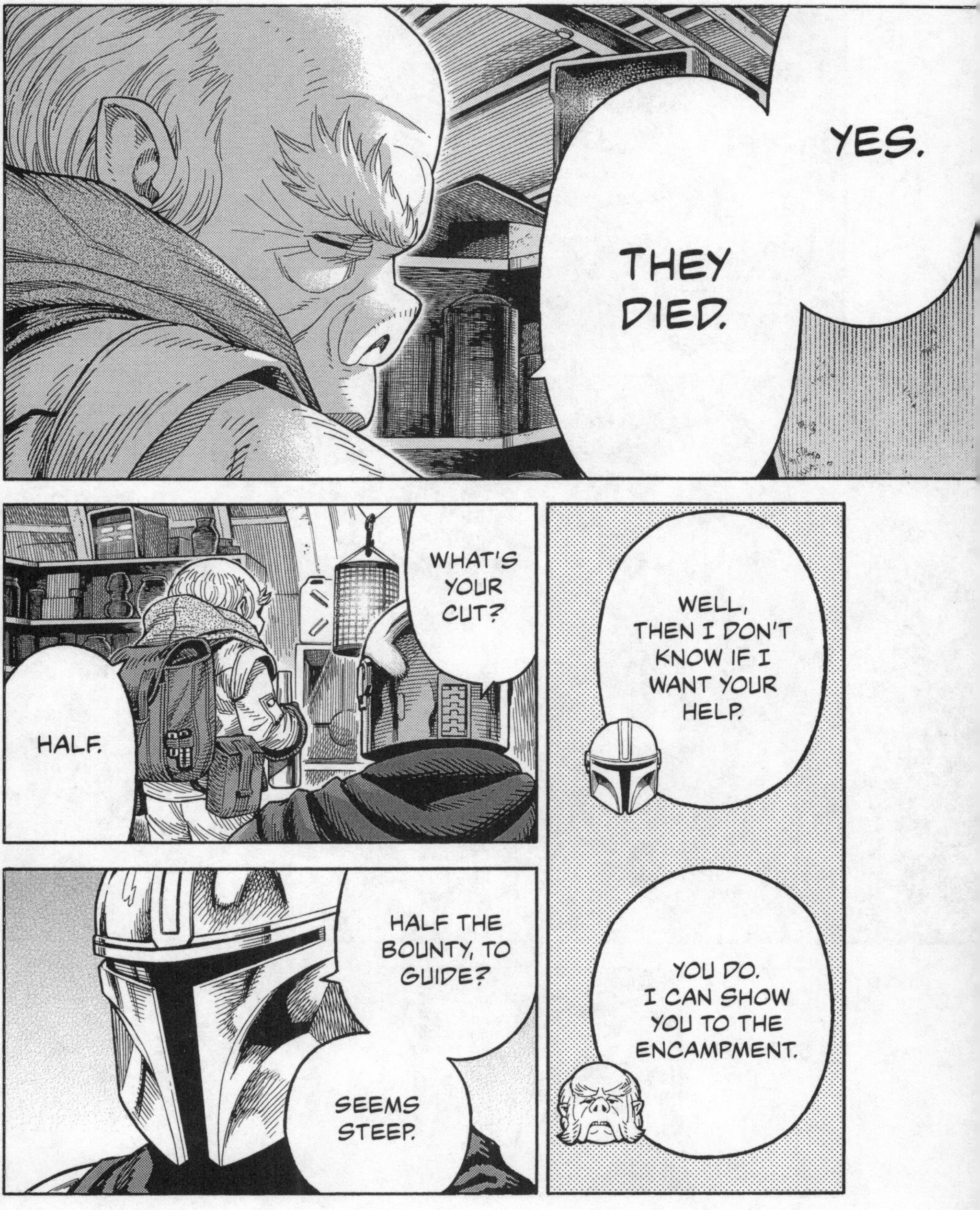
YES.
THEY DIED.
WELL, THEN I DON'T KNOW IF I WANT YOUR HELP.
YOU DO. I CAN SHOW YOU TO THE ENCAMPMENT.
WHAT'S YOUR CUT?
HALF.
HALF THE BOUNTY, TO GUIDE?
SEEMS STEEP.

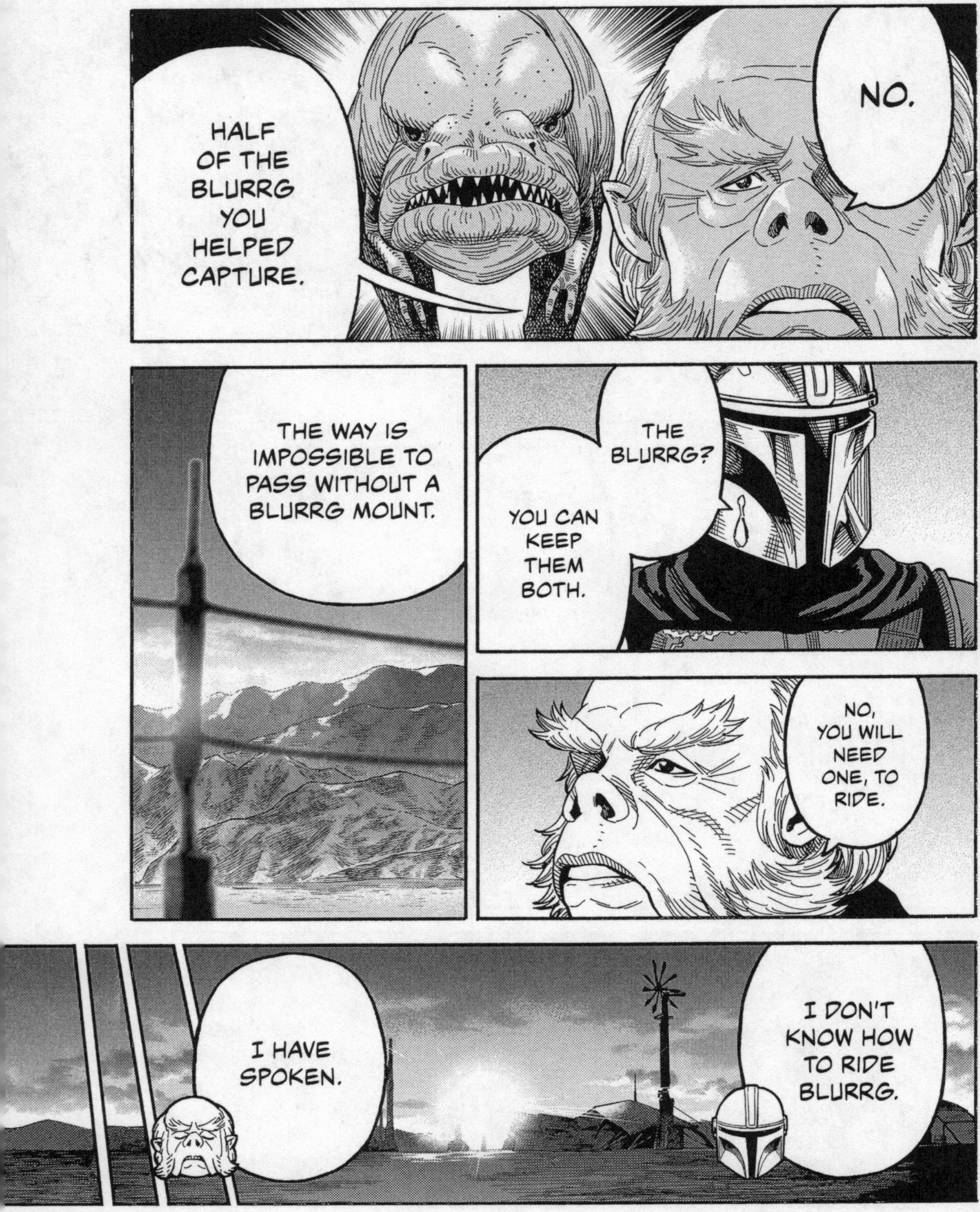
NO.
HALF OF THE BLURRG YOU HELPED CAPTURE.
THE BLURRG?
YOU CAN KEEP THEM BOTH.
NO, YOU WILL NEED ONE, TO RIDE.
THE WAY IS IMPOSSIBLE TO PASS WITHOUT A BLURRG MOUNT.
I DON'T KNOW HOW TO RIDE BLURRG.
I HAVE SPOKEN.

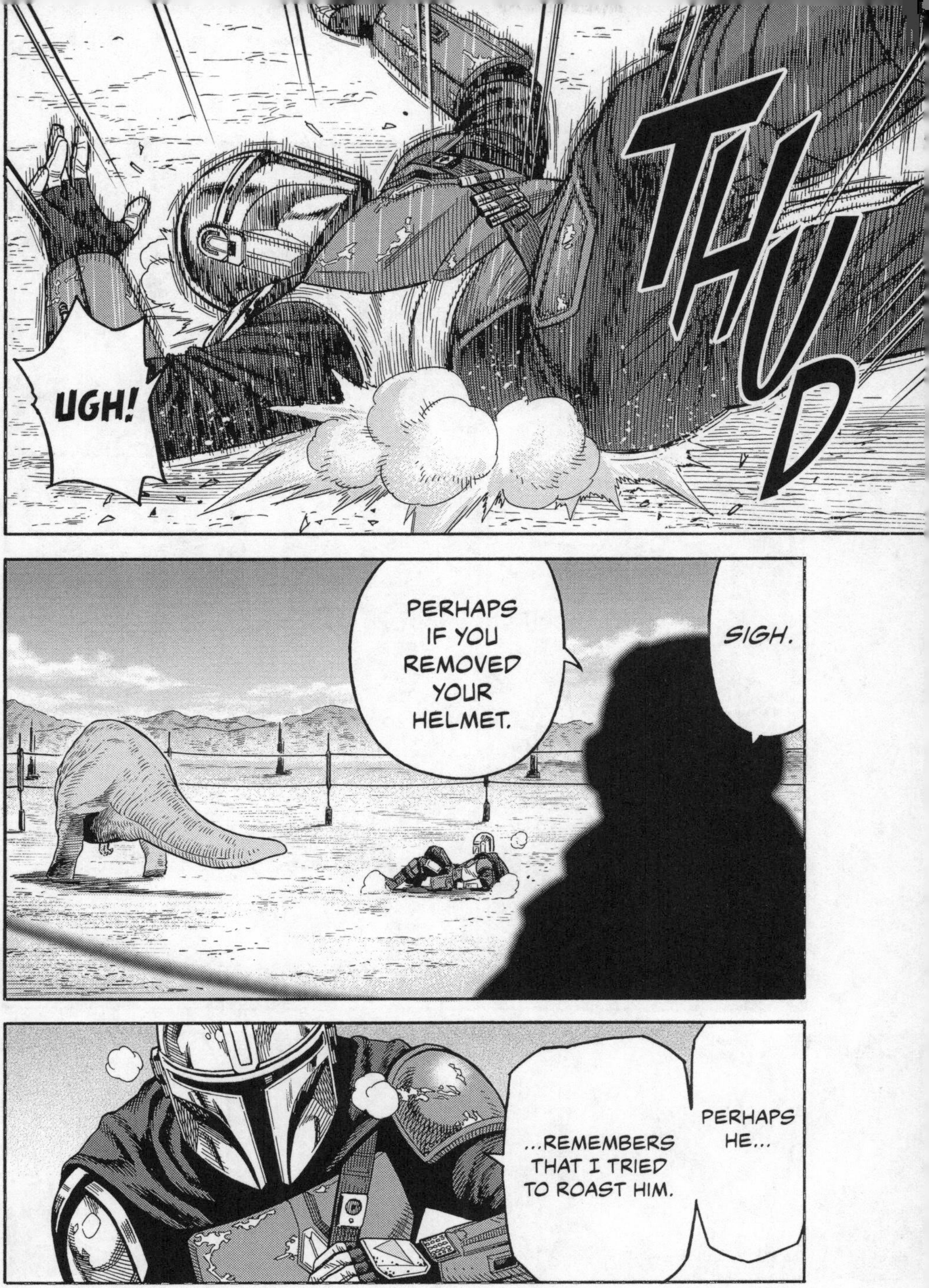
THUD
UGH!
SIGH.
PERHAPS IF YOU REMOVED YOUR HELMET.
PERHAPS HE...
...REMEMBERS THAT I TRIED TO ROAST HIM.

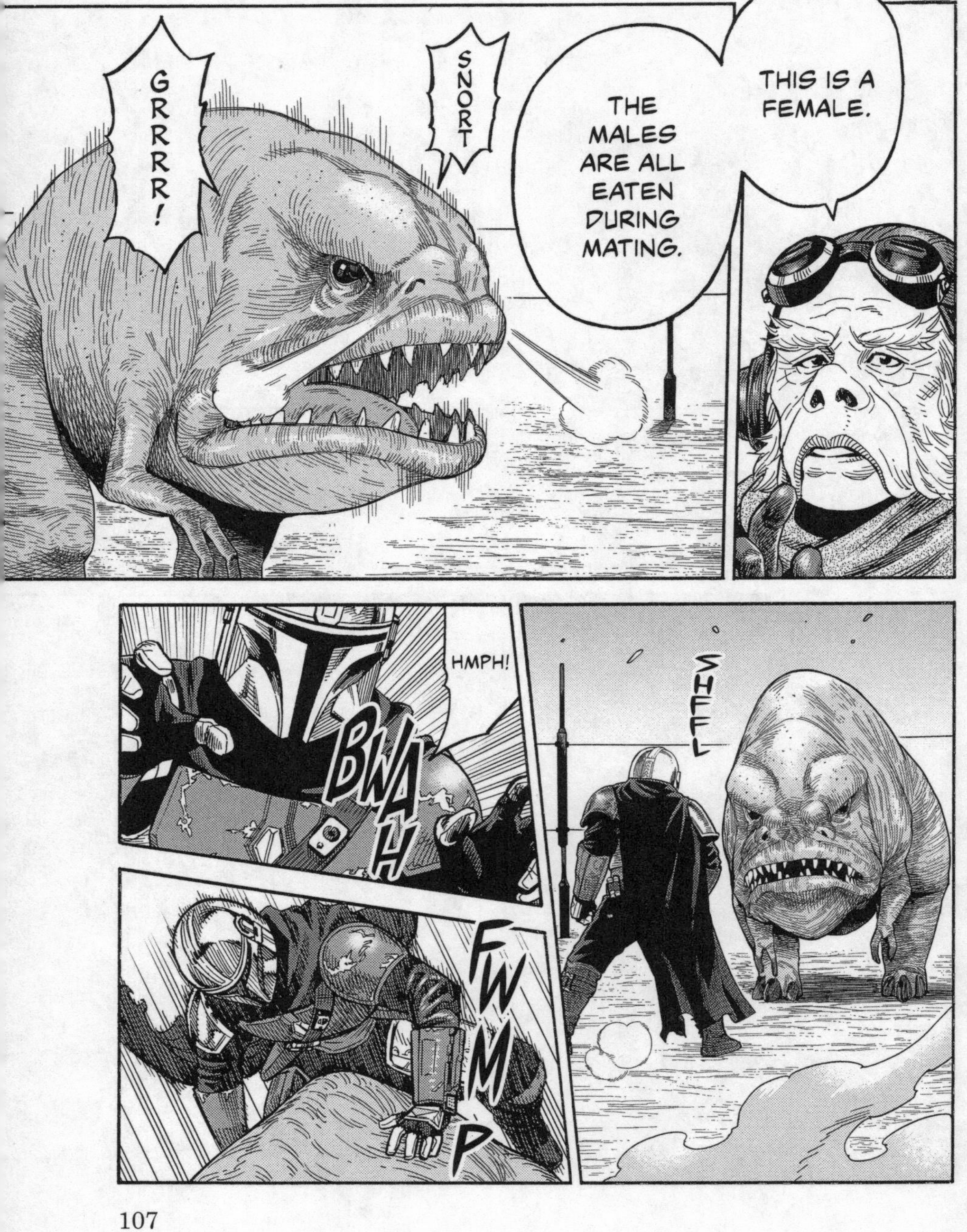
THIS IS A FEMALE.
THE MALES ARE ALL EATEN DURING MATING.
SNORT
GRRRR!
SHFFL
HMPH!
BWAH
FWMP

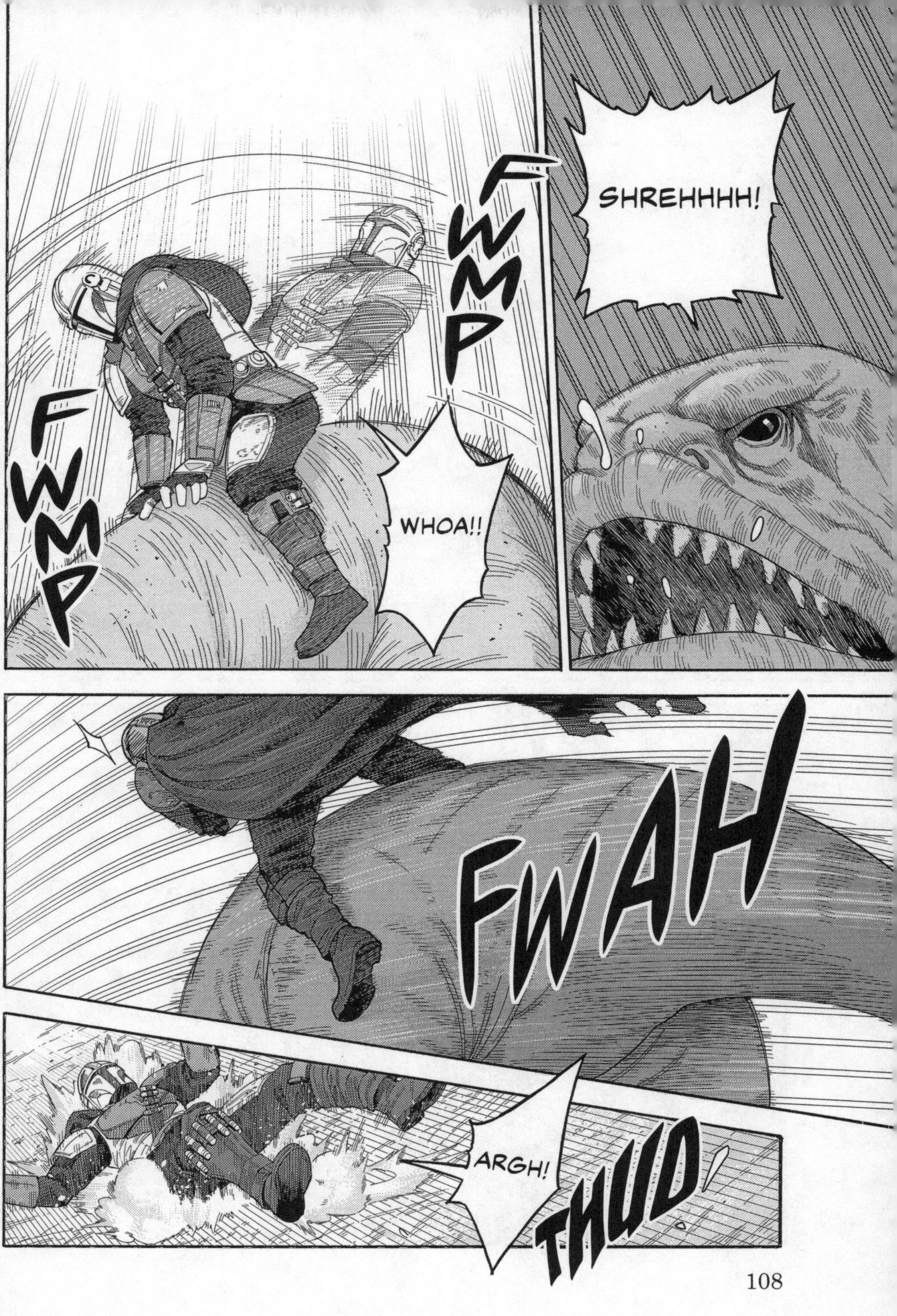
SHREHHHH!
FWMP
WHOA!!
FWMP
FWAH
ARGH!
THUD

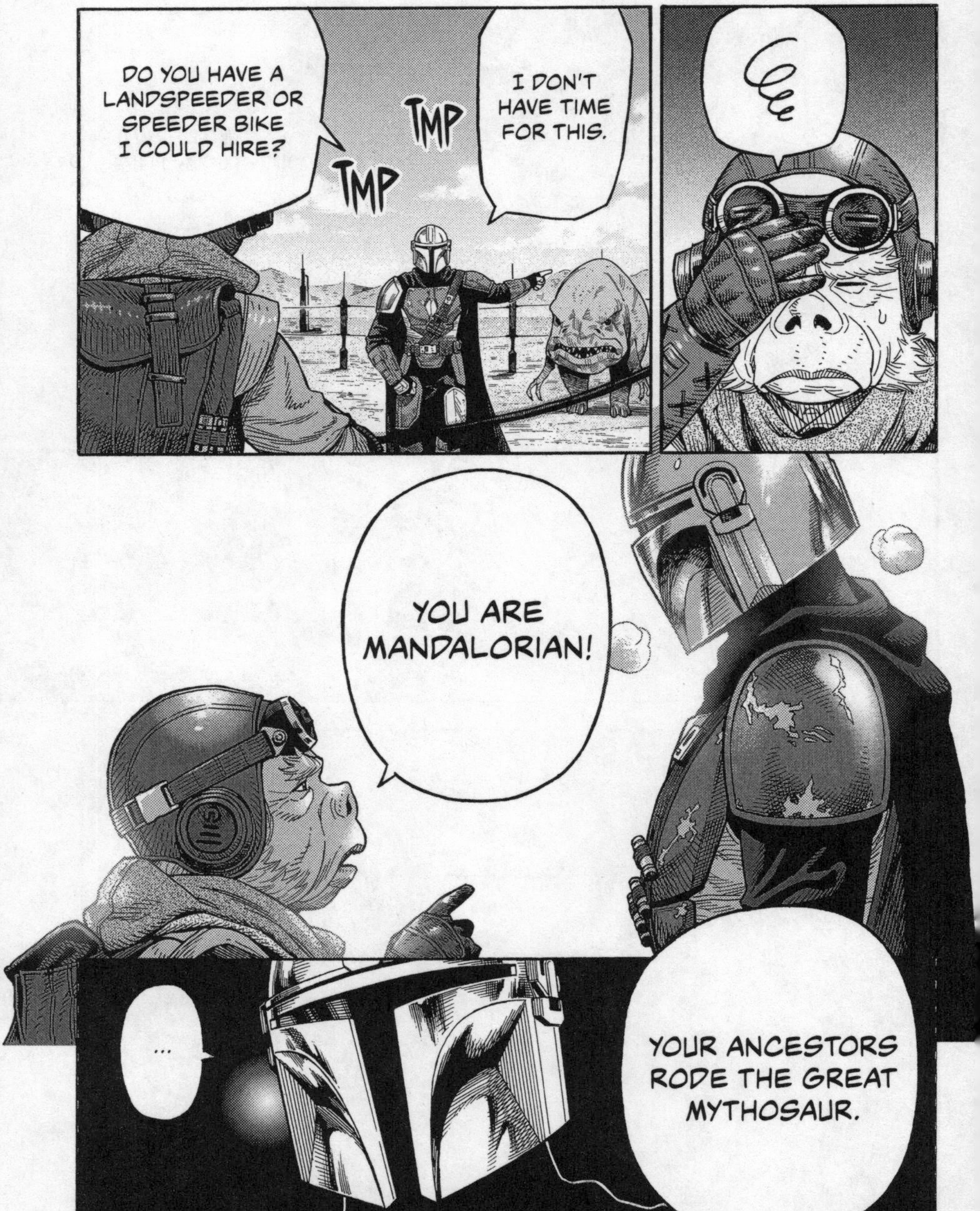

DO YOU HAVE A LANDSPEEDER OR SPEEDER BIKE I COULD HIRE?
TMP
TMP
I DON'T HAVE TIME FOR THIS.
YOU ARE MANDALORIAN!
...
YOUR ANCESTORS RODE THE GREAT MYTHOSAUR.

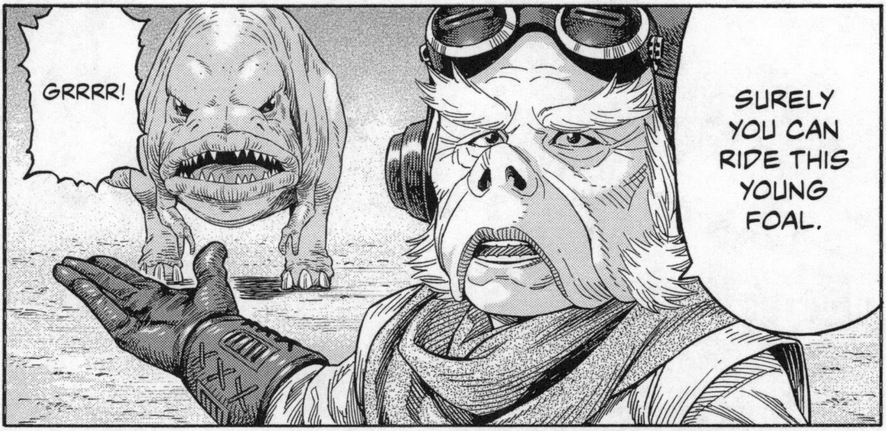
SURELY YOU CAN RIDE THIS YOUNG FOAL.
GRRRR!

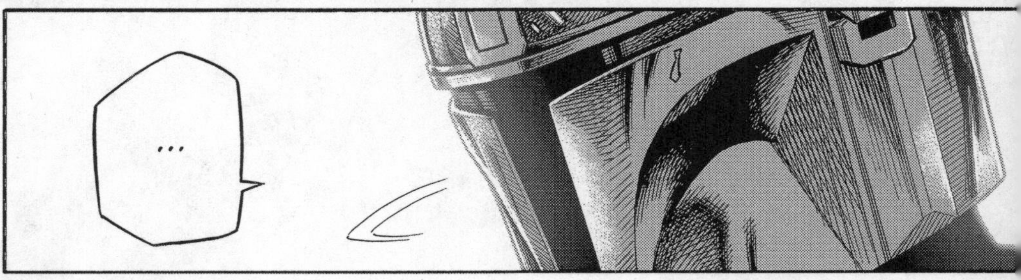
...

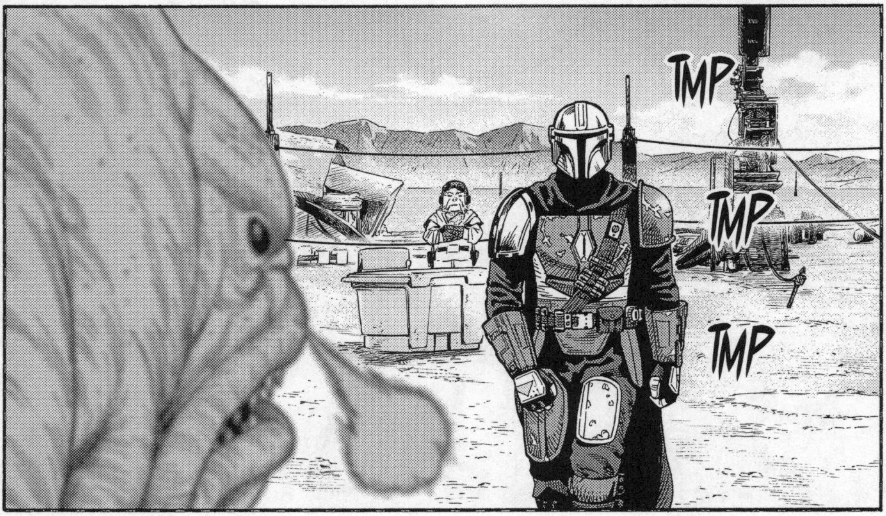
TMP
TMP
TMP

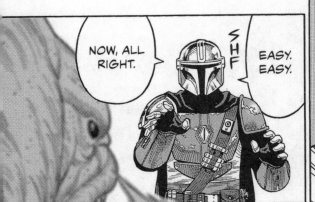

NOW, ALL RIGHT.

SHF

EASY. EASY.

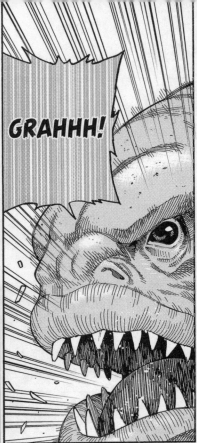

GRAHHH!

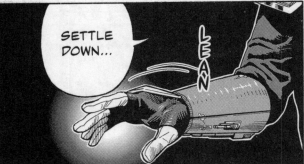

SETTLE DOWN...

LEAN

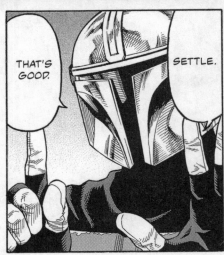

THAT'S GOOD.

SETTLE.

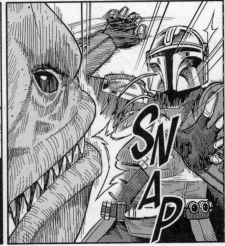

SNAP

EASY...
OKAY.
GRRR...
!
THAT'S GOOD.
ALL RIGHT.

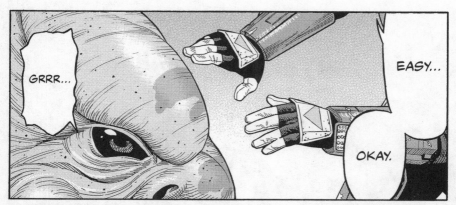

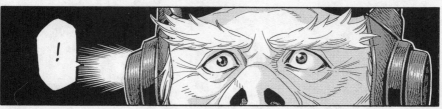

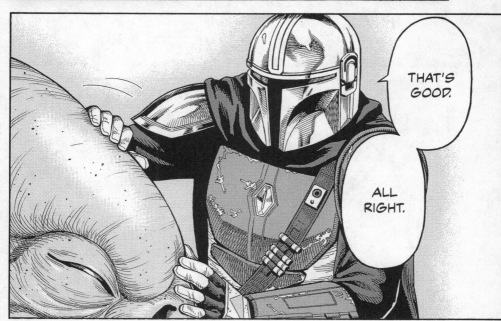

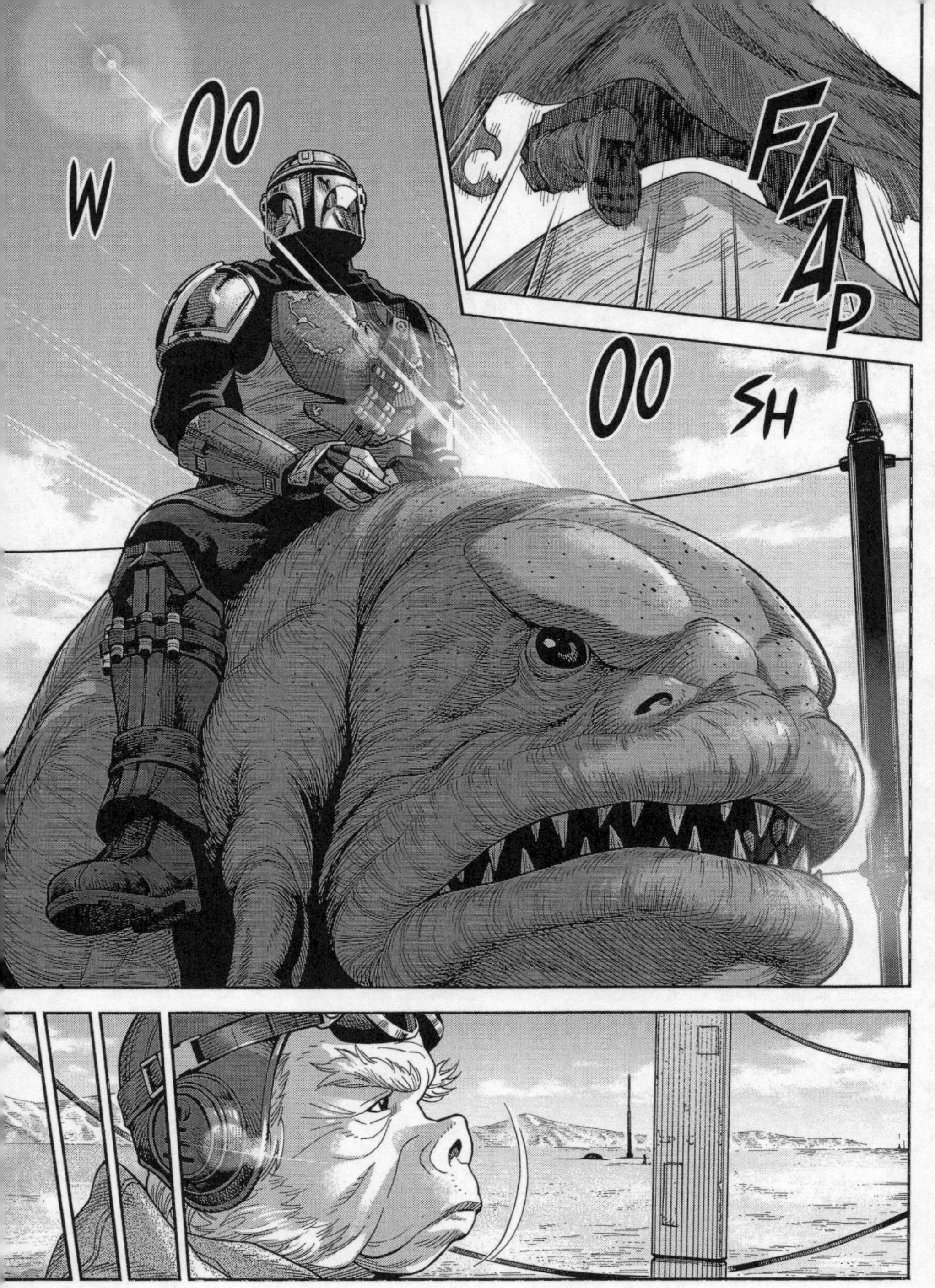
FLAP
W OO OO SH

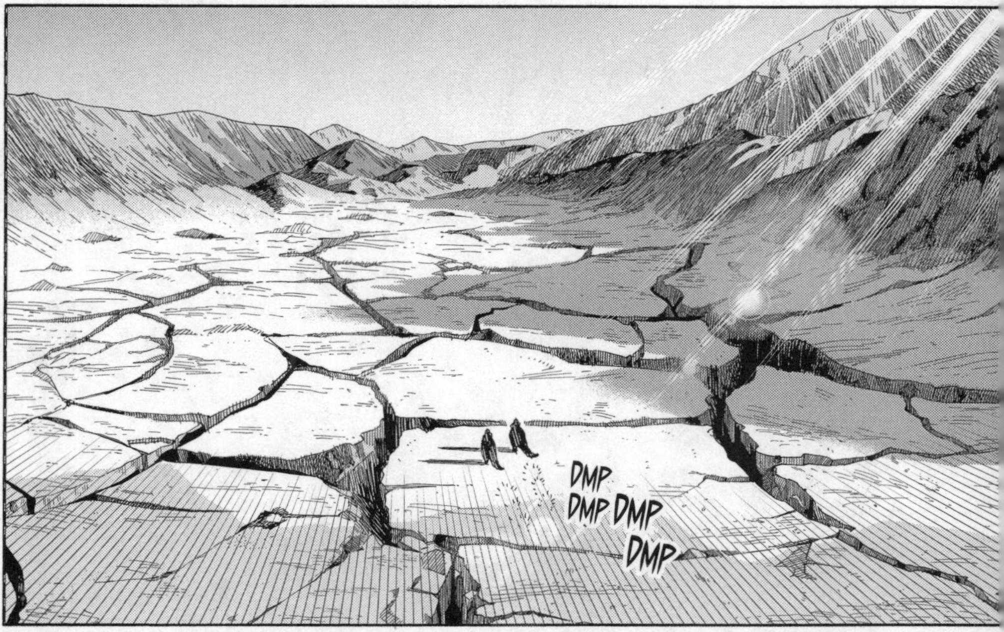
DMP
DMP DMP
DMP
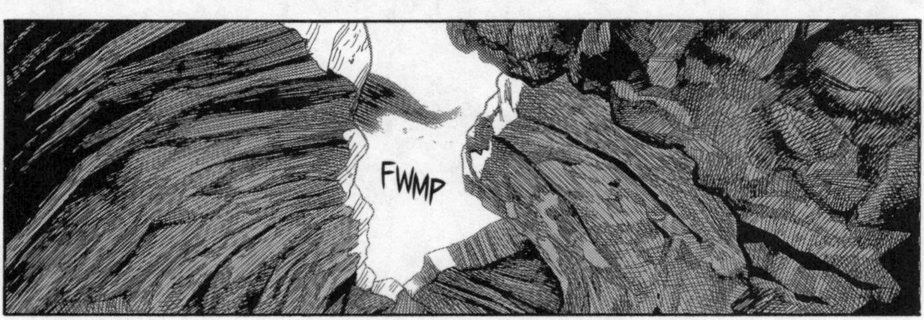
FWMP
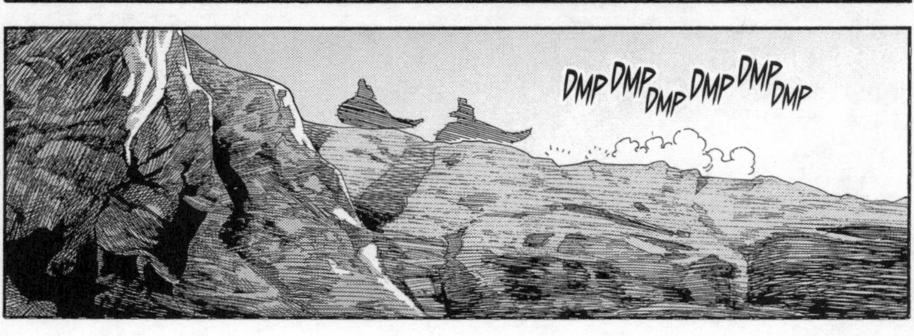
DMP DMP DMP DMP DMP DMP

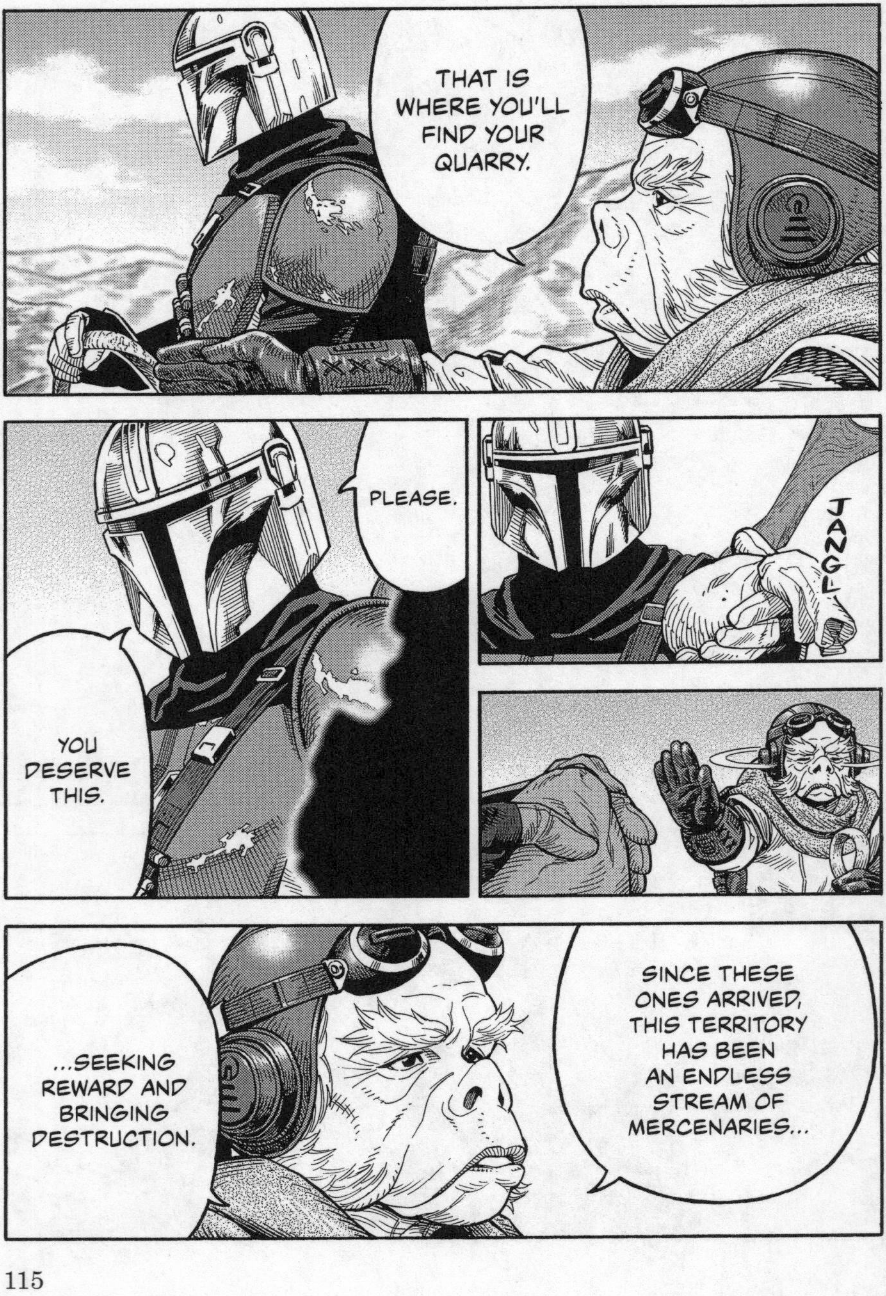
THAT IS WHERE YOU'LL FIND YOUR QUARRY.
JANGL
PLEASE.
YOU DESERVE THIS.
SINCE THESE ONES ARRIVED, THIS TERRITORY HAS BEEN AN ENDLESS STREAM OF MERCENARIES...
...SEEKING REWARD AND BRINGING DESTRUCTION.

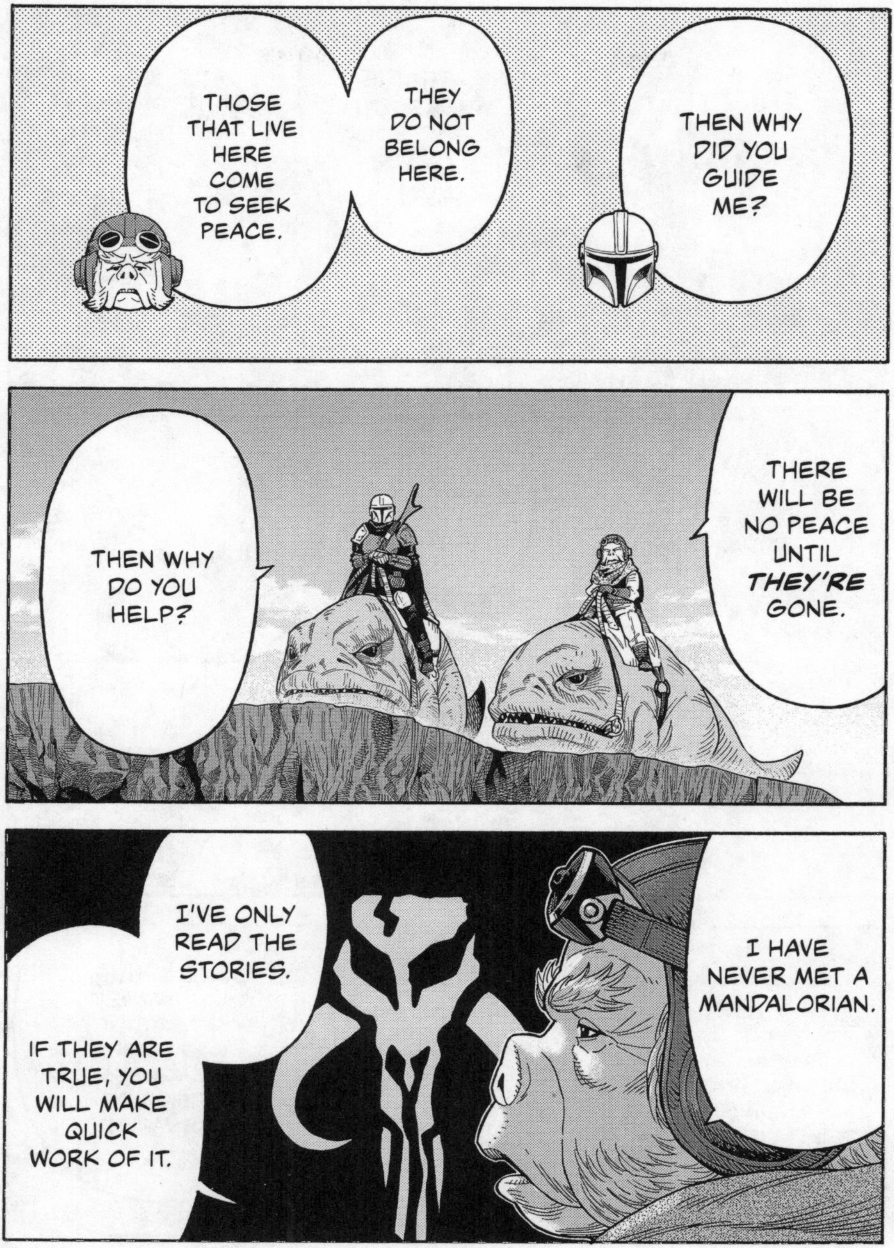
THEY DO NOT BELONG HERE.
THOSE THAT LIVE HERE COME TO SEEK PEACE.
THEN WHY DID YOU GUIDE ME?
THERE WILL BE NO PEACE UNTIL *THEY'RE* GONE.
THEN WHY DO YOU HELP?
I HAVE NEVER MET A MANDALORIAN.
I'VE ONLY READ THE STORIES.
IF THEY ARE TRUE, YOU WILL MAKE QUICK WORK OF IT.

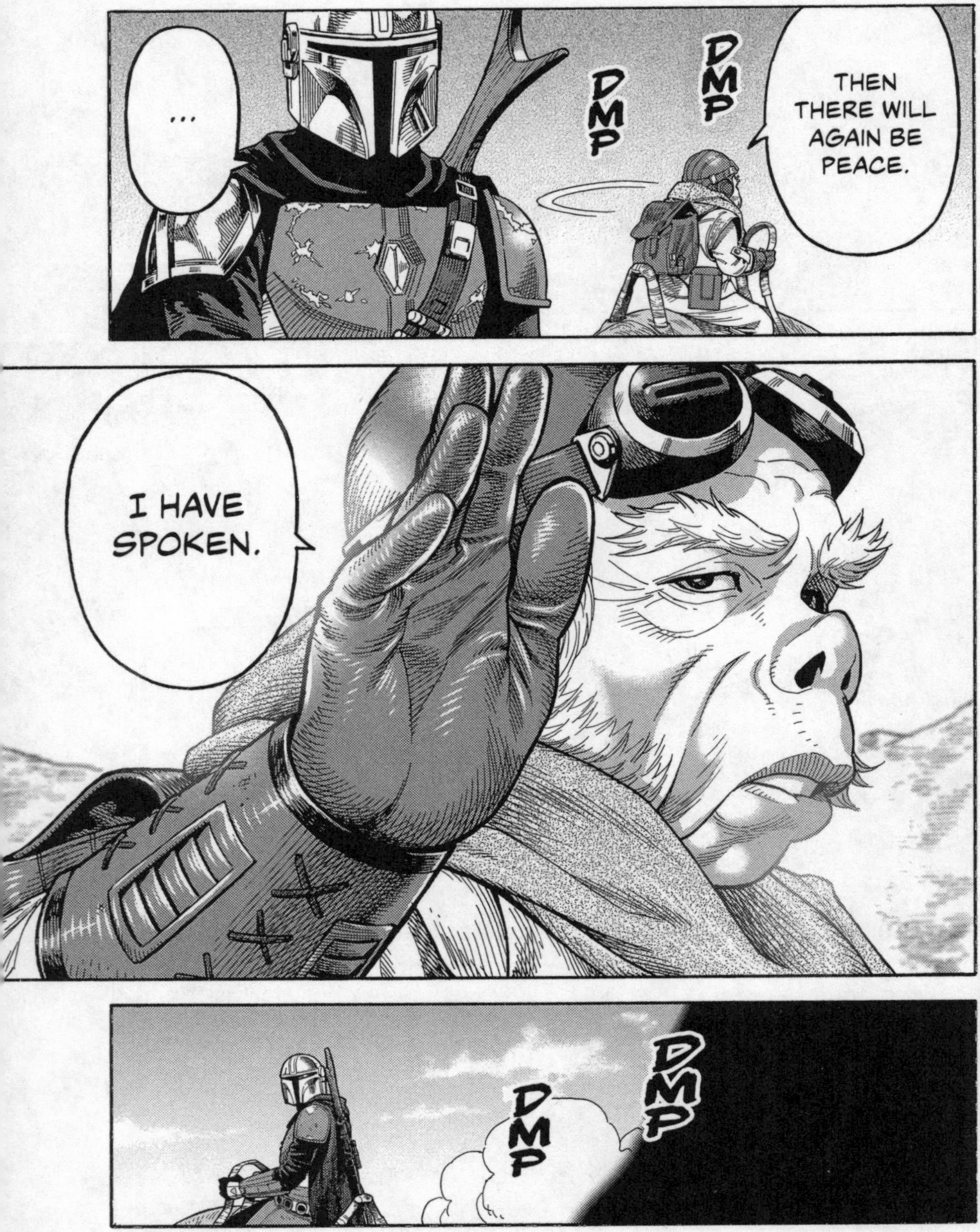
THEN THERE WILL AGAIN BE PEACE.
DMP DMP
DMP DMP
...
I HAVE SPOKEN.
DMP DMP
DMP DMP

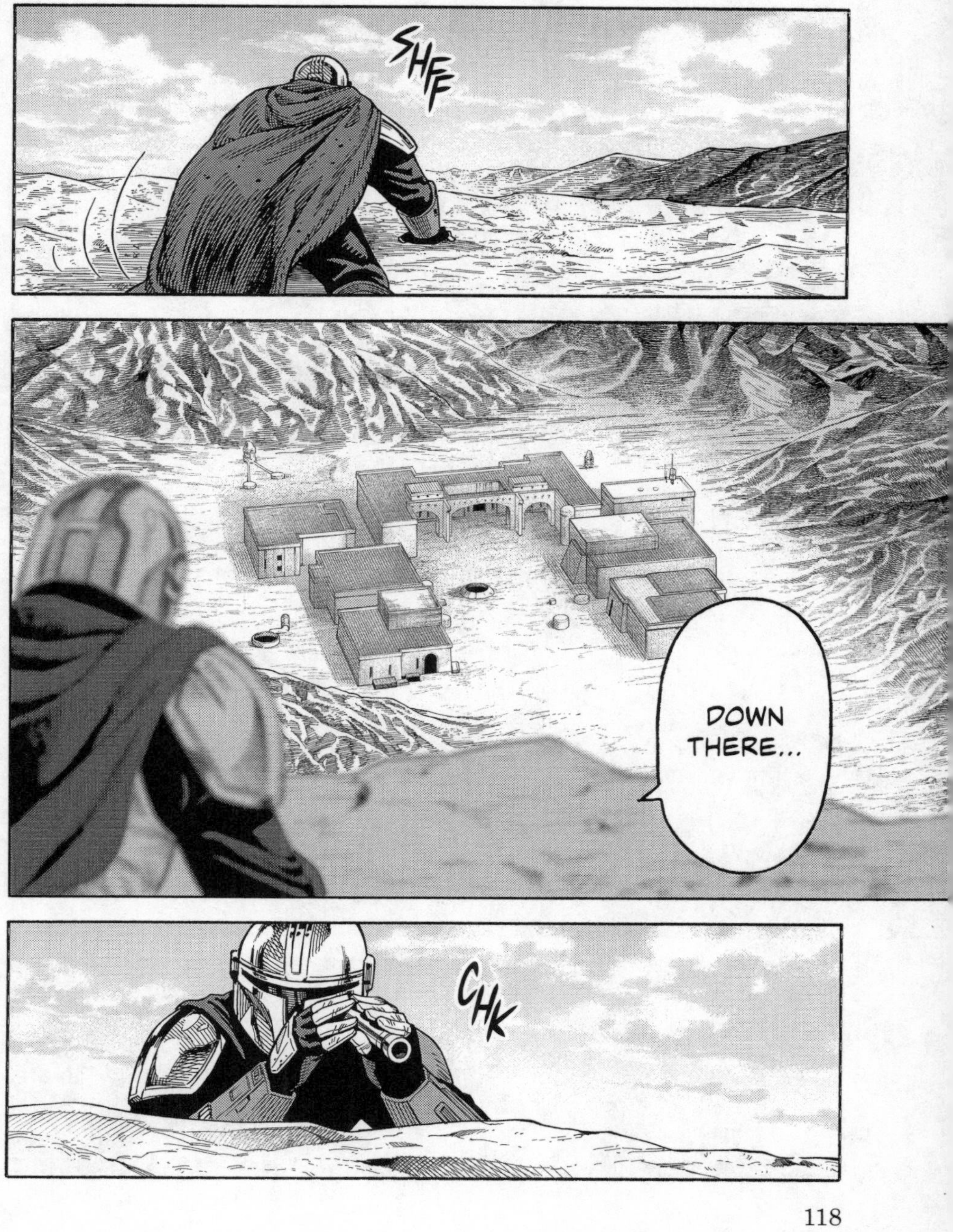
SHFF
DOWN THERE...
CHK

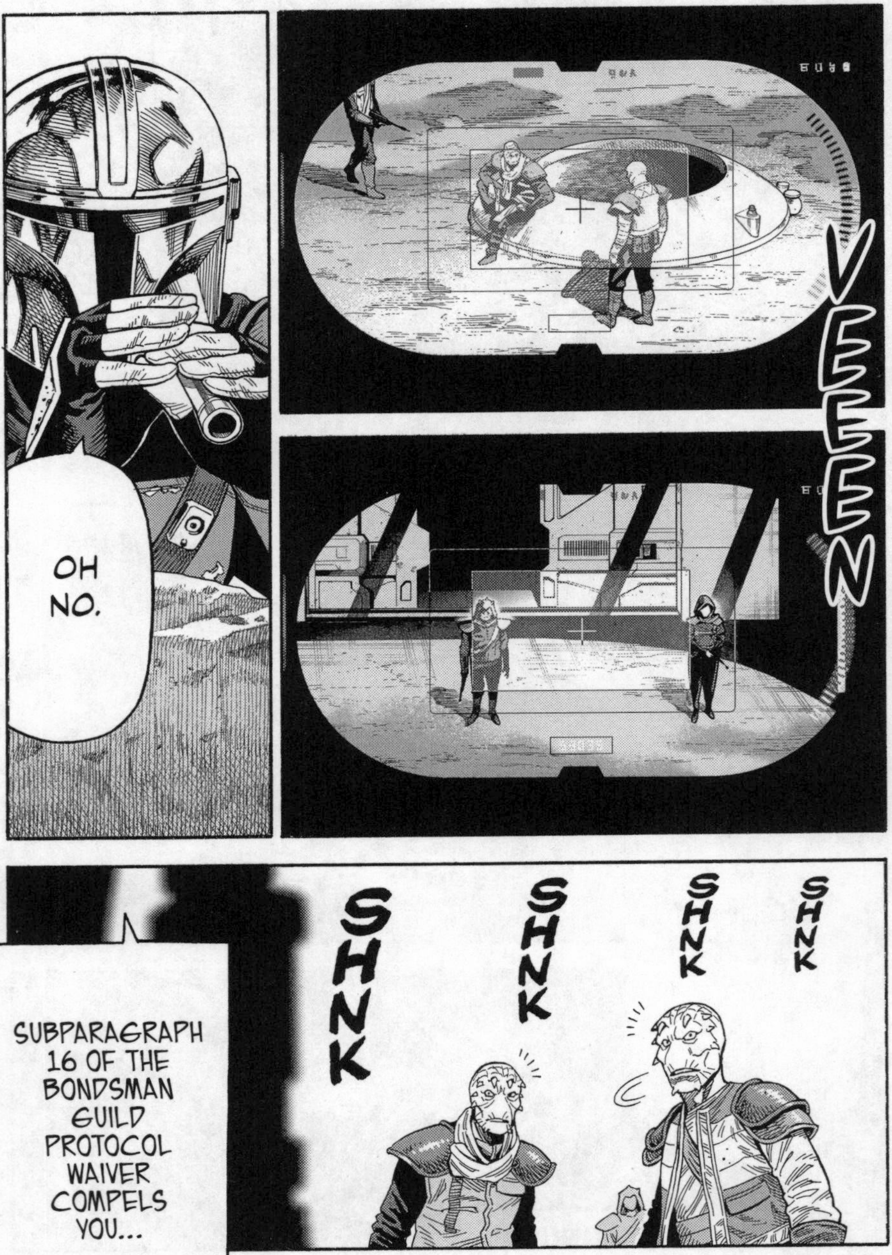
VEEEEN
OH NO.
SHNK
SHNK
SHNK
SHNK
SUBPARAGRAPH 16 OF THE BONDSMAN GUILD PROTOCOL WAIVER COMPELS YOU...

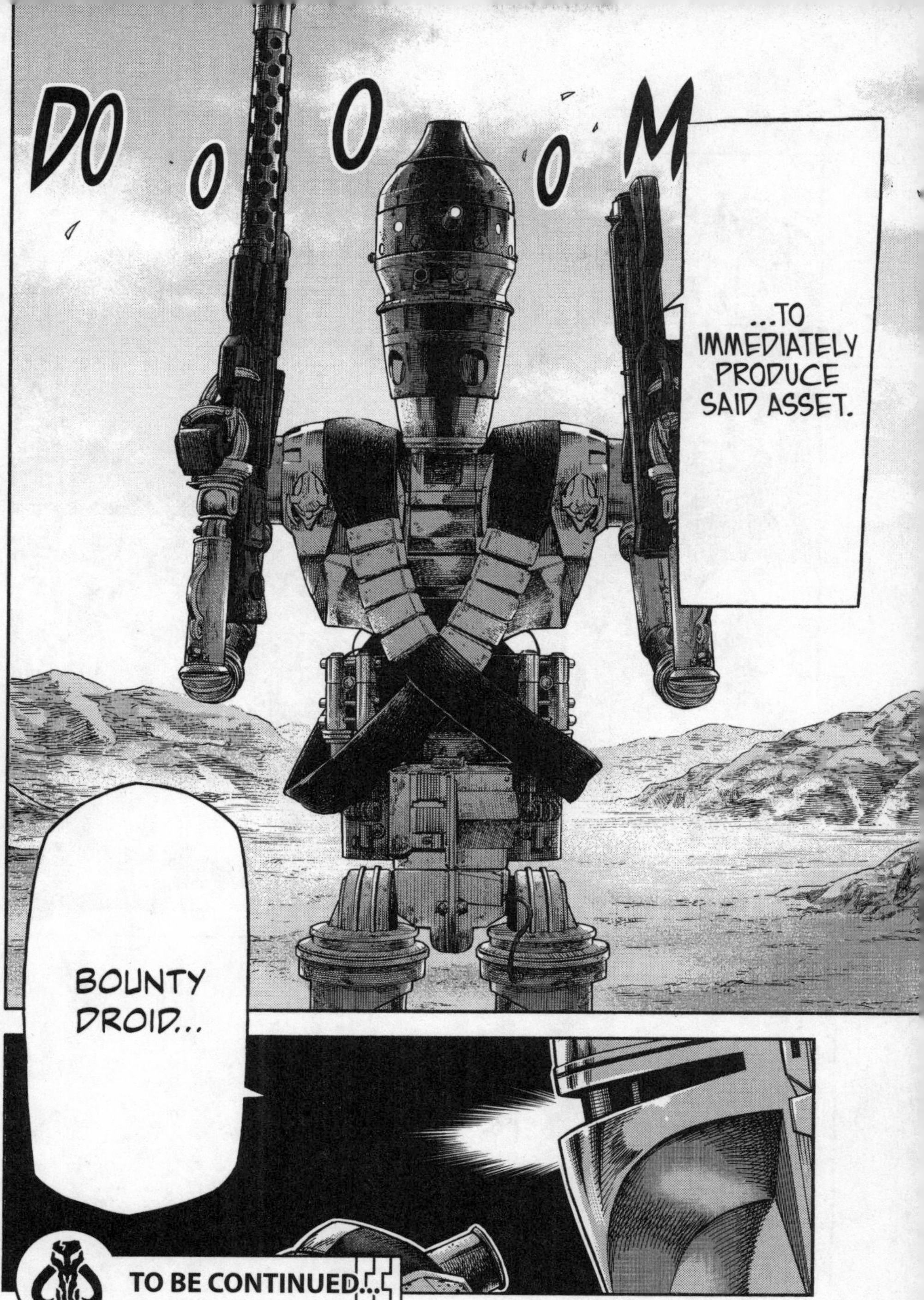

...TO IMMEDIATELY PRODUCE SAID ASSET.
DOoOoOM
BOUNTY DROID...
TO BE CONTINUED...

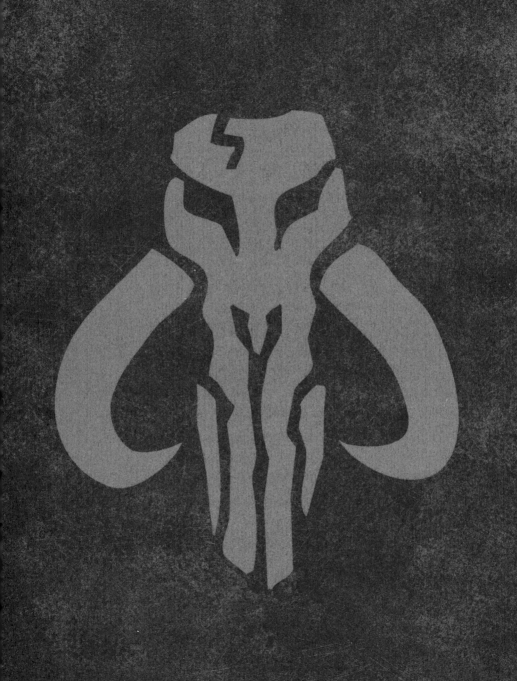

STAR WARS

THE

MANDALORIAN

THE MANGA

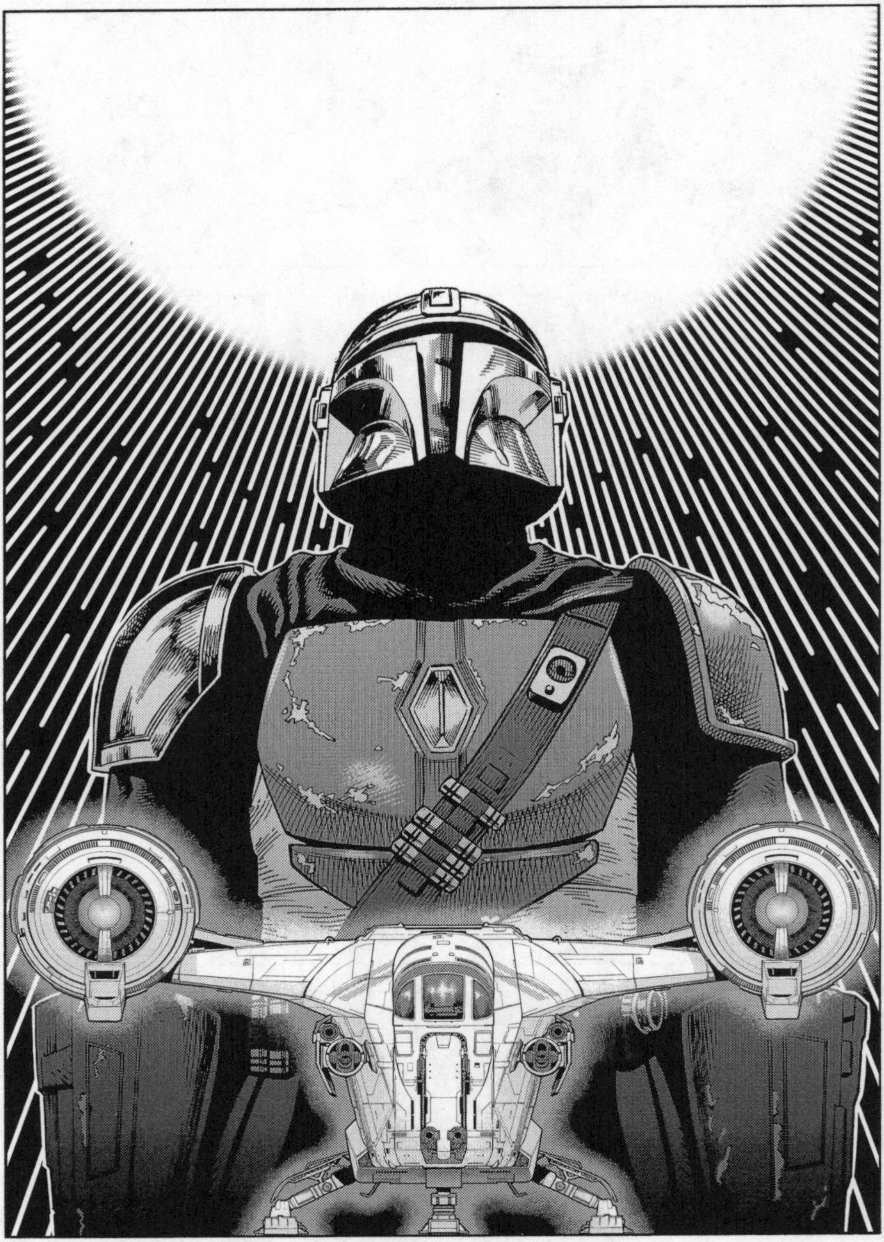

Episode. 04

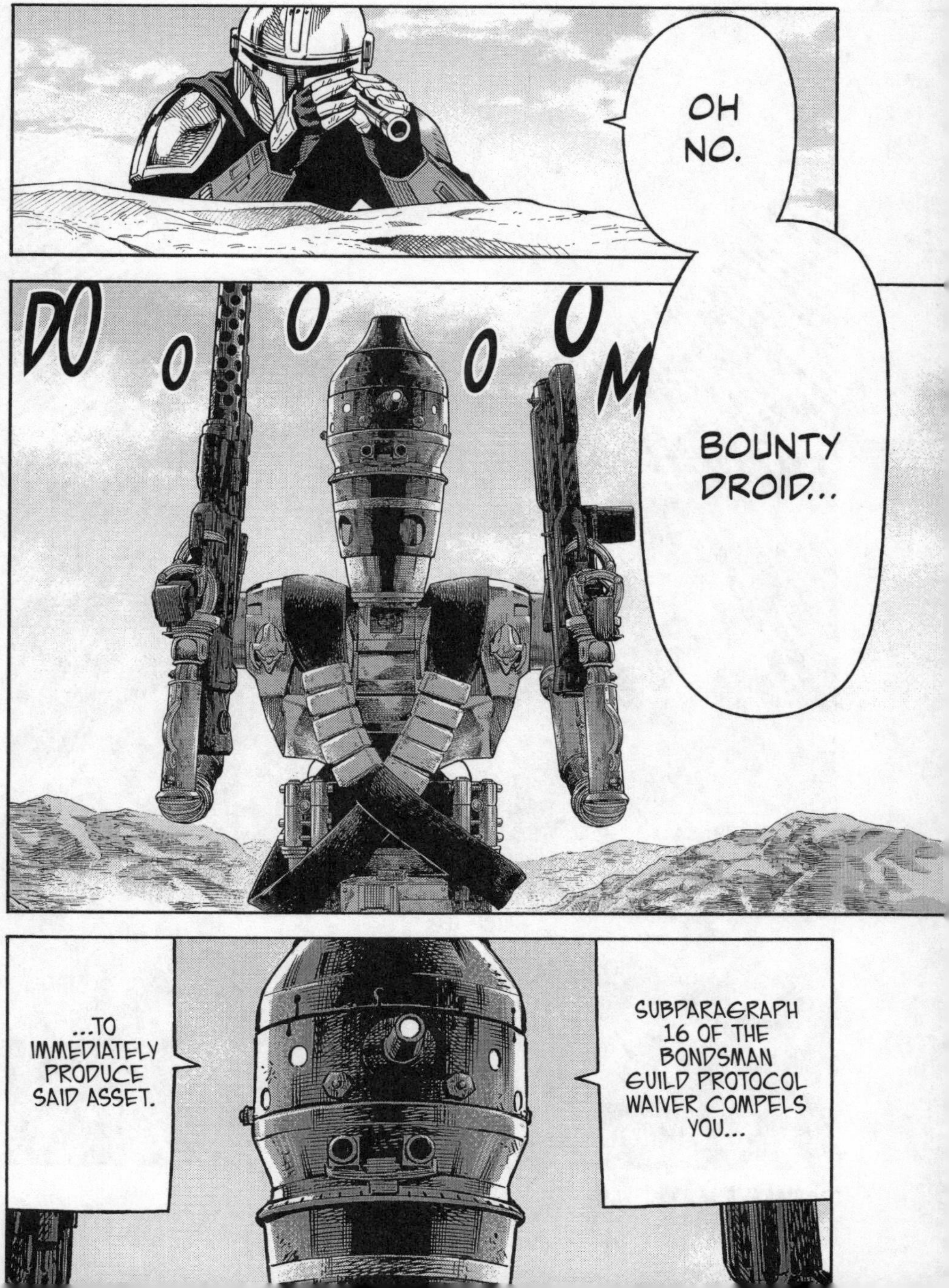
OH NO.
BOUNTY DROID...
DOOOOOM
SUBPARAGRAPH 16 OF THE BONDSMAN GUILD PROTOCOL WAIVER COMPELS YOU...
...TO IMMEDIATELY PRODUCE SAID ASSET.

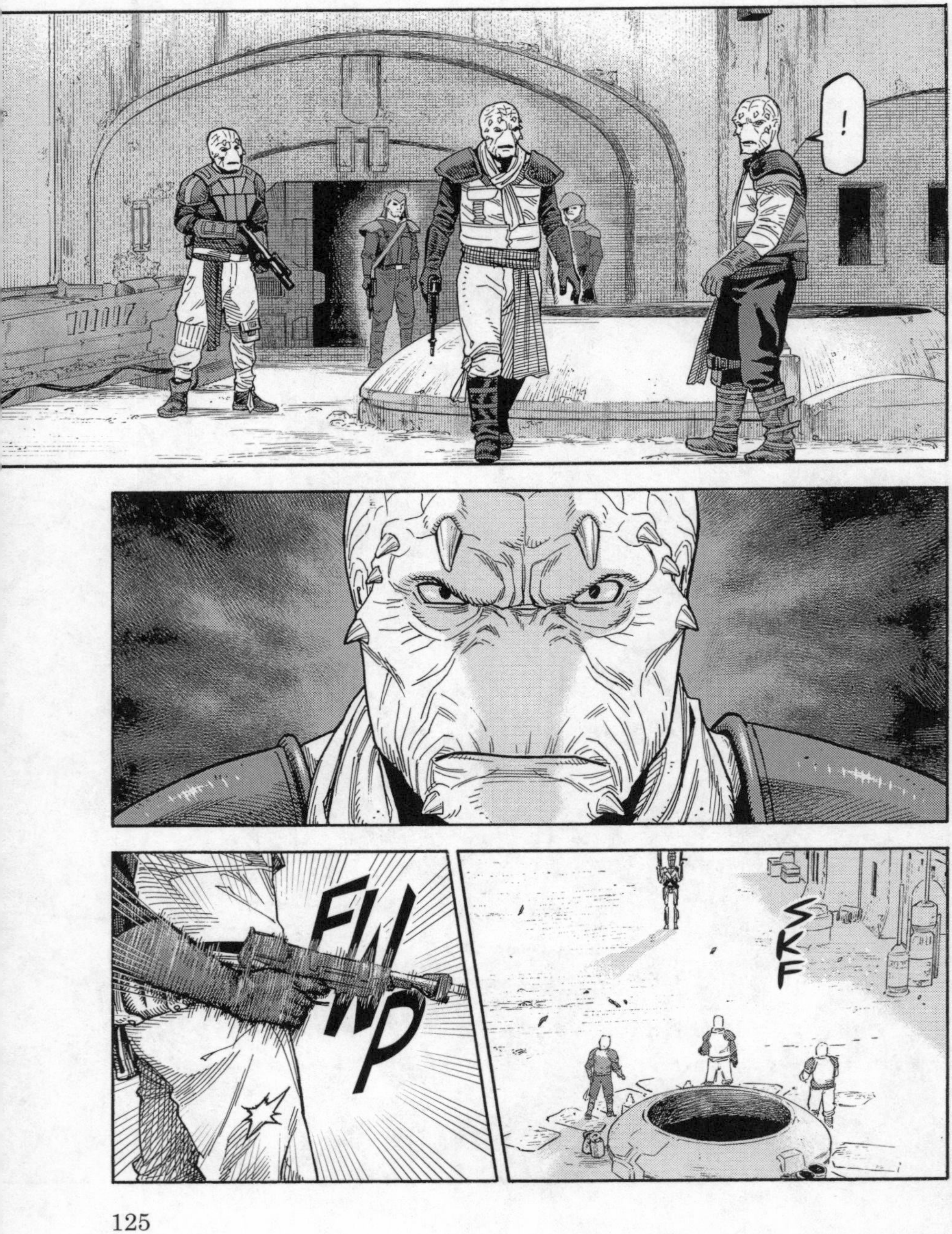
!
SKF
FWP

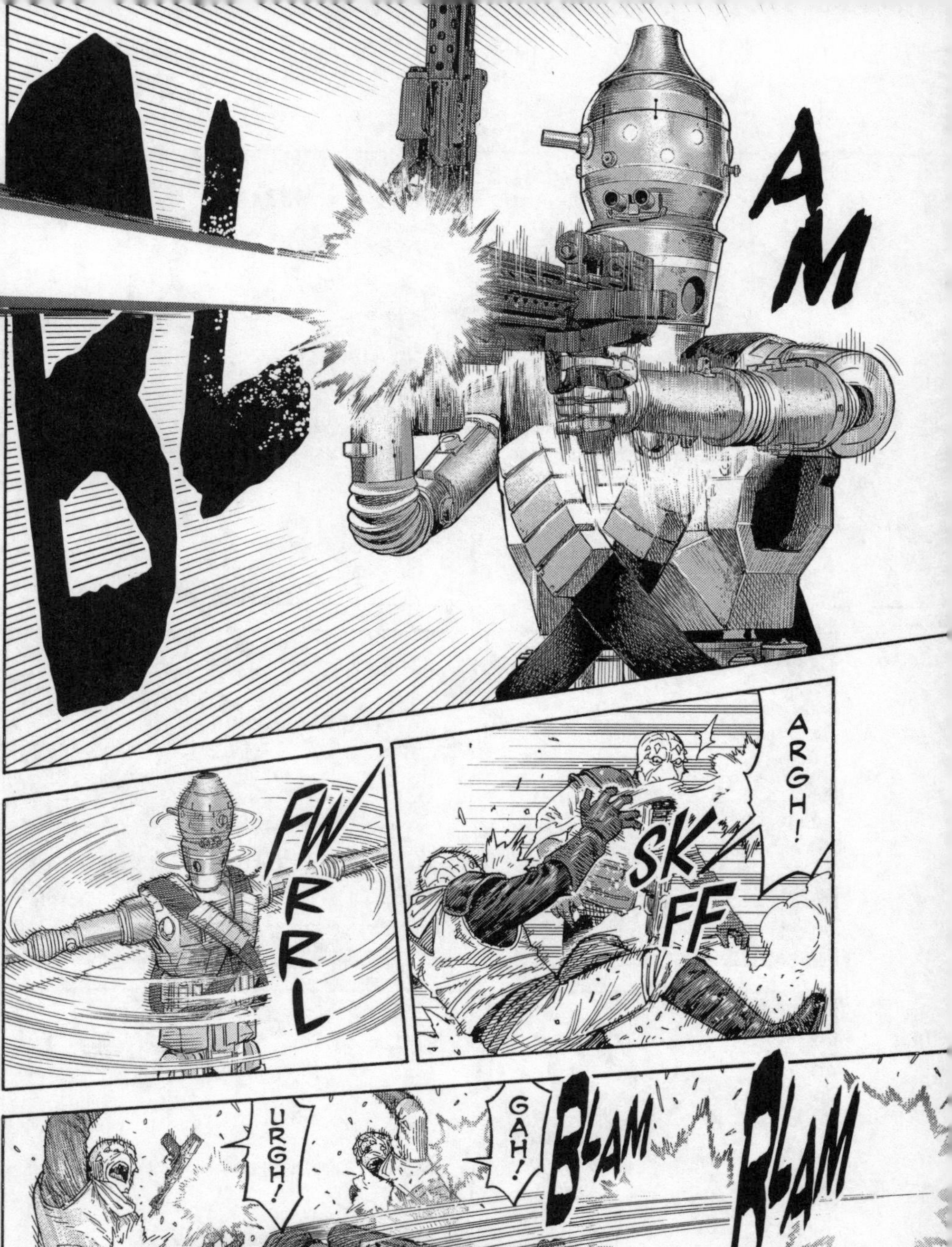
BLAM
ARGH!
SKFF
FWRRL
BLAM
BLAM
GAH!
URGH!

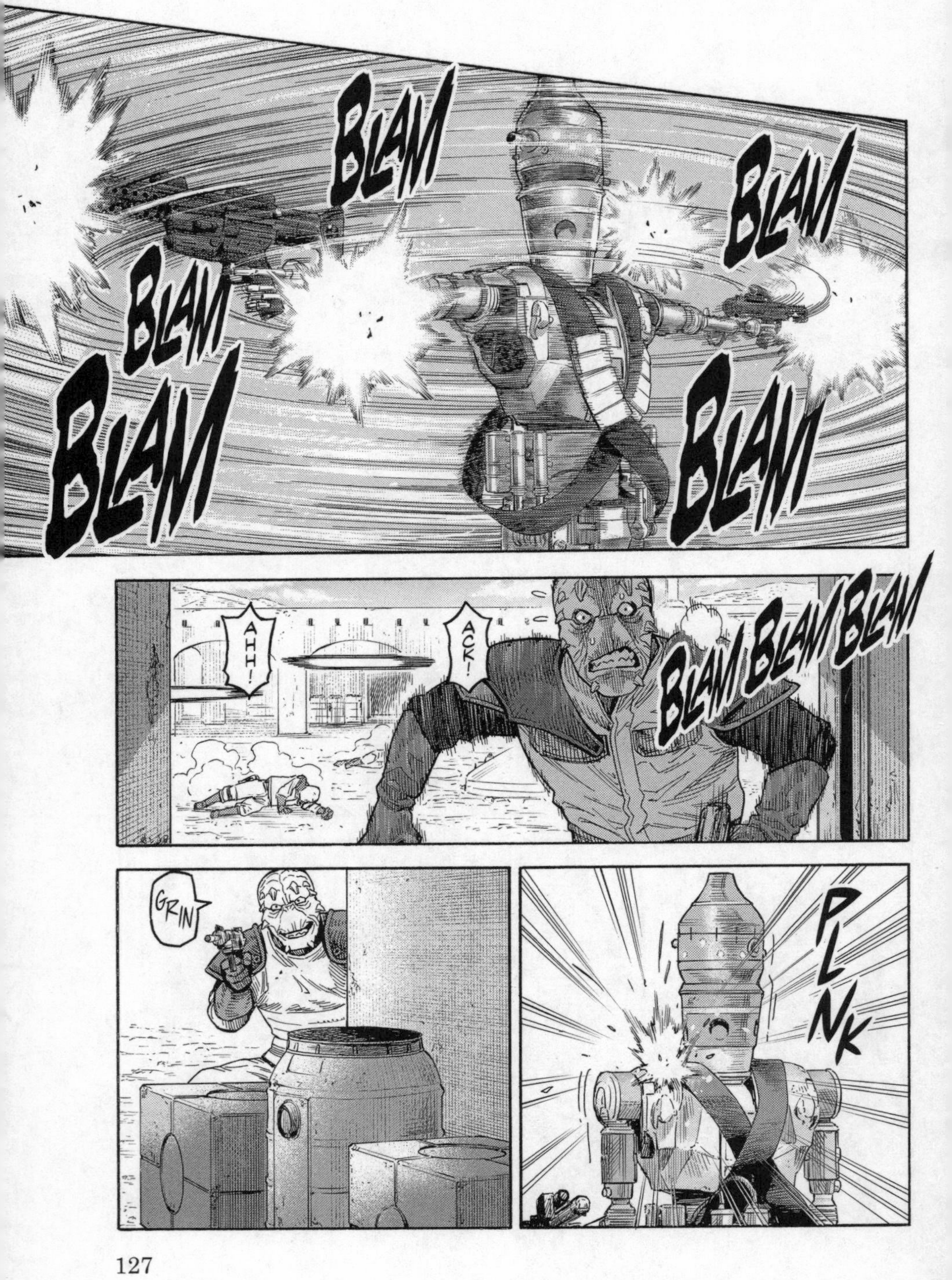
BLAM
BLAM
BLAM
BLAM
BLAM
BLAM
BLAM BLAM BLAM
ACK!
AHH!
PLINK
GRIN

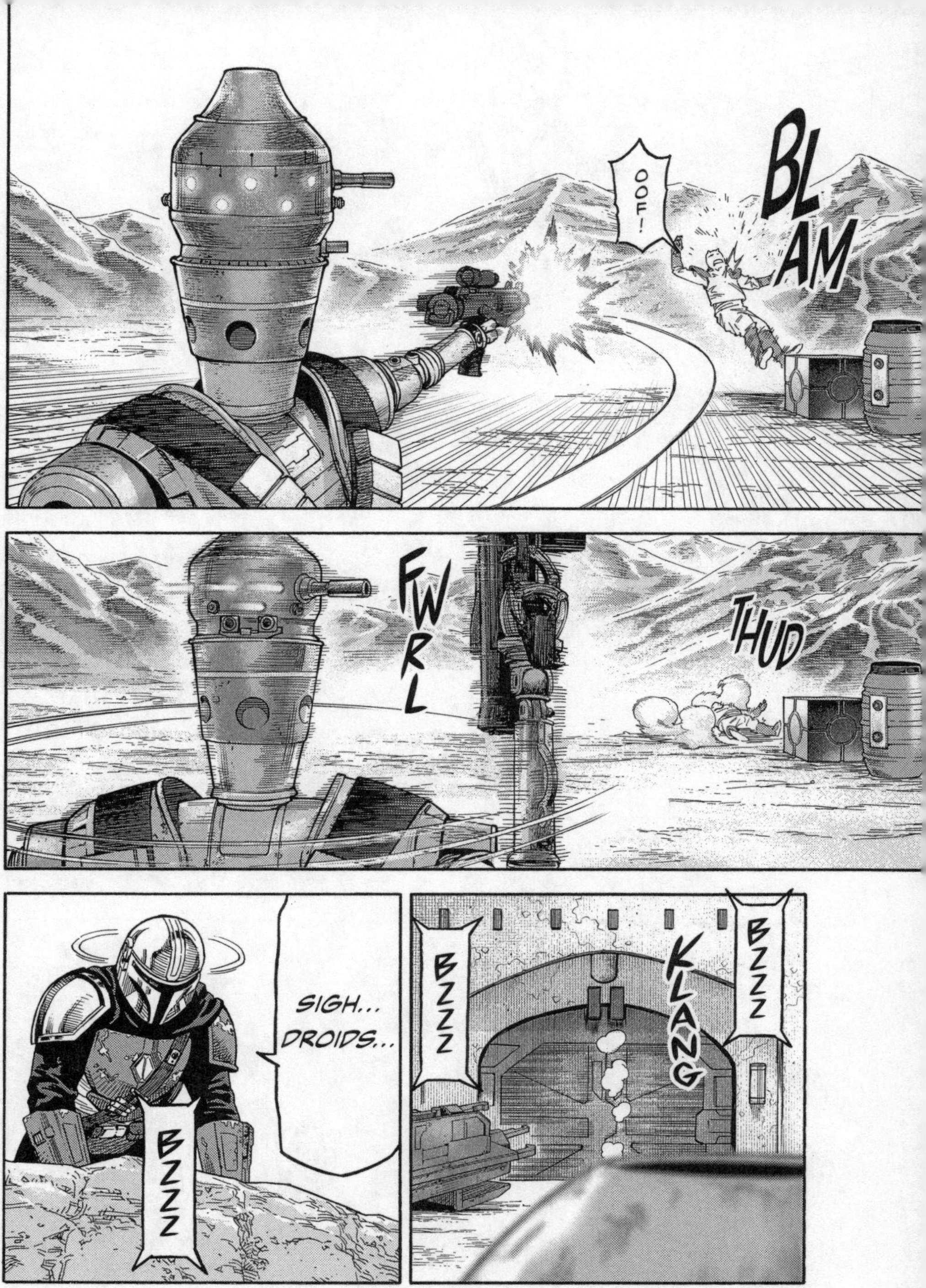
BLAM
OOF!
THUD
FWRL
BZZZ
KLANG
BZZZ
SIGH... DROIDS...
BZZZ

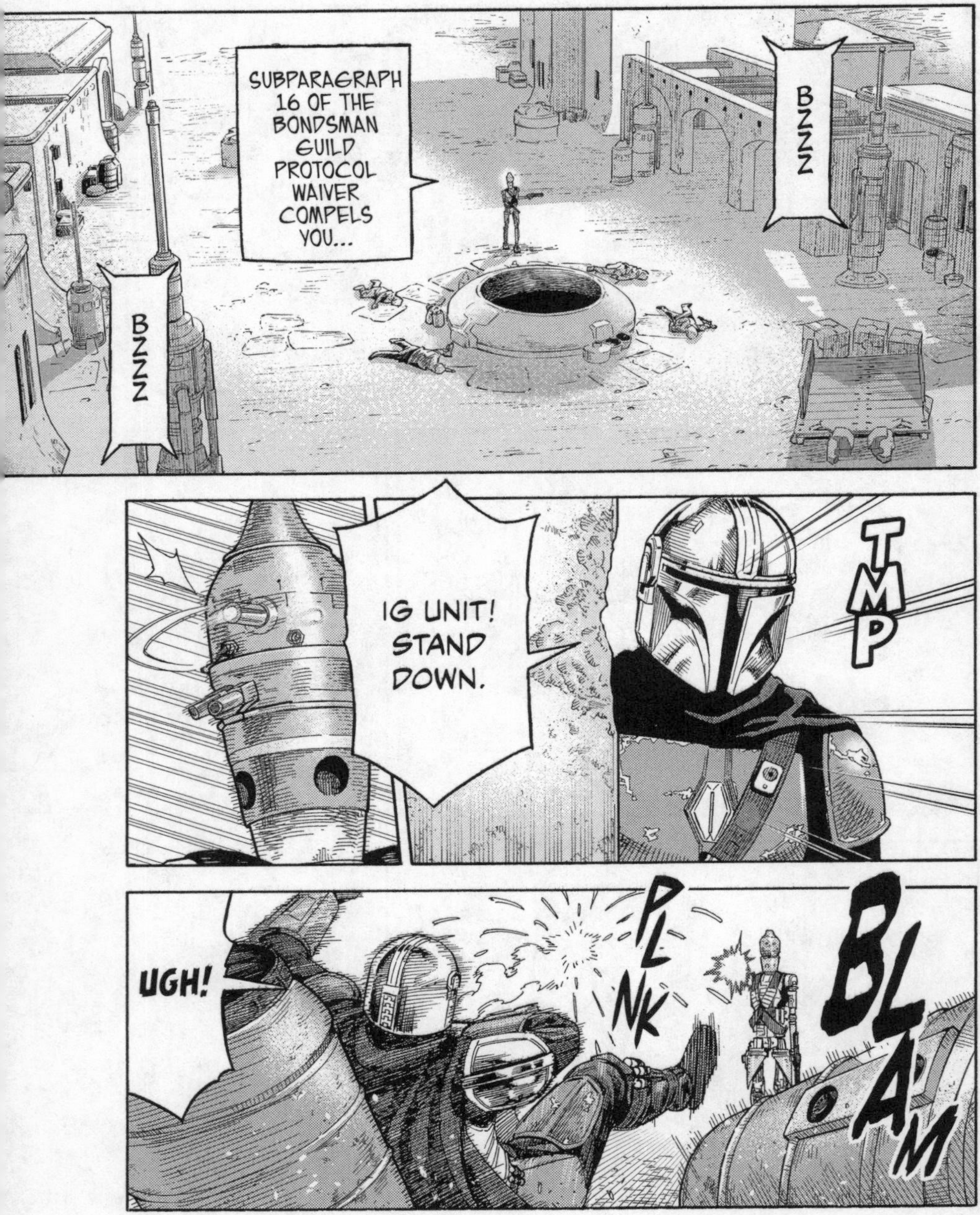
BZZZ
SUBPARAGRAPH 16 OF THE BONDSMAN GUILD PROTOCOL WAIVER COMPELS YOU...
BZZZ
TMP
IG UNIT! STAND DOWN.
BLAM
PLNK
UGH!

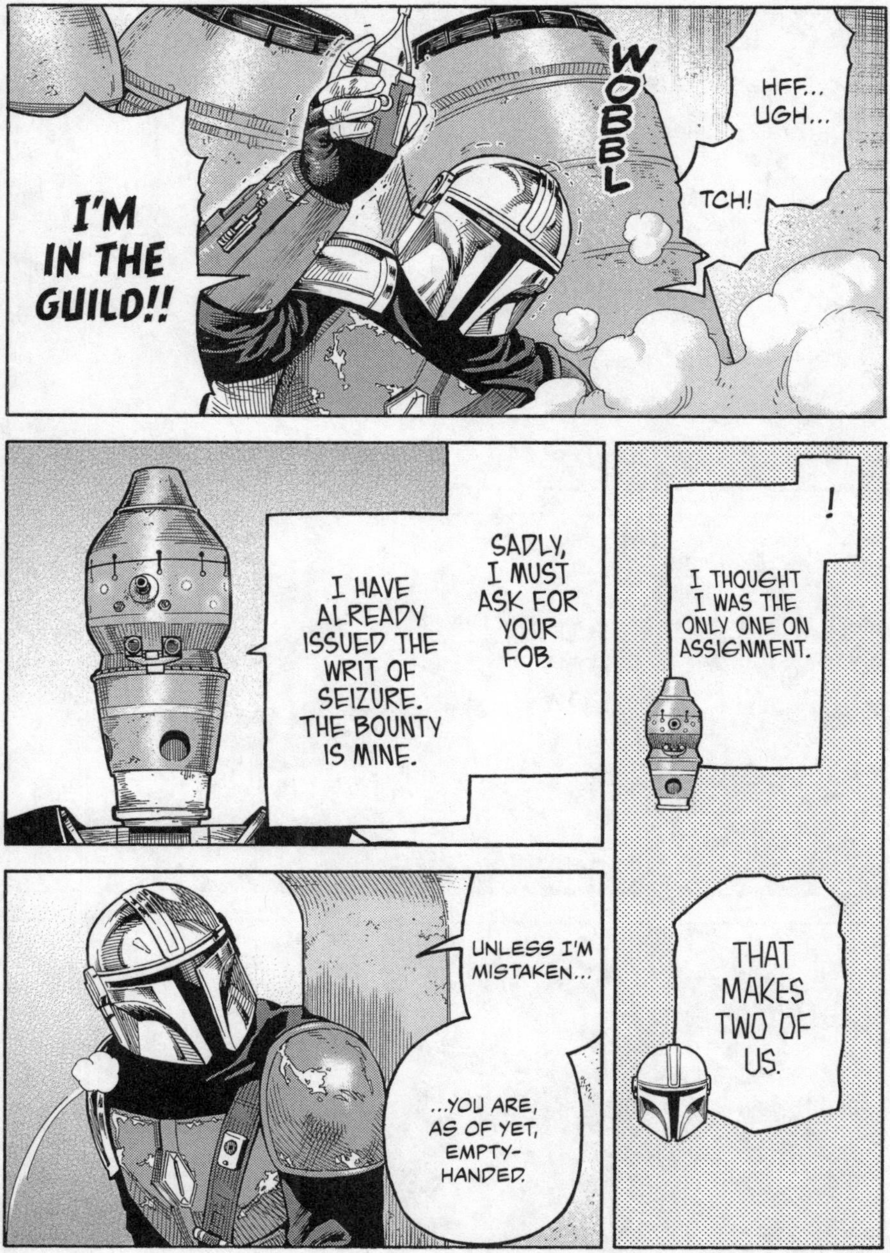
HFF... UGH...
WOBBL
TCH!
I'M IN THE GUILD!!
!
I THOUGHT I WAS THE ONLY ONE ON ASSIGNMENT.
THAT MAKES TWO OF US.
SADLY, I MUST ASK FOR YOUR FOB.
I HAVE ALREADY ISSUED THE WRIT OF SEIZURE. THE BOUNTY IS MINE.
UNLESS I'M MISTAKEN...
...YOU ARE, AS OF YET, EMPTY-HANDED.

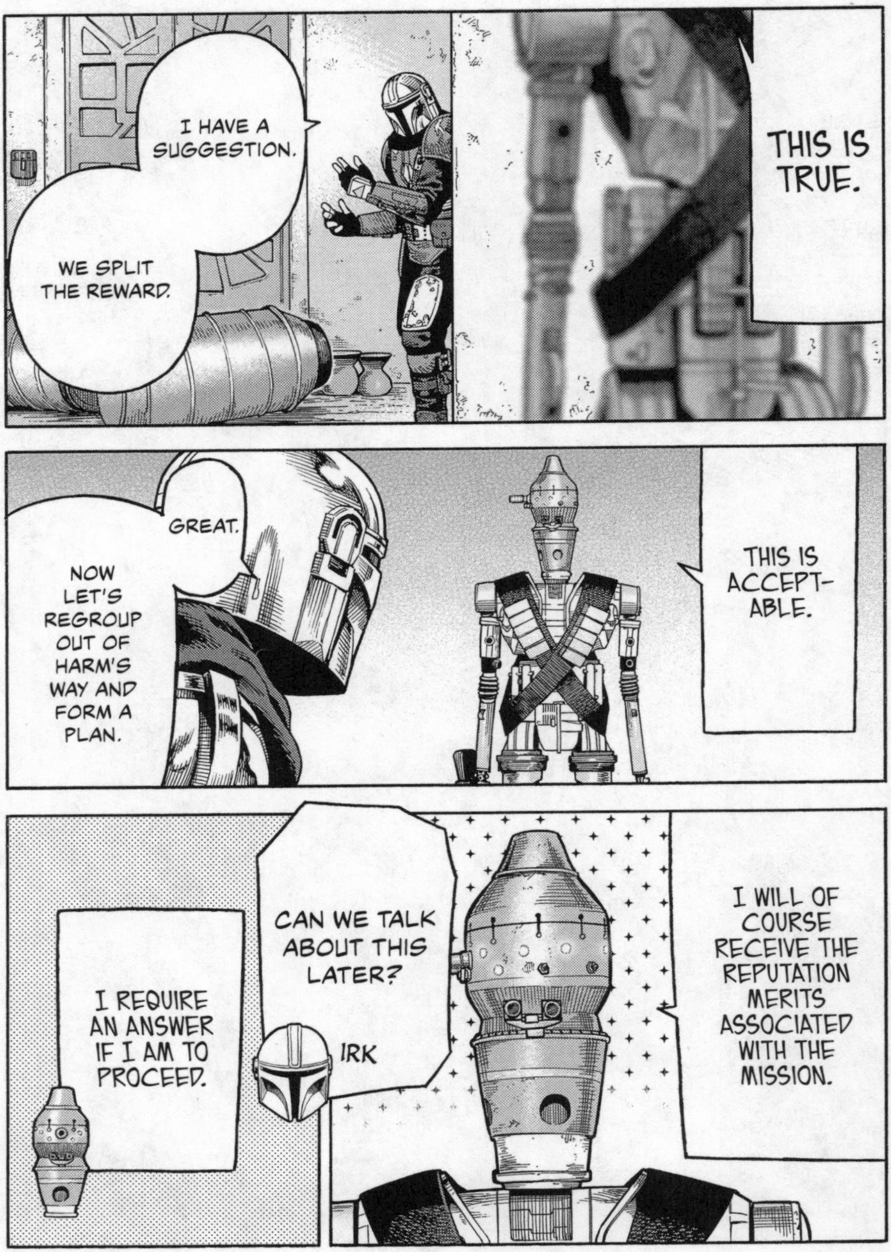
THIS IS TRUE.
I HAVE A SUGGESTION.
WE SPLIT THE REWARD.
THIS IS ACCEPT-ABLE.
GREAT.
NOW LET'S REGROUP OUT OF HARM'S WAY AND FORM A PLAN.
I WILL OF COURSE RECEIVE THE REPUTATION MERITS ASSOCIATED WITH THE MISSION.
CAN WE TALK ABOUT THIS LATER?
IRK
I REQUIRE AN ANSWER IF I AM TO PROCEED.

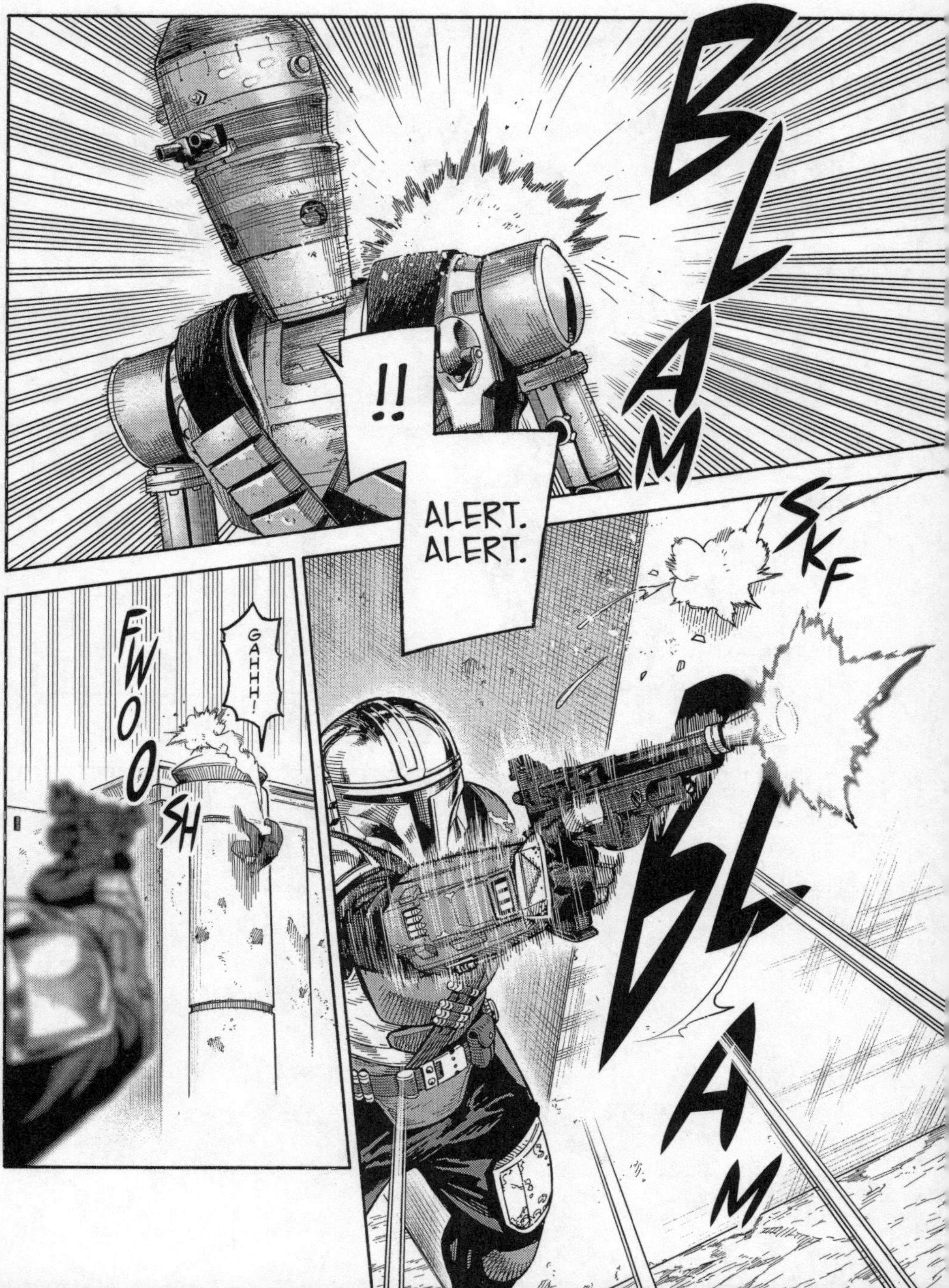
BLAM
!!
ALERT. ALERT.
SKF
BLAM
GAHHH!
FWOOSH

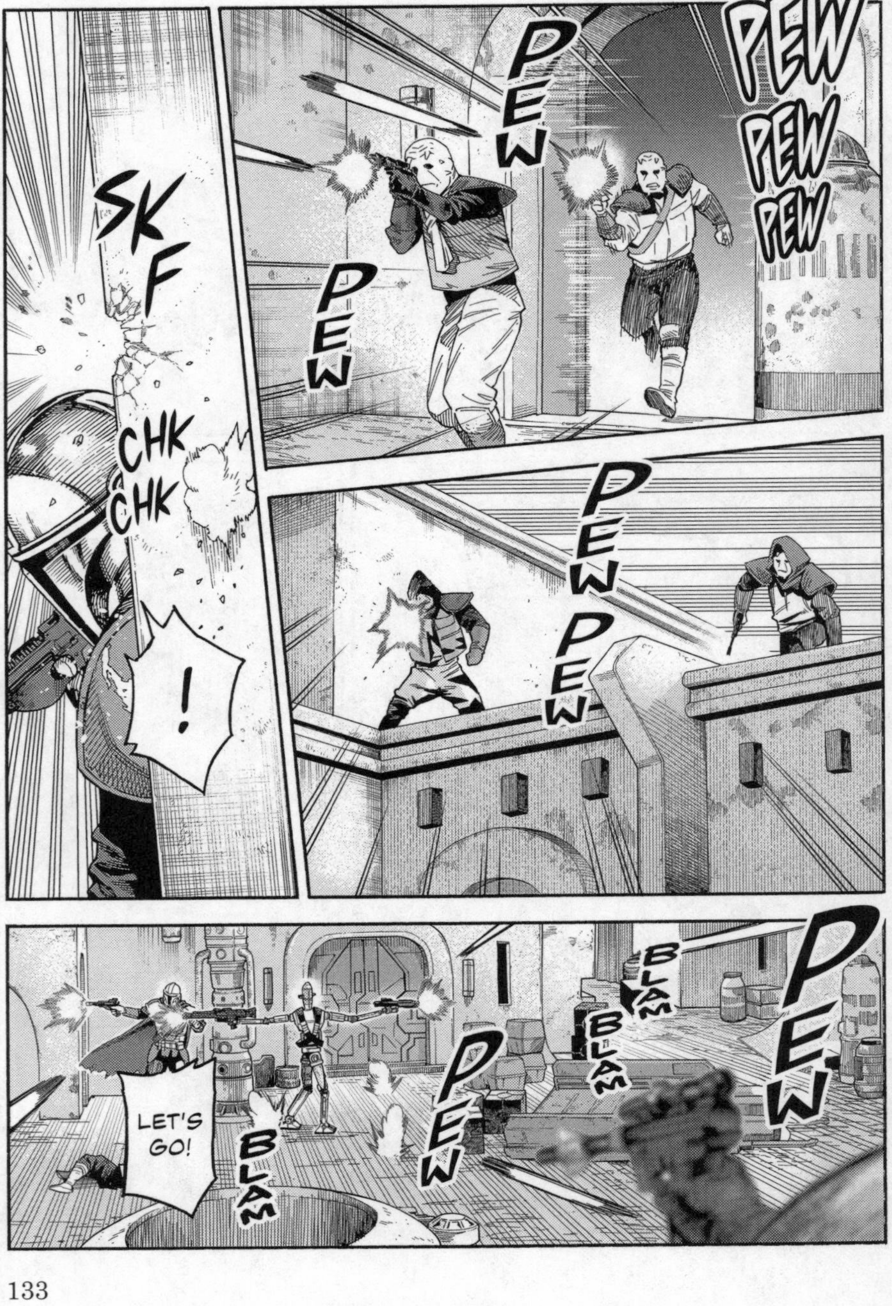
PEW
PEW
PEW
PEW
PEW
PEW
PEW
SKF
CHK
CHK
!
PEW
BLAM
BLAM
BLAM
PEW
LET'S GO!
BLAM

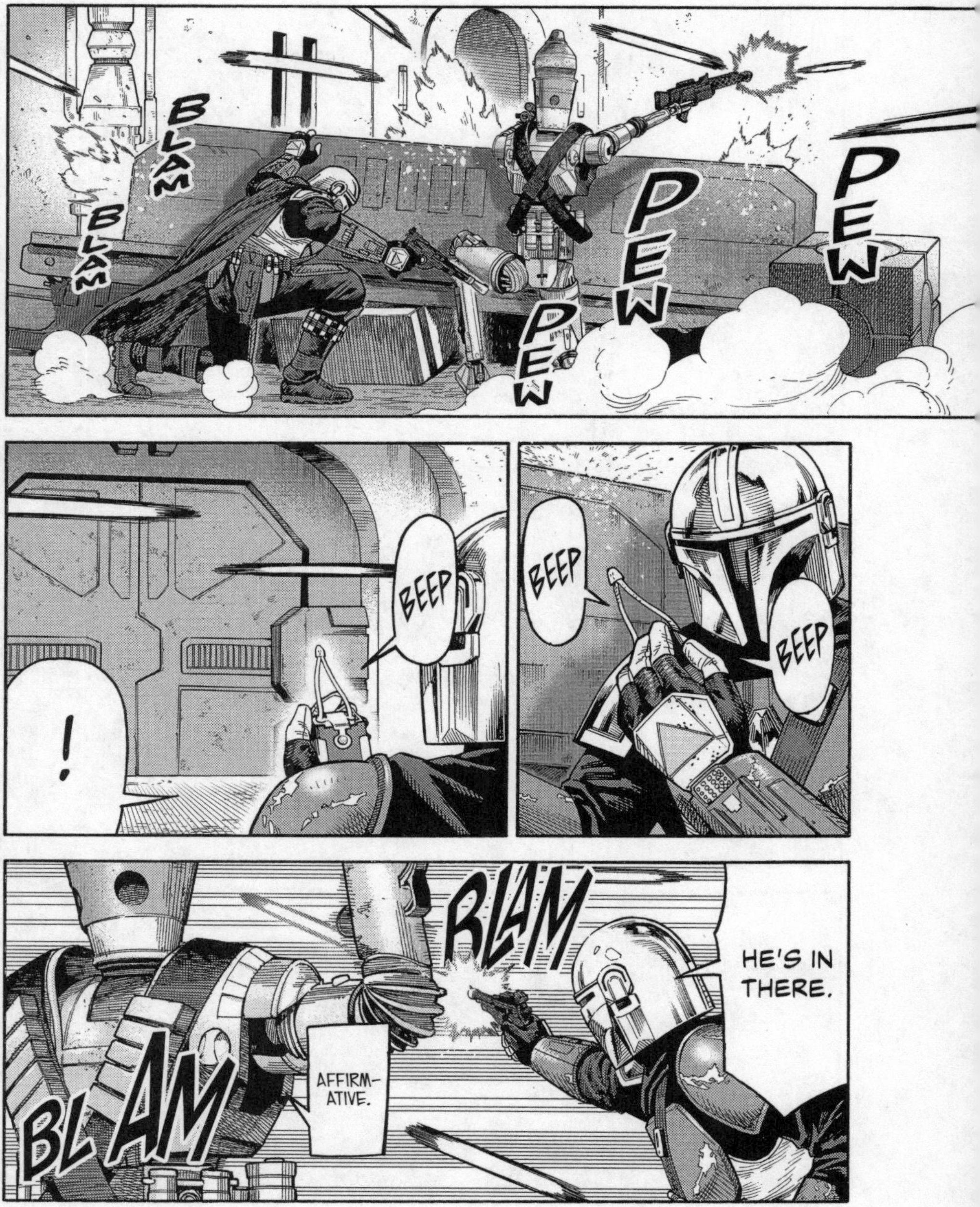
PEW
PEW
PEW
BLAM
BLAM
BEEP
BEEP
BEEP
!
BLAM
HE'S IN THERE.
AFFIRM-
ATIVE.
BLAM

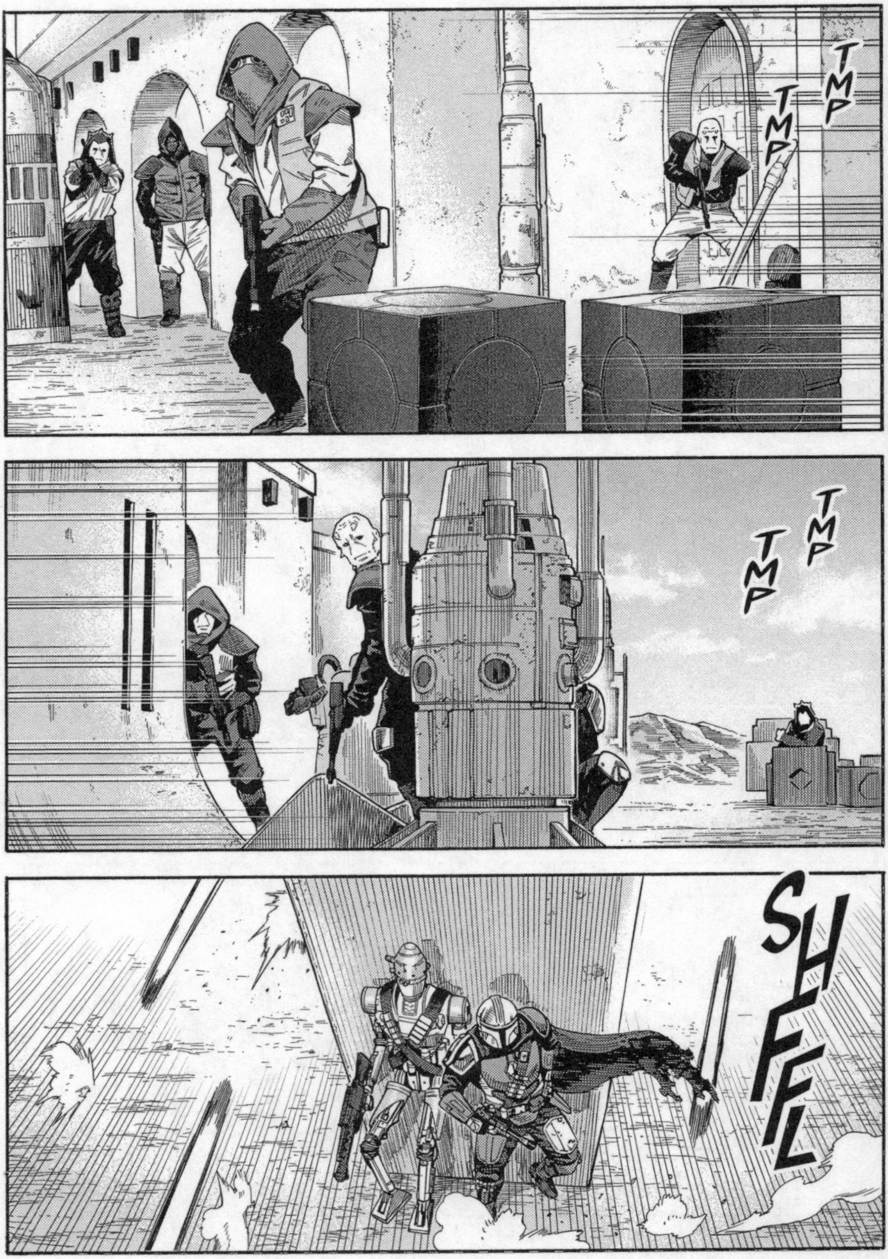
TMP TMP
TMP TMP
SHFFL

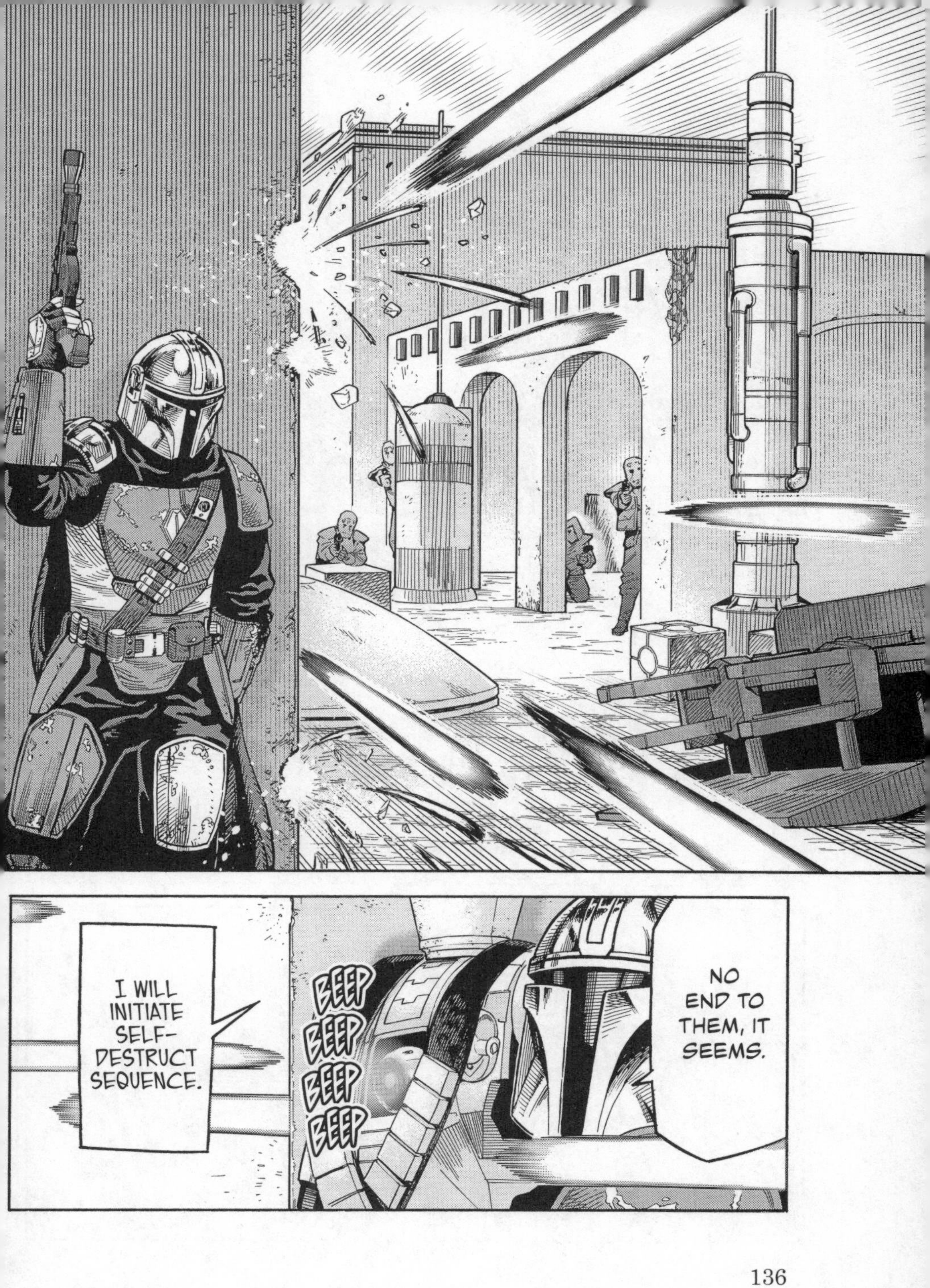
NO END TO THEM, IT SEEMS.
BEEP BEEP BEEP BEEP
I WILL INITIATE SELF-DESTRUCT SEQUENCE.

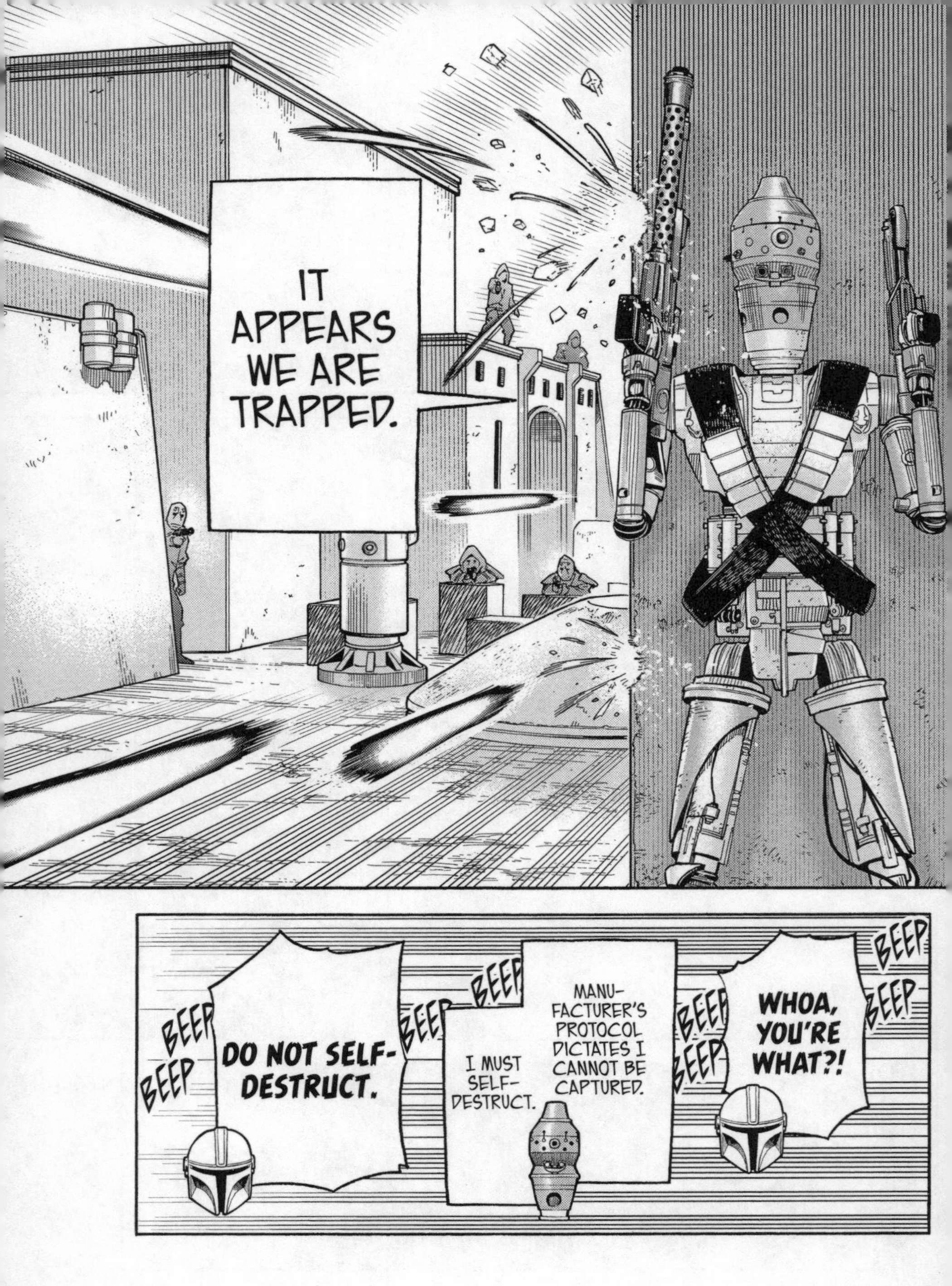
IT APPEARS WE ARE TRAPPED.
BEEP BEEP
WHOA, YOU'RE WHAT?!
BEEP BEEP
MANU-FACTURER'S PROTOCOL DICTATES I CANNOT BE CAPTURED.
I MUST SELF-DESTRUCT.
BEEP BEEP
DO NOT SELF-DESTRUCT.
BEEP BEEP

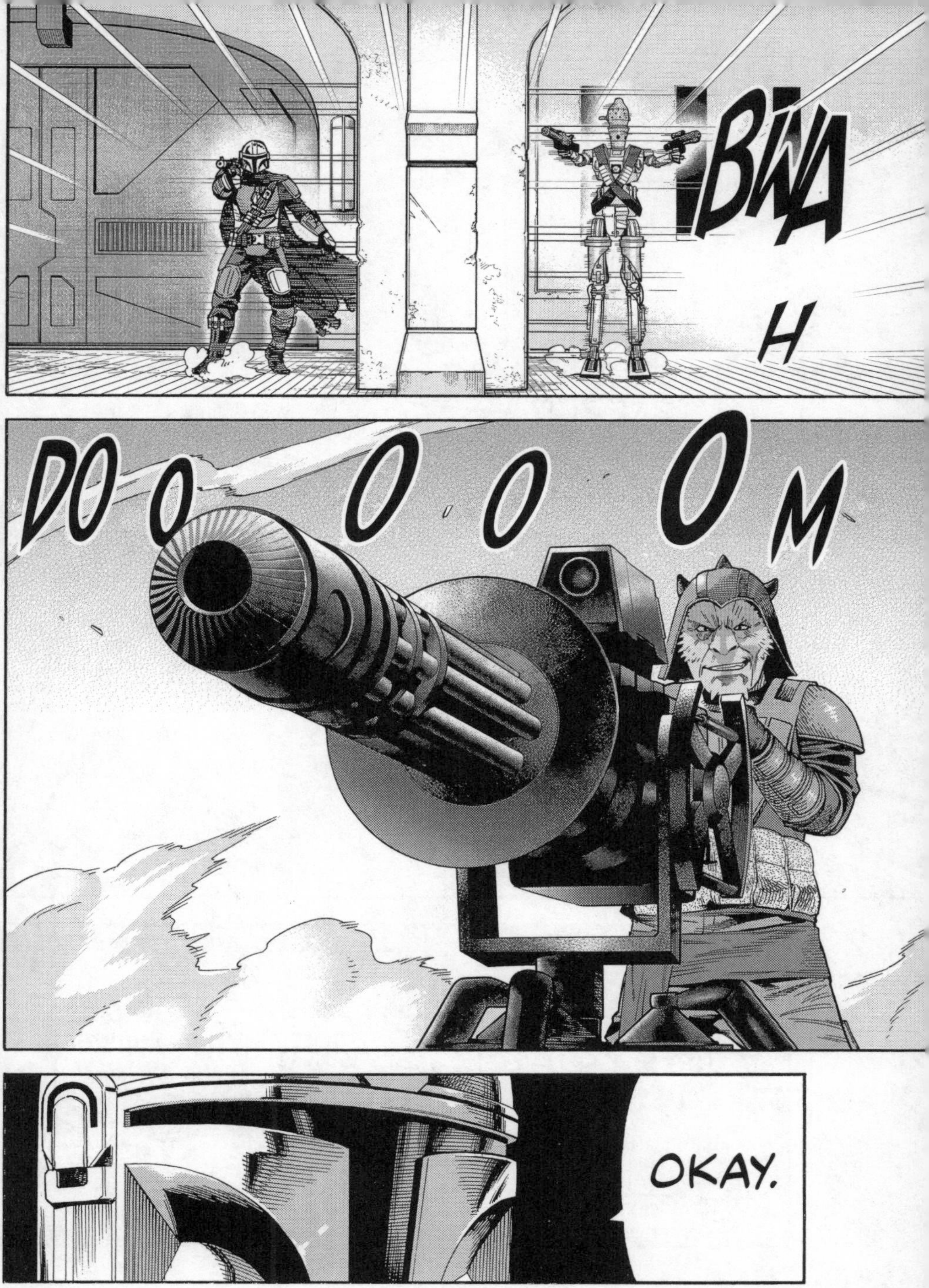
BWAH
DOOOOOM
OKAY.

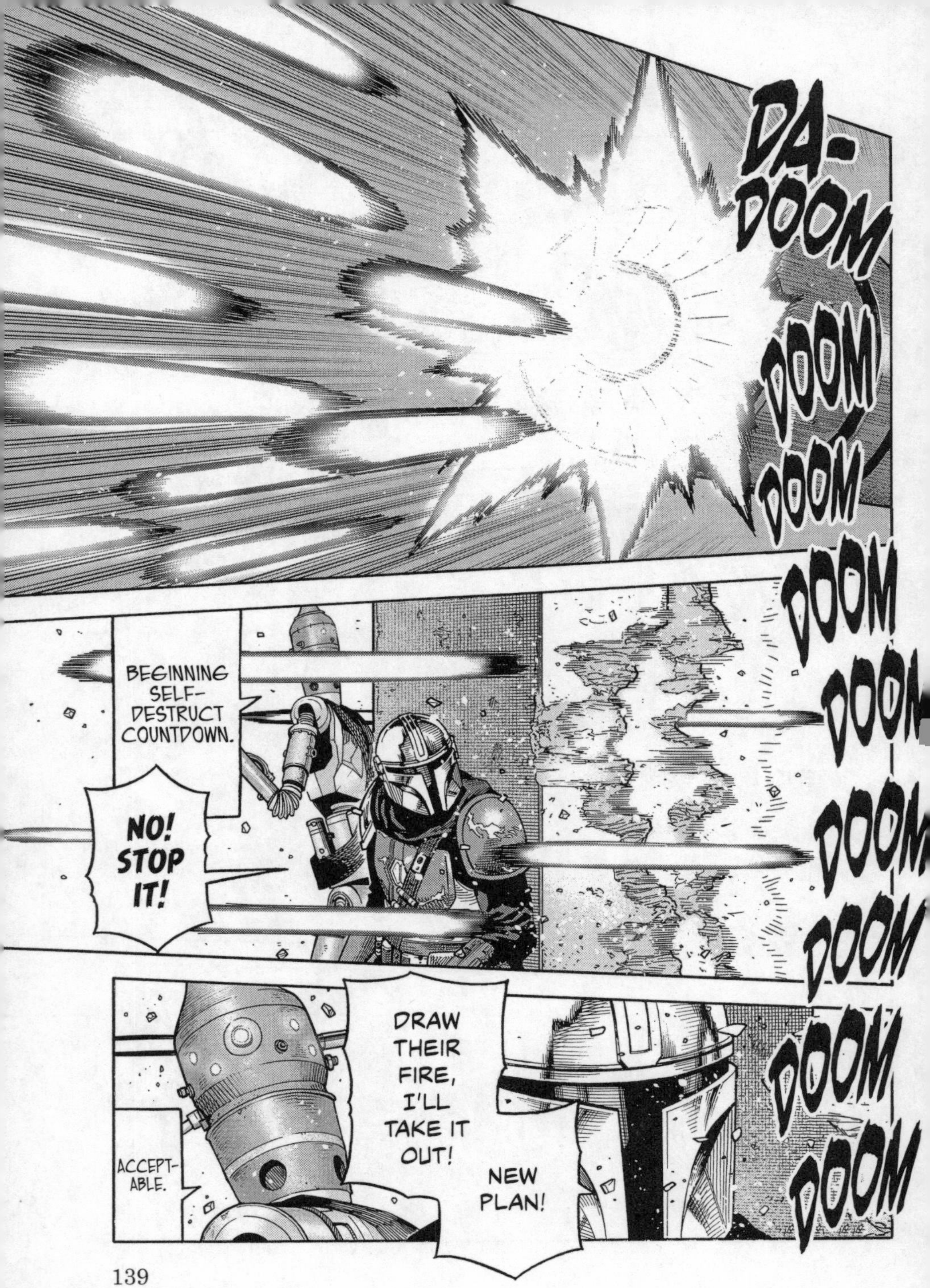
DA-DOOM DOOM DOOM DOOM DOOM DOOM DOOM DOOM DOOM
BEGINNING SELF-DESTRUCT COUNTDOWN.
NO! STOP IT!
NEW PLAN!
DRAW THEIR FIRE, I'LL TAKE IT OUT!
ACCEPTABLE.

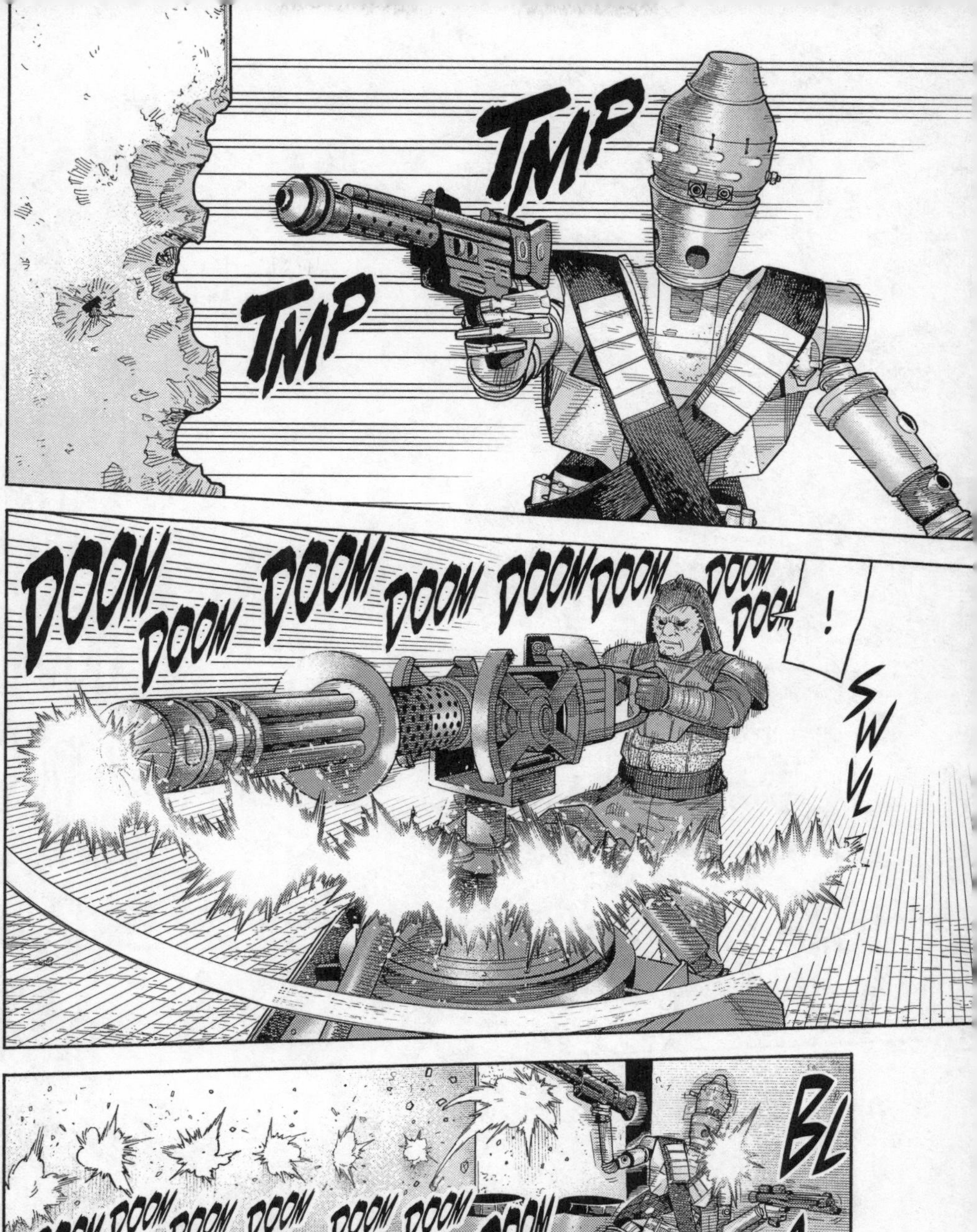
TMP
TMP
!
SWVL
DOOM
DOOM
DOOM
DOOM
DOOM
DOOM
DOOM
DOOM
BLAM
DOOM
DOOM
DOOM
DOOM
DOOM
DOOM
DOOM

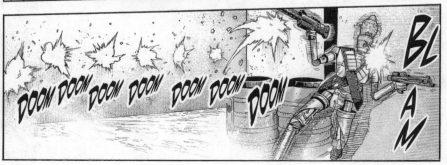

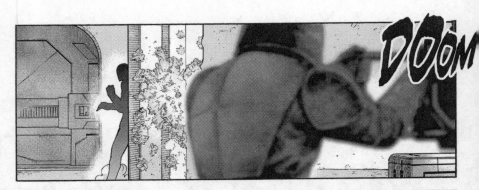

DOOM

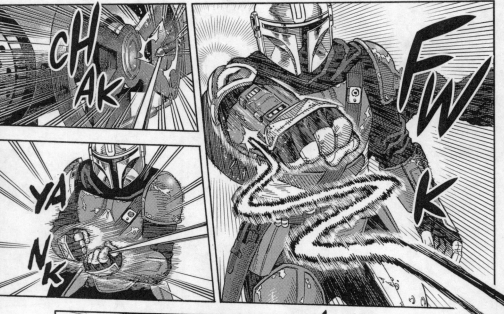

CH AK

YA NK

FW K

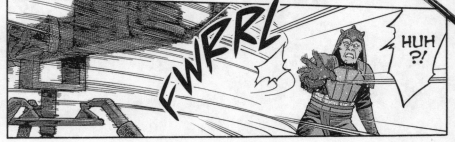

FWRRL

HUH ?!

141

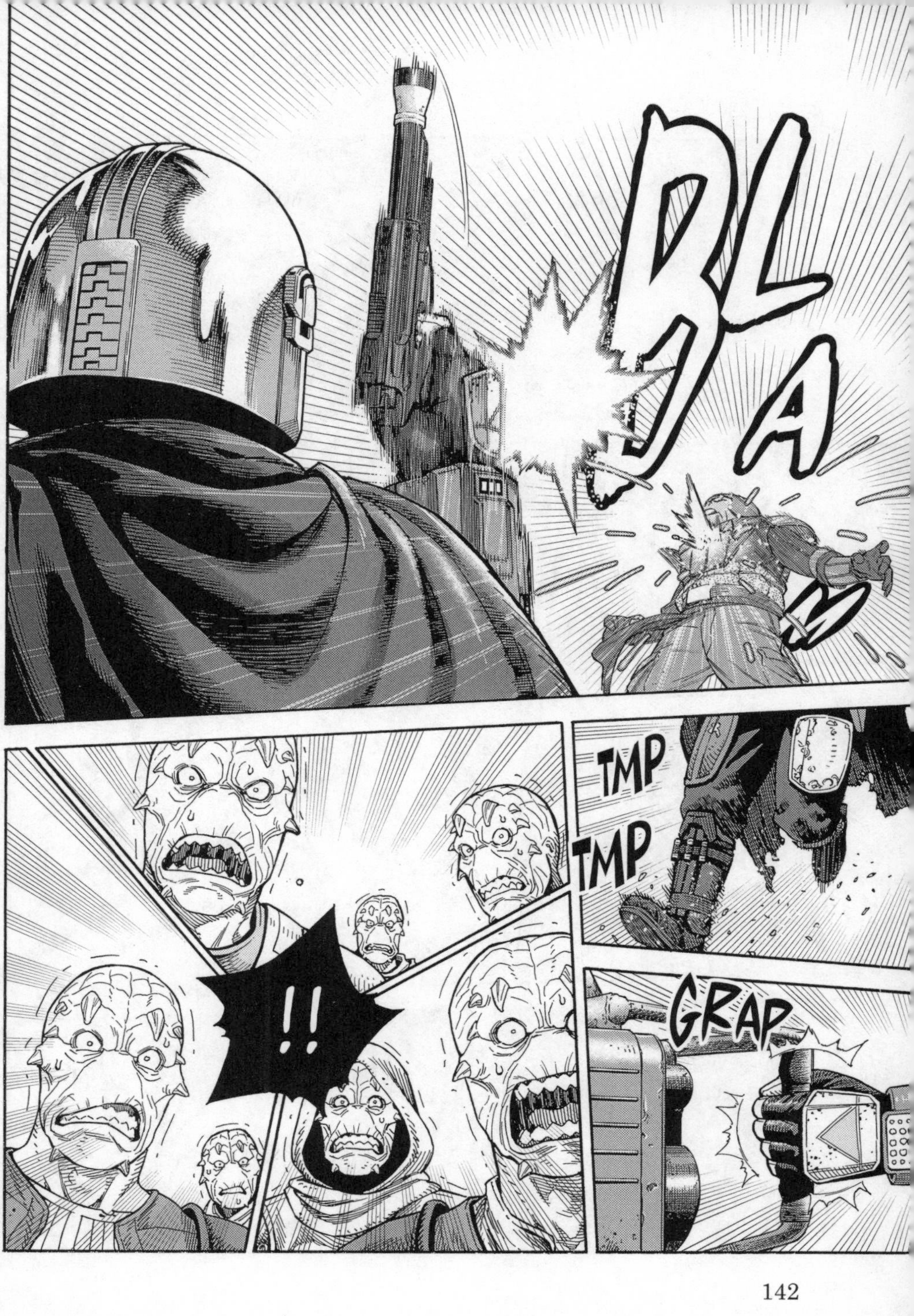
BLAM
TMP
TMP
GRAP
!!

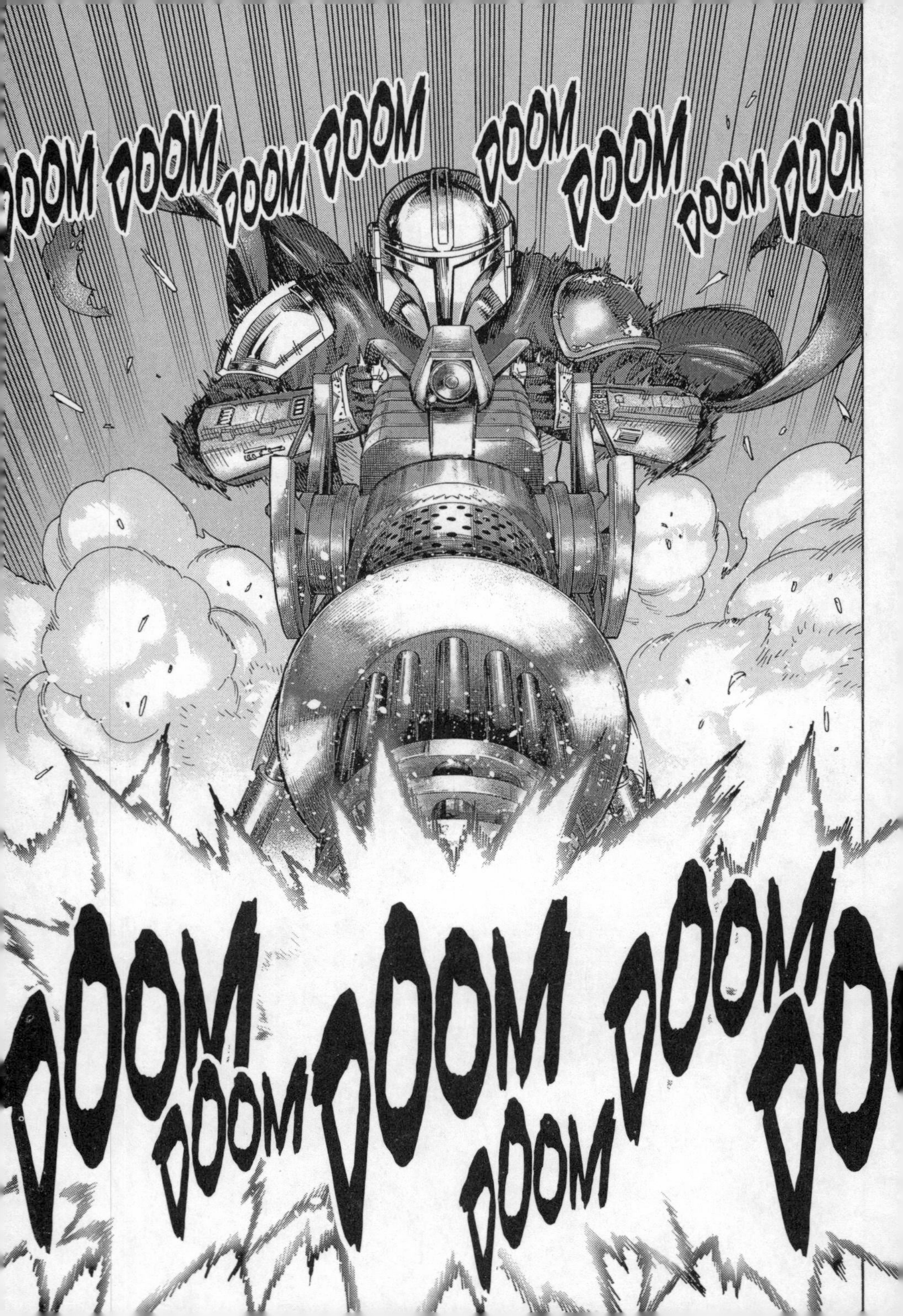
DOOM
DOOM
DOOM
DOOM
DOOM
DOOM
DOOM
DOOM
DOOM
DOOM
DOOM
DOOM
DOOM
DOOM

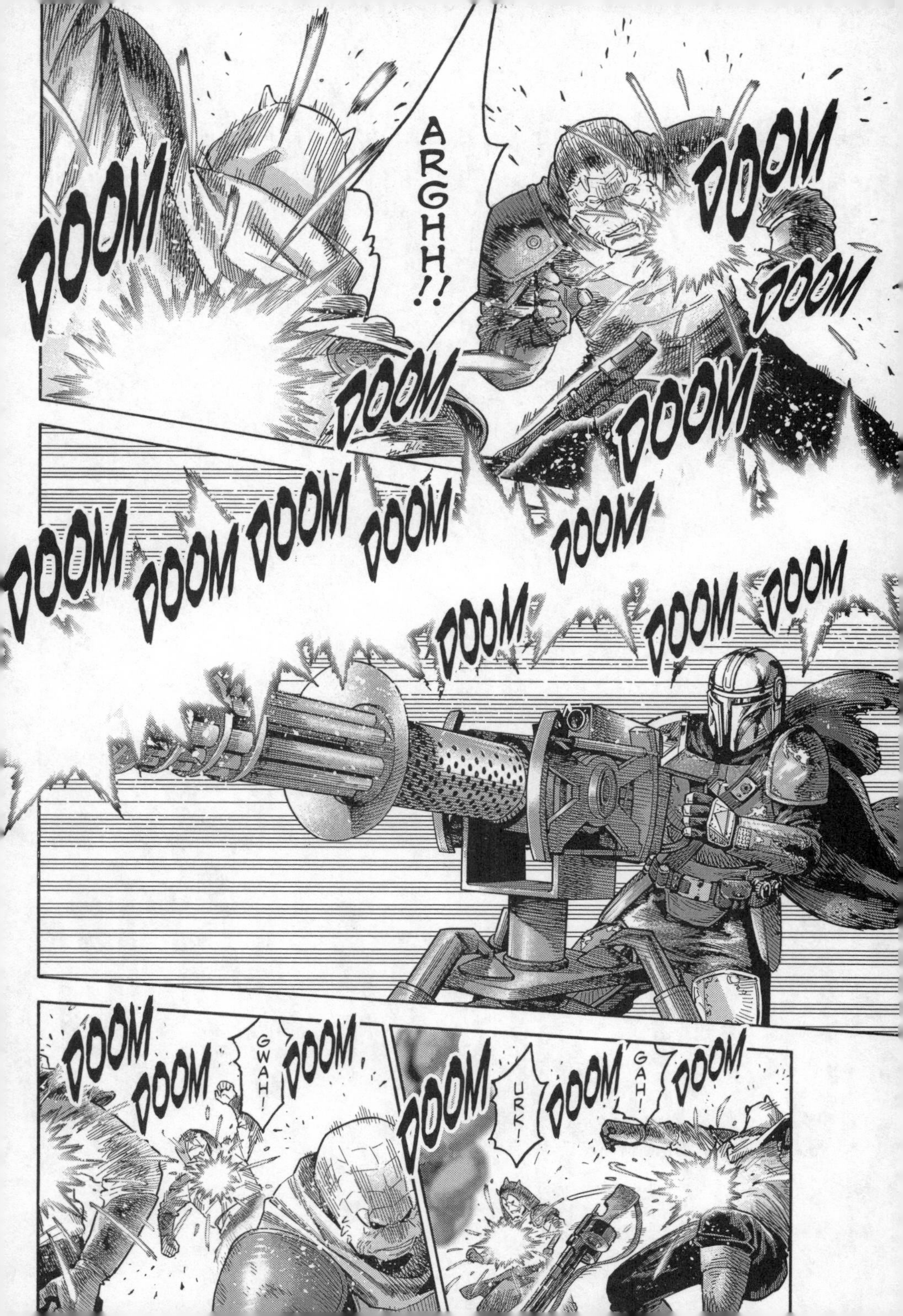
DOOM
DOOM
DOOM
DOOM
ARGHH!!
DOOM
DOOM
DOOM
DOOM
DOOM
DOOM
DOOM
DOOM
DOOM DOOM
DOOM
DOOM
DOOM
GAH!
DOOM
URK!
DOOM
DOOM
GWAH!
DOOM
DOOM

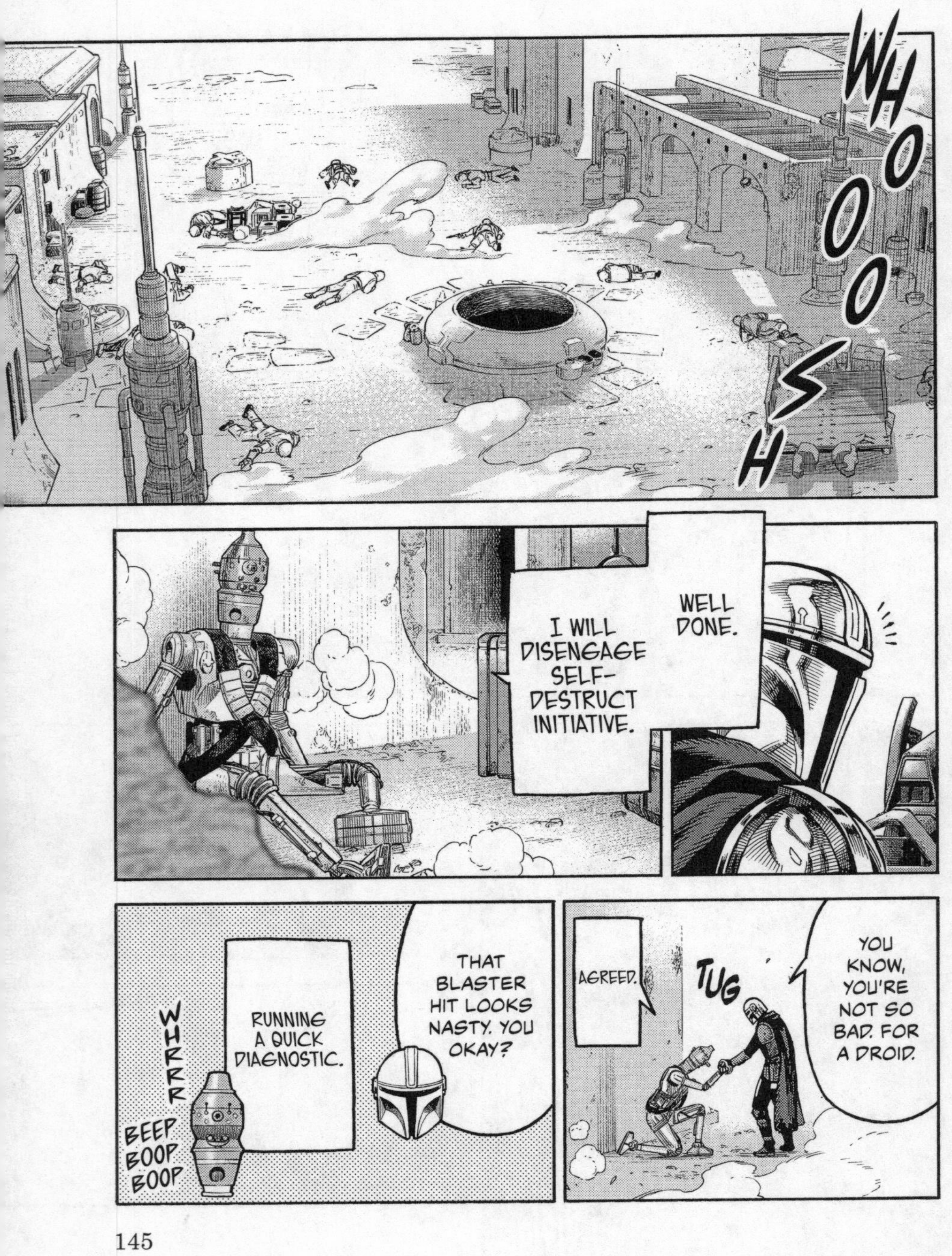
WHOOOOSH
WELL DONE.
I WILL DISENGAGE SELF-DESTRUCT INITIATIVE.
YOU KNOW, YOU'RE NOT SO BAD. FOR A DROID.
TUG
AGREED.
THAT BLASTER HIT LOOKS NASTY. YOU OKAY?
RUNNING A QUICK DIAGNOSTIC.
WHRRR
BEEP BOOP BOOP

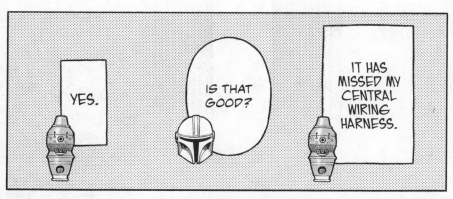

YES.

IS THAT GOOD?

IT HAS MISSED MY CENTRAL WIRING HARNESS.

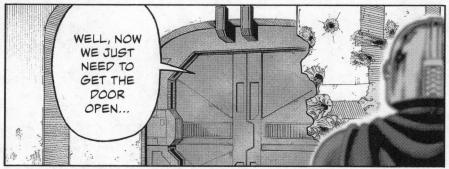

WELL, NOW WE JUST NEED TO GET THE DOOR OPEN...

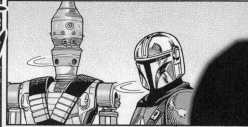

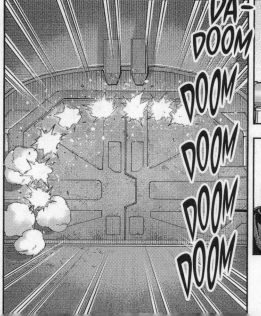

DA-DOOM

DOOM

DOOM

DOOM

DOOM

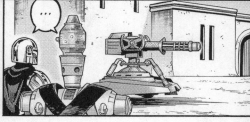

...

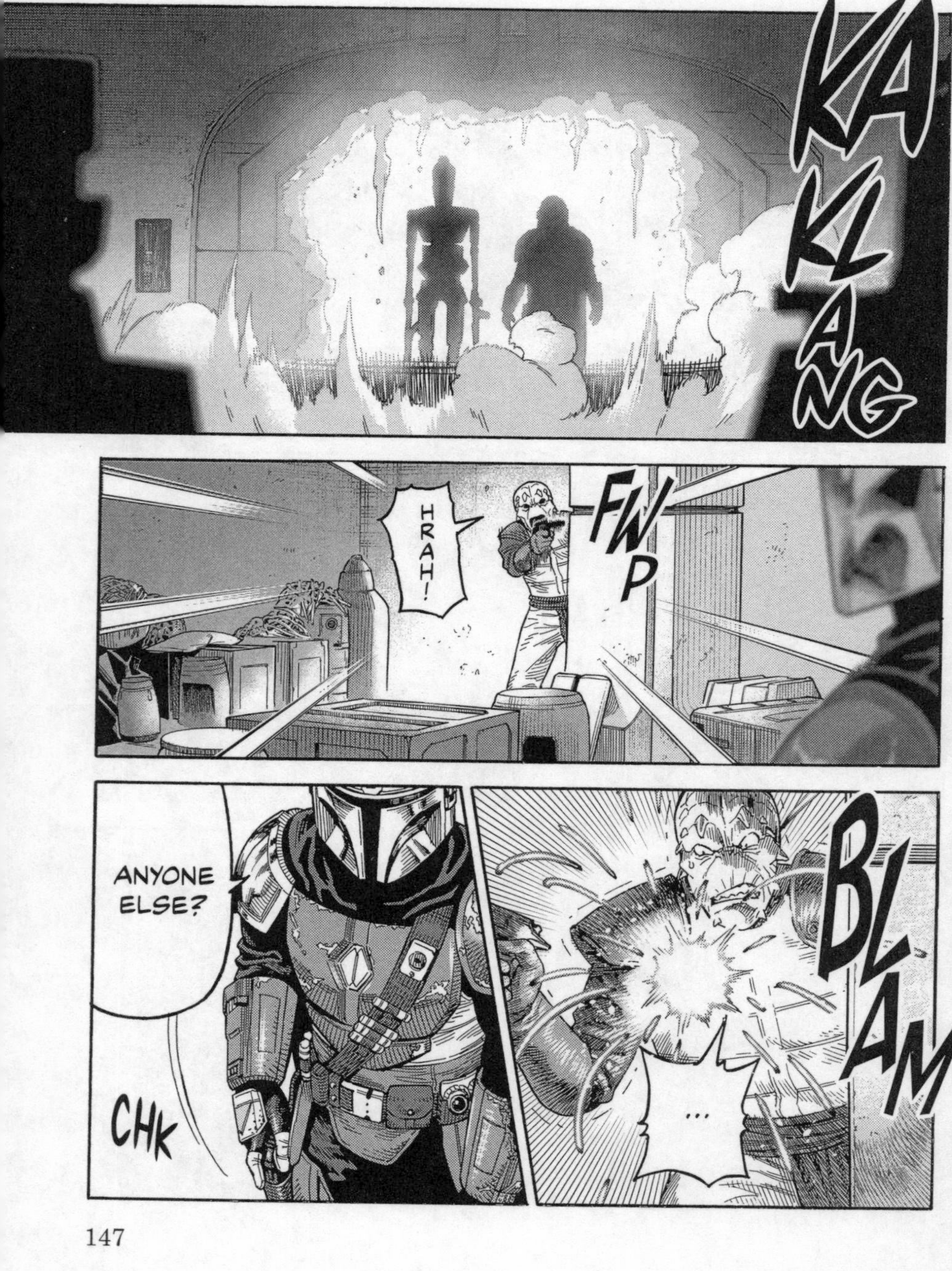
KA KLANG
FWP
HRAH!
BLAM
...
ANYONE ELSE?
CHK

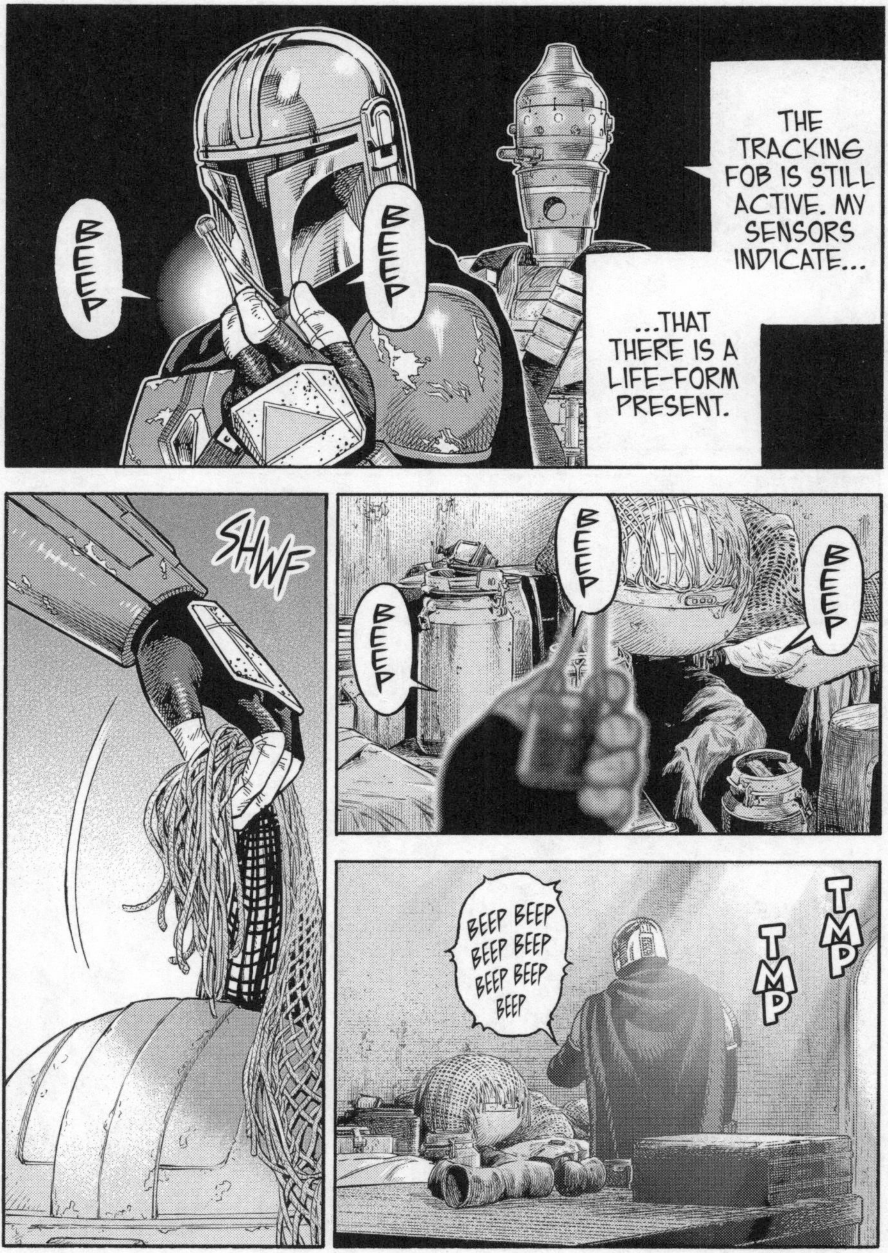
THE TRACKING FOB IS STILL ACTIVE. MY SENSORS INDICATE...
...THAT THERE IS A LIFE-FORM PRESENT.
BEEP
BEEP
BEEP
BEEP
BEEP
TMP
TMP
BEEP BEEP BEEP BEEP BEEP BEEP BEEP
SHWF

CLK
VWRRR
!
WAIT...
HOW CAN THIS BE?
SKWEEZ

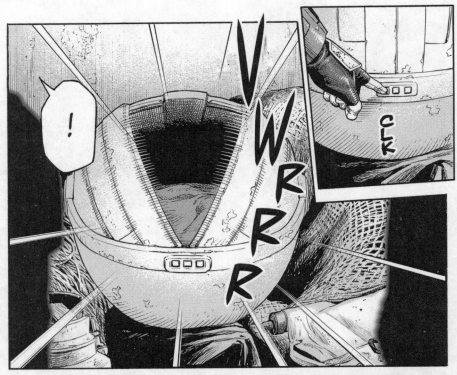

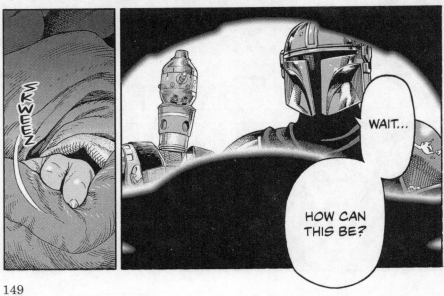

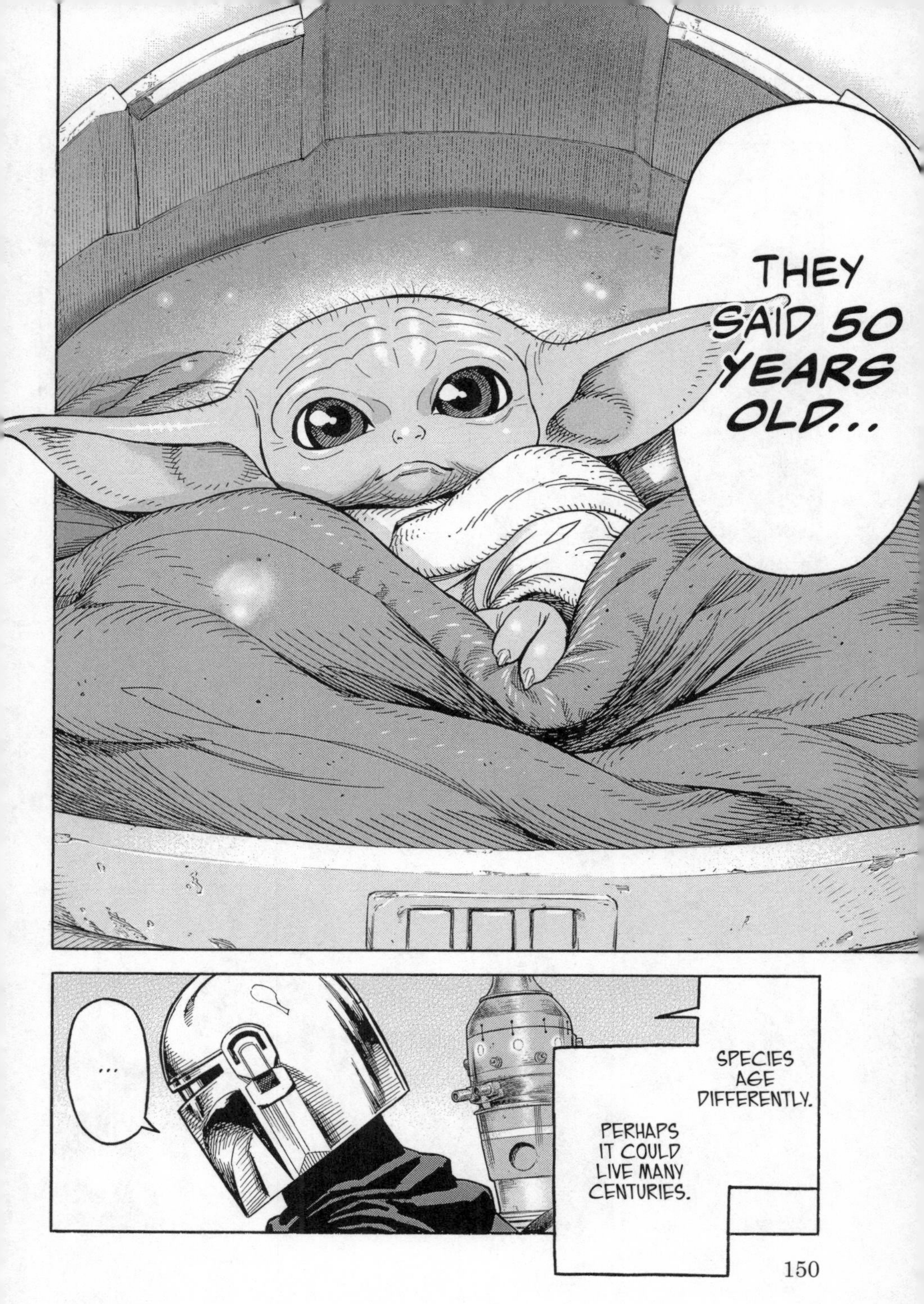
THEY SAID 50 YEARS OLD...
SPECIES AGE DIFFERENTLY.
PERHAPS IT COULD LIVE MANY CENTURIES.
...

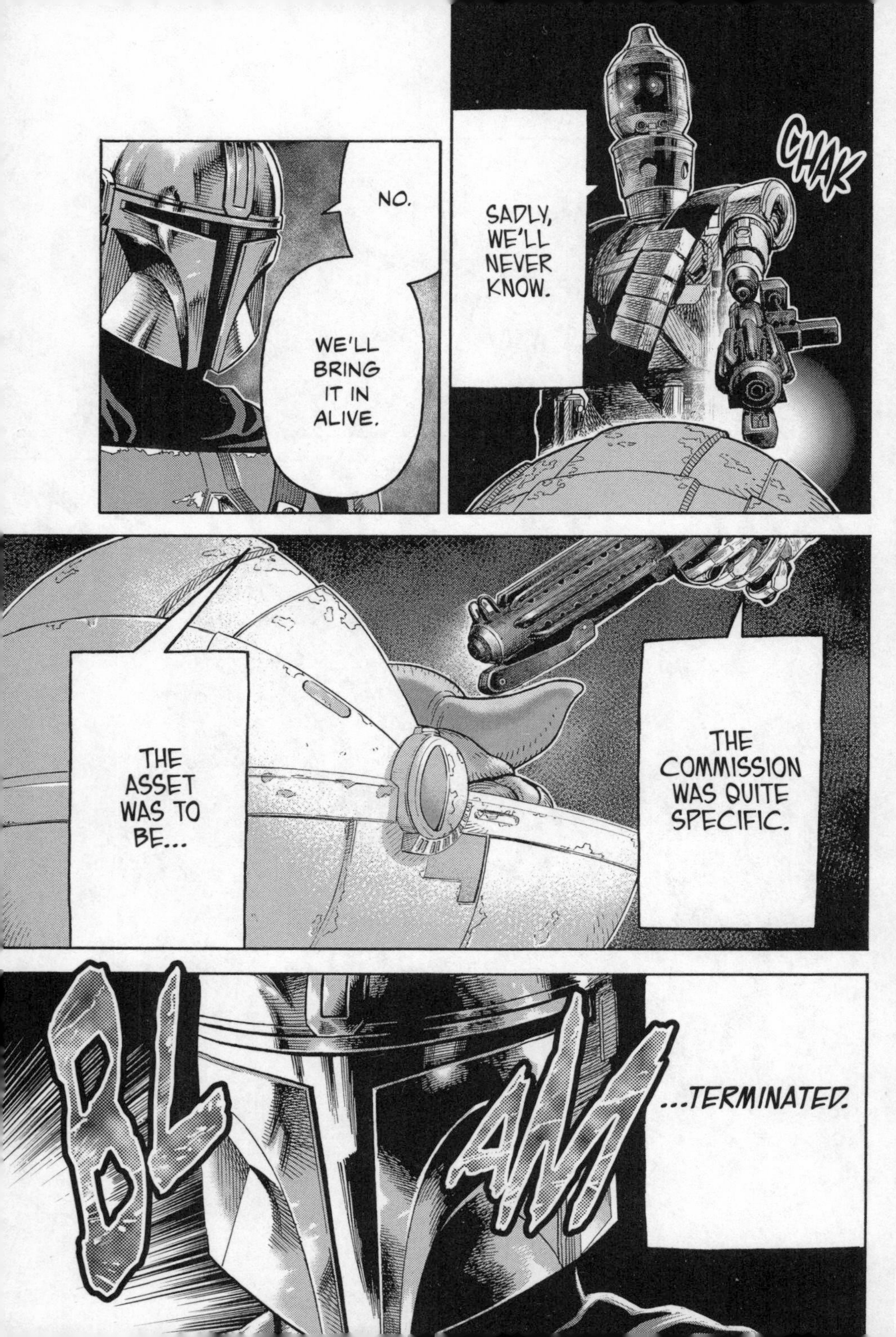
CHAK
SADLY, WE'LL NEVER KNOW.
NO.
WE'LL BRING IT IN ALIVE.
THE COMMISSION WAS QUITE SPECIFIC.
THE ASSET WAS TO BE...
...TERMINATED.
BLAM

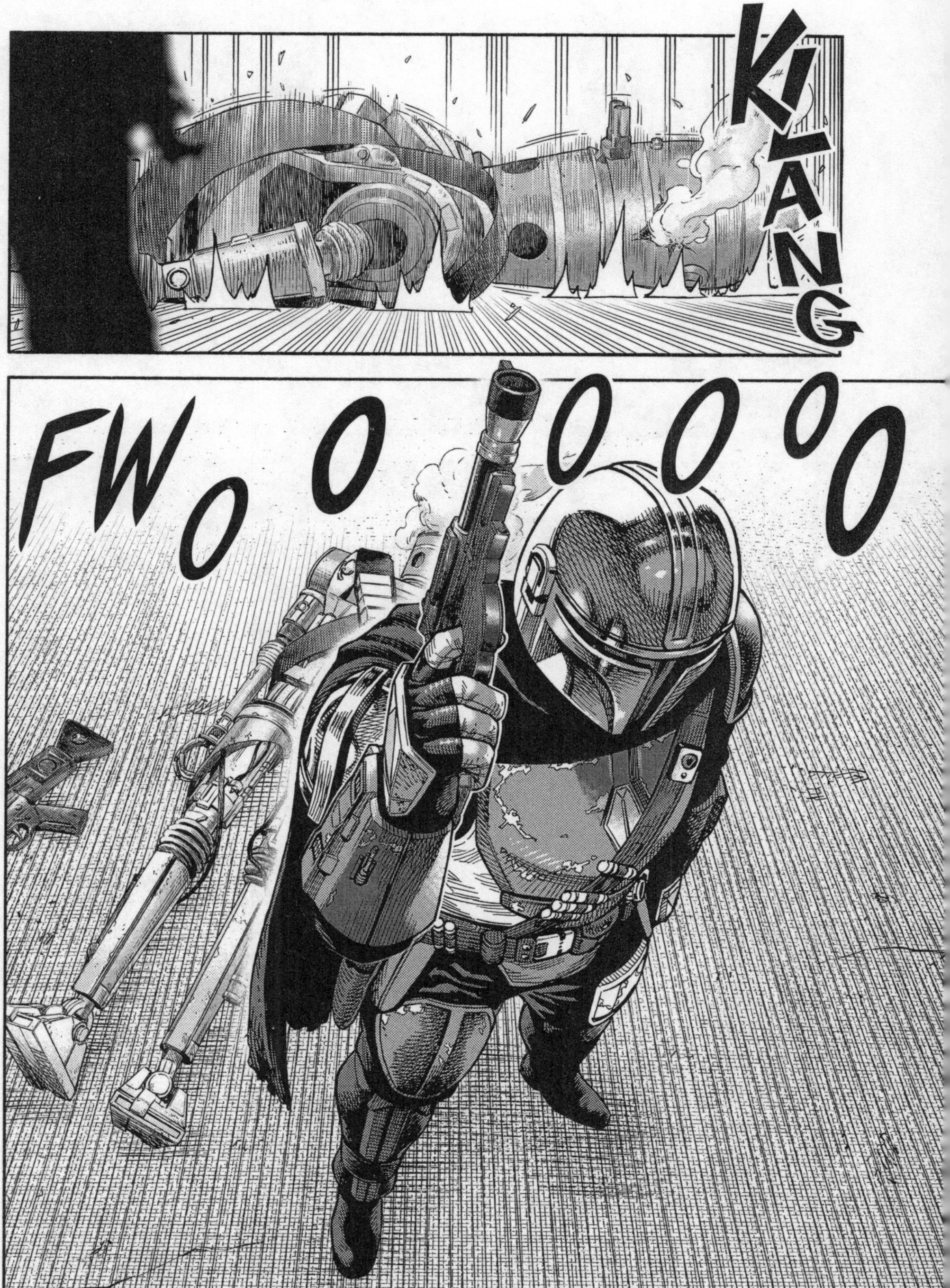
KLANG
FWOOOOOO

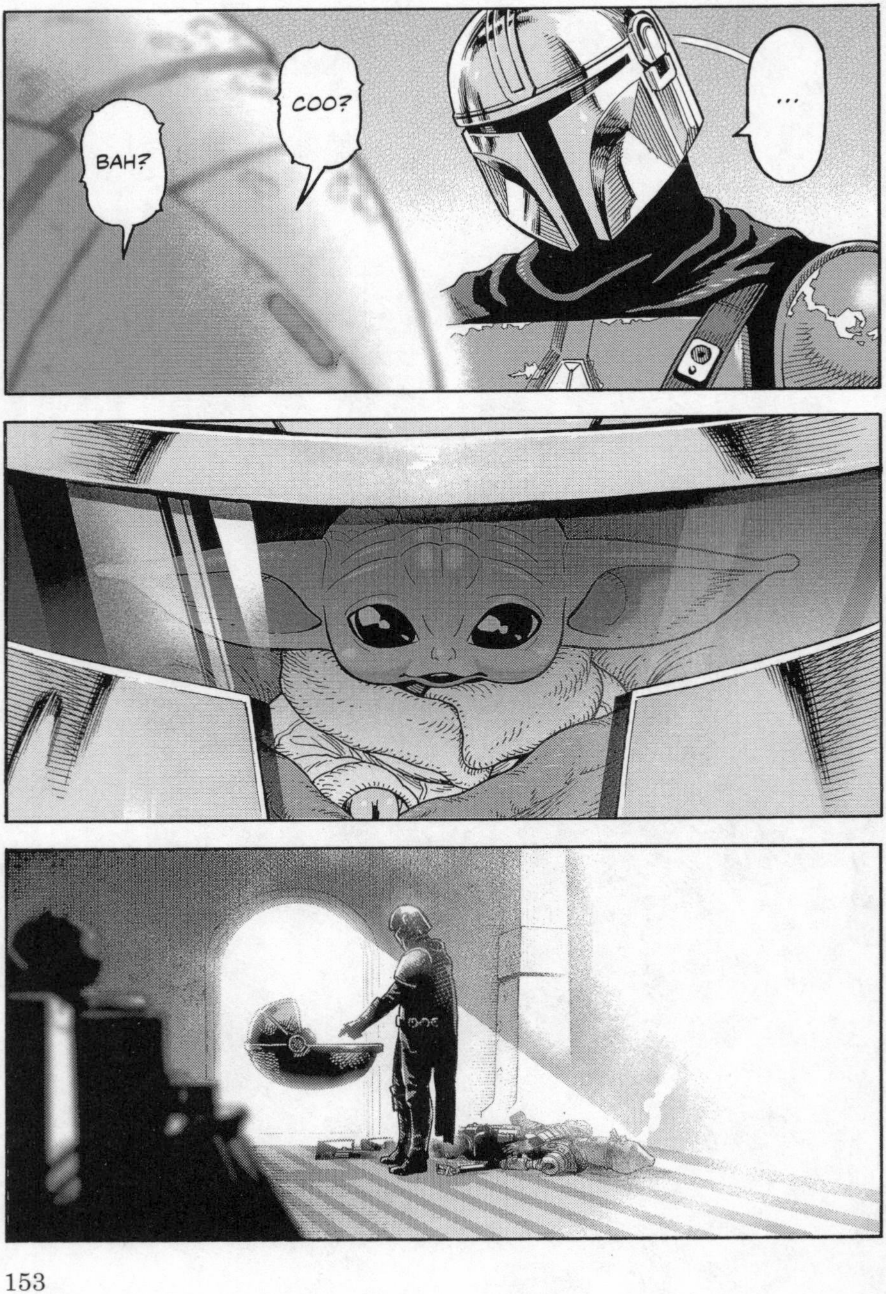
...
COO?
BAH?

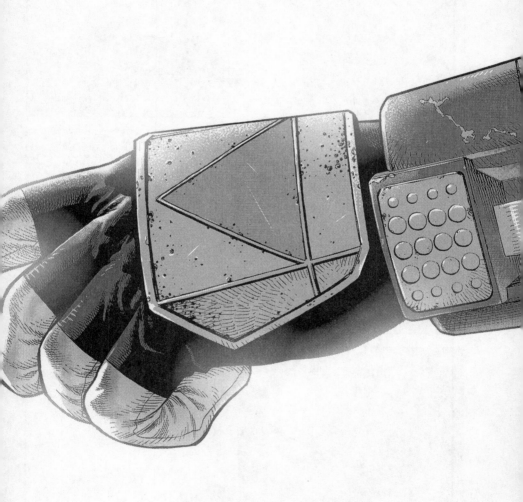

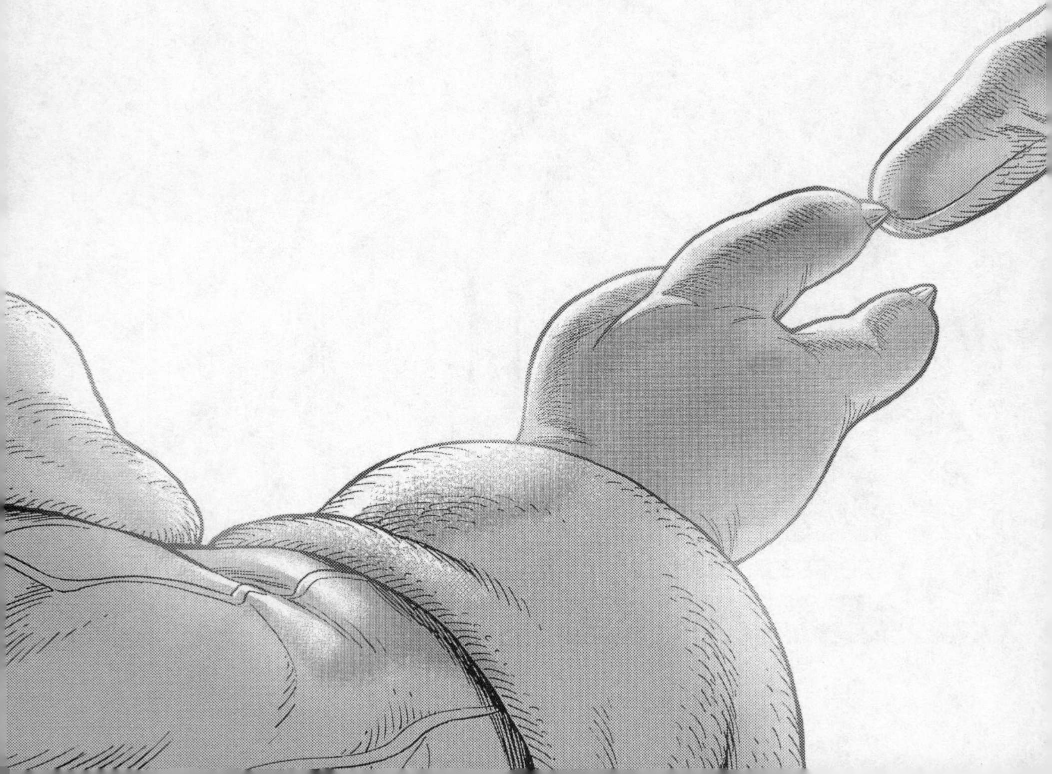

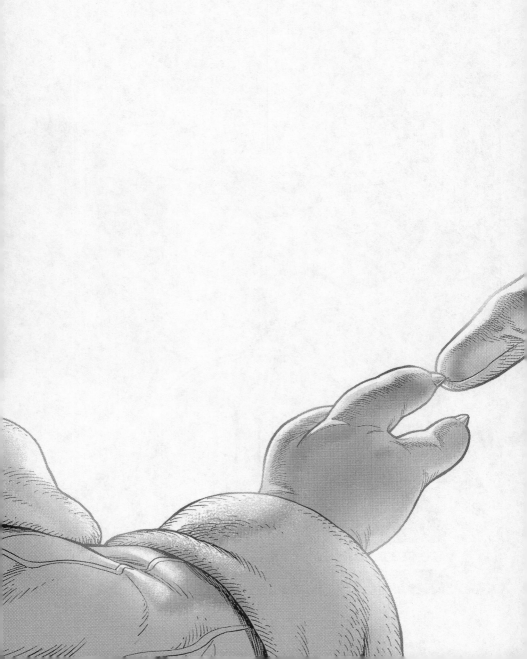

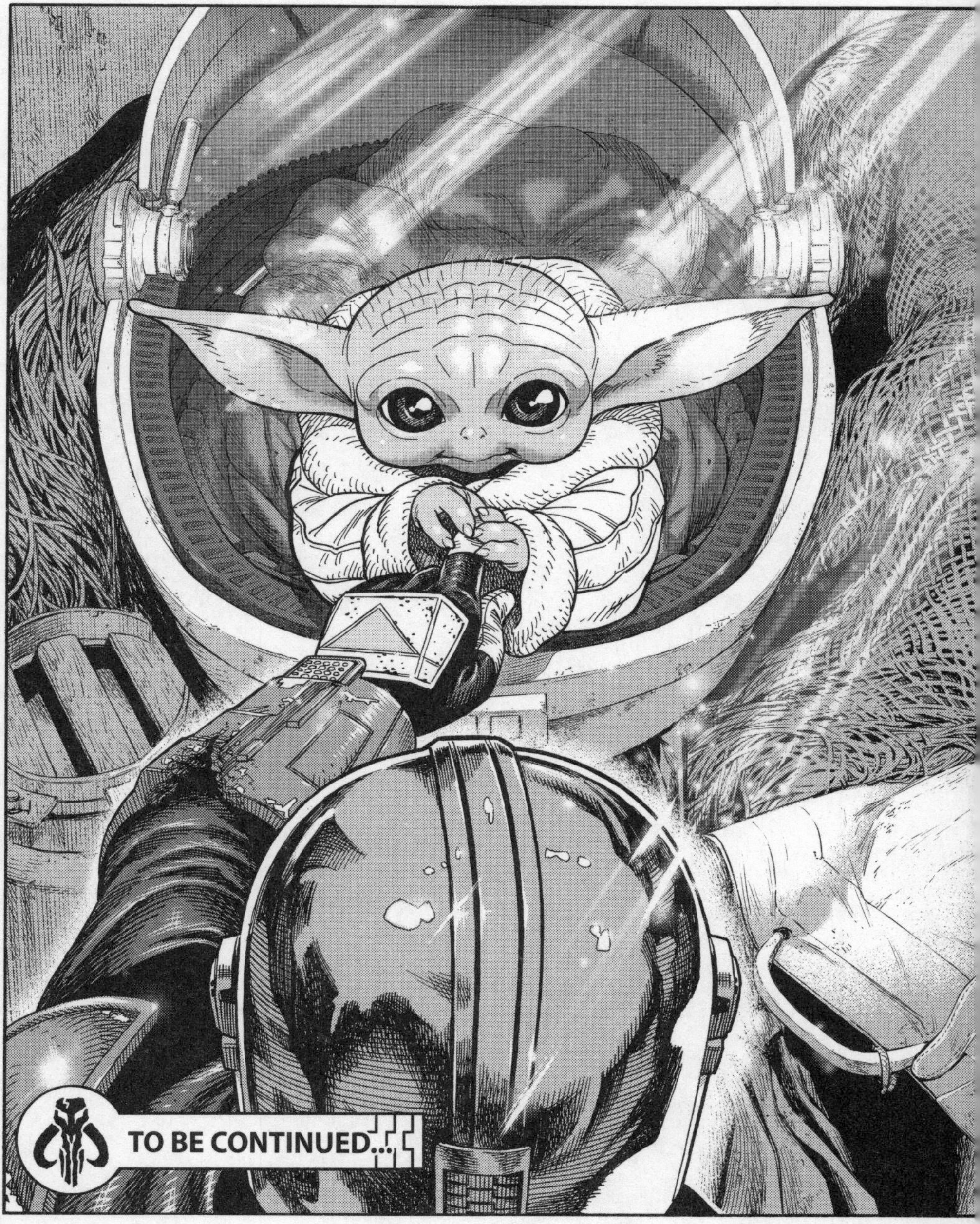
TO BE CONTINUED...

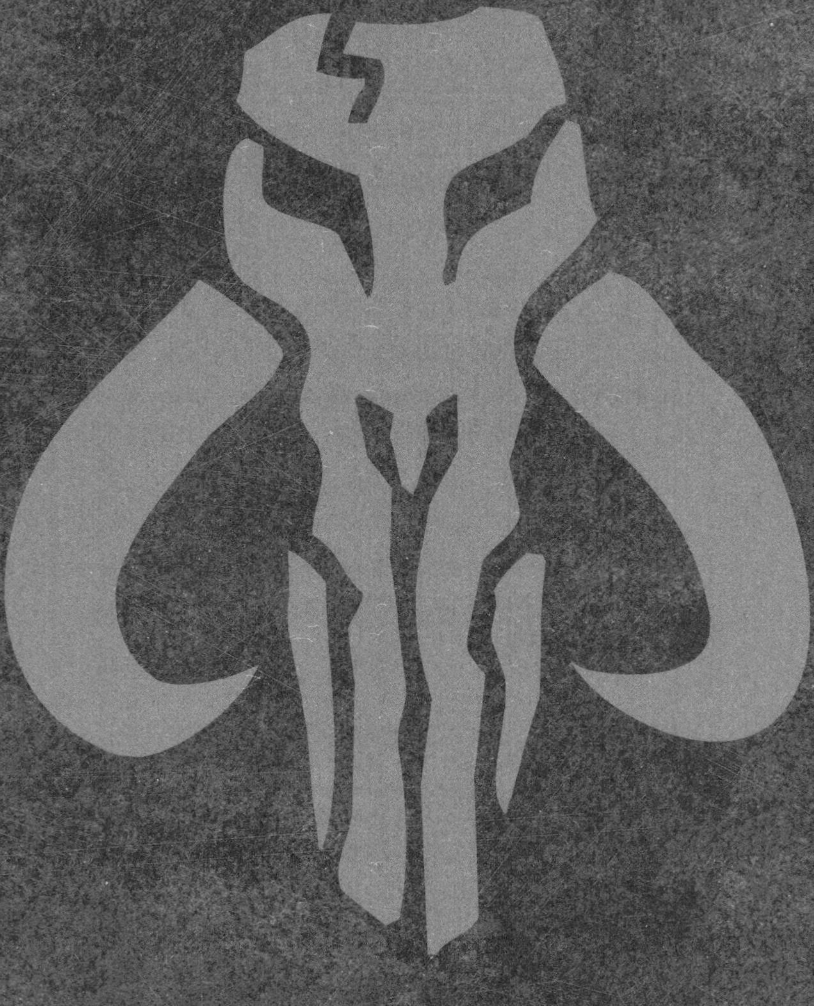

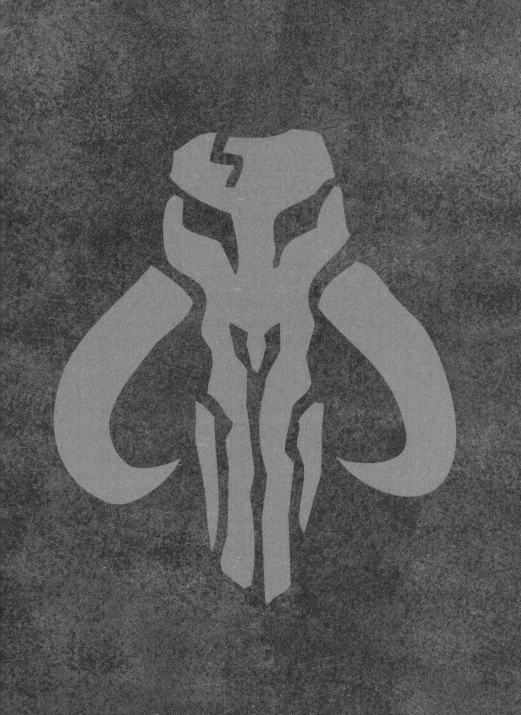

RAZOR CREST

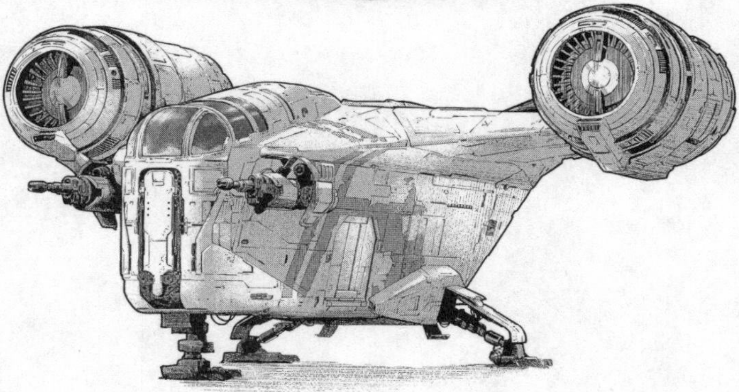

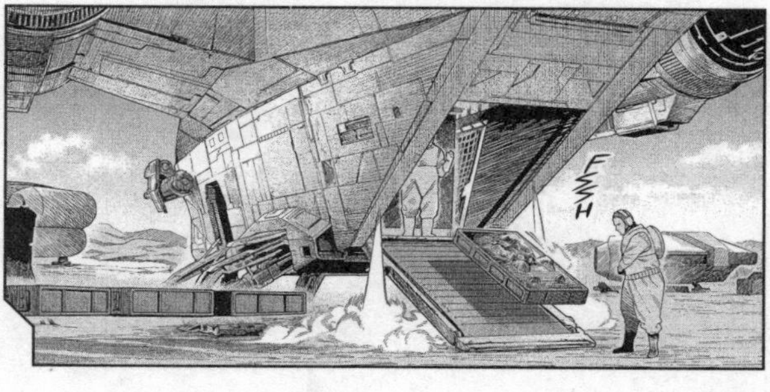
FSSH

Mando's gunship, equipped with two laser cannons. This class of military vessel predates the Galactic Empire and was used for local patrols in remote zones. The *Razor Crest* is outfitted with a refresher, sleeping quarters, carbon-freezing equipment, and an escape pod in the upper section.

AMBAN SNIPER RIFLE

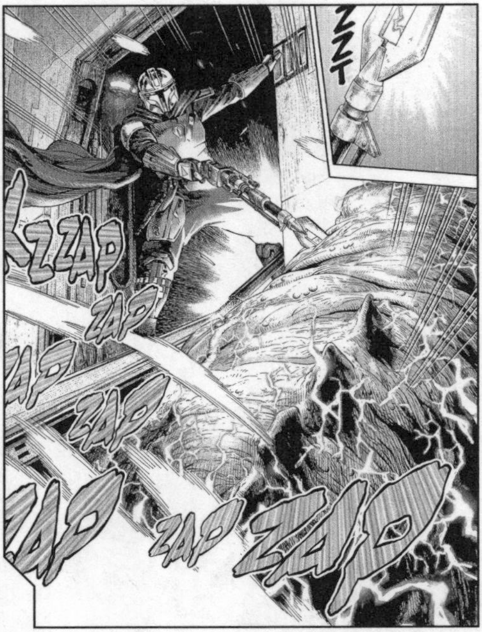
ZZZT
KZZAP
ZAP
ZAP
ZAP
ZAP
ZAP
ZAP
ZAP

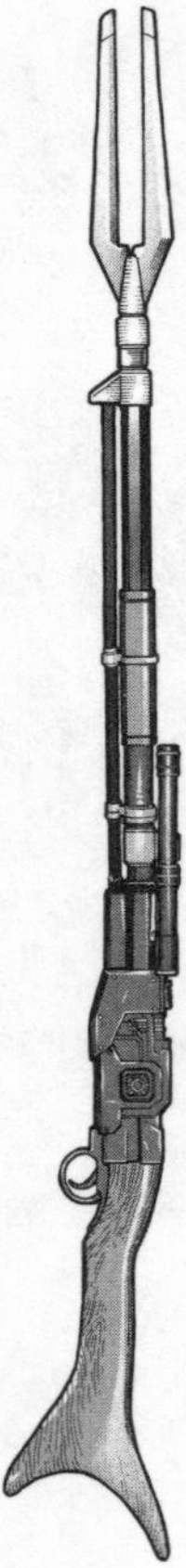

Mando's preferred disruptor sniper rifle. Disruptors employ deadly phase-pulse energy to break down its targets to the molecular level. This rifle also features a forked ion prod electro-bayonet for stunning targets.

IB-94 BLASTER

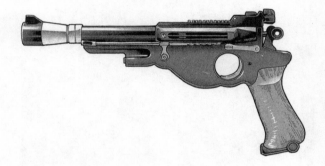

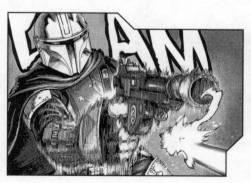

A blaster pistol made by BlasTech Industries. The IB-94 is a rare model that packs a surprising punch for its small size.

GONK DROID

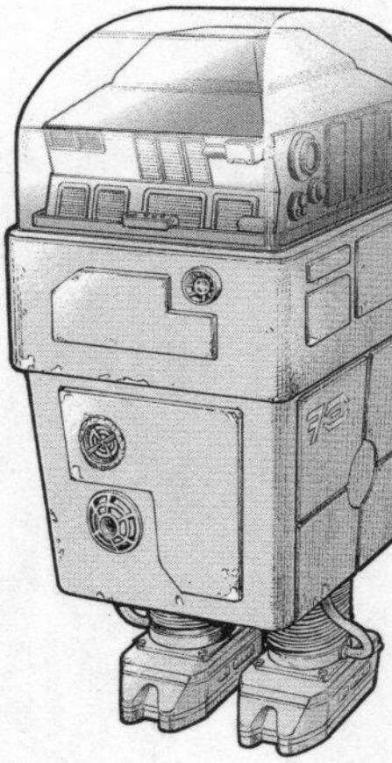

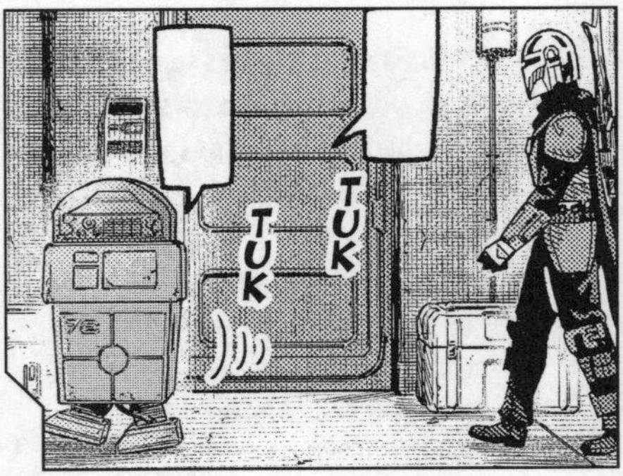
TUK
TUK

Common throughout the galaxy, these droids are essentially mobile batteries that follow their owners' directives or programming to travel to and power vehicles and other machinery. The colloquial "gonk" nickname came about as a result of their distinctive utterances.

CARBON-FREEZING

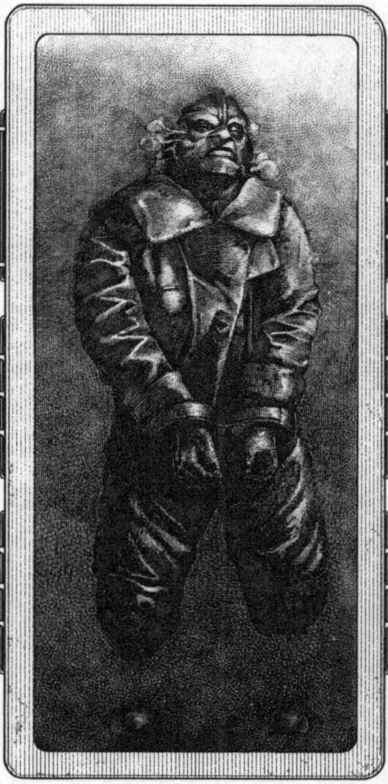

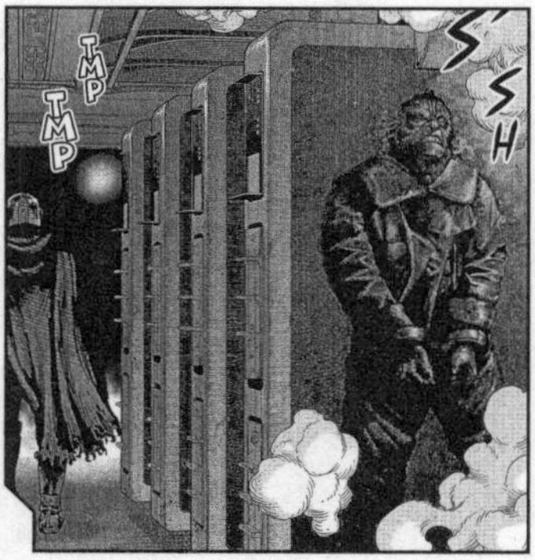

SSH
TMP
TMP

An industrial process that combines high-strength carbonite with high-pressure gas to trap and preserve otherwise unstable materials. The technology was not originally developed to be used on living, sentient organisms, but when it is, the target is perfectly preserved (assuming it does not die in the process).

Thank you to all the Force-sensitive readers
who picked up the *Mandalorian* manga.

My goal in life is to stay alive long enough
to portray that one scene from season 2 (you know the one)
in the manga, so I really appreciate your support.

"This is the Way!"
—Yusuke Osawa

—Special Thanks—

(Assistants)
Waa, Mitomo Sasako, Hitoshi Uchiyama, Nakamura

(Editor)
Shion Takahashi

(Walt Disney Japan)
Kohei Hijikata

AND YOU!

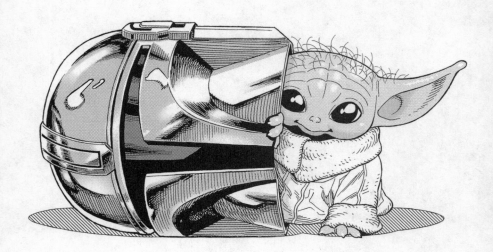

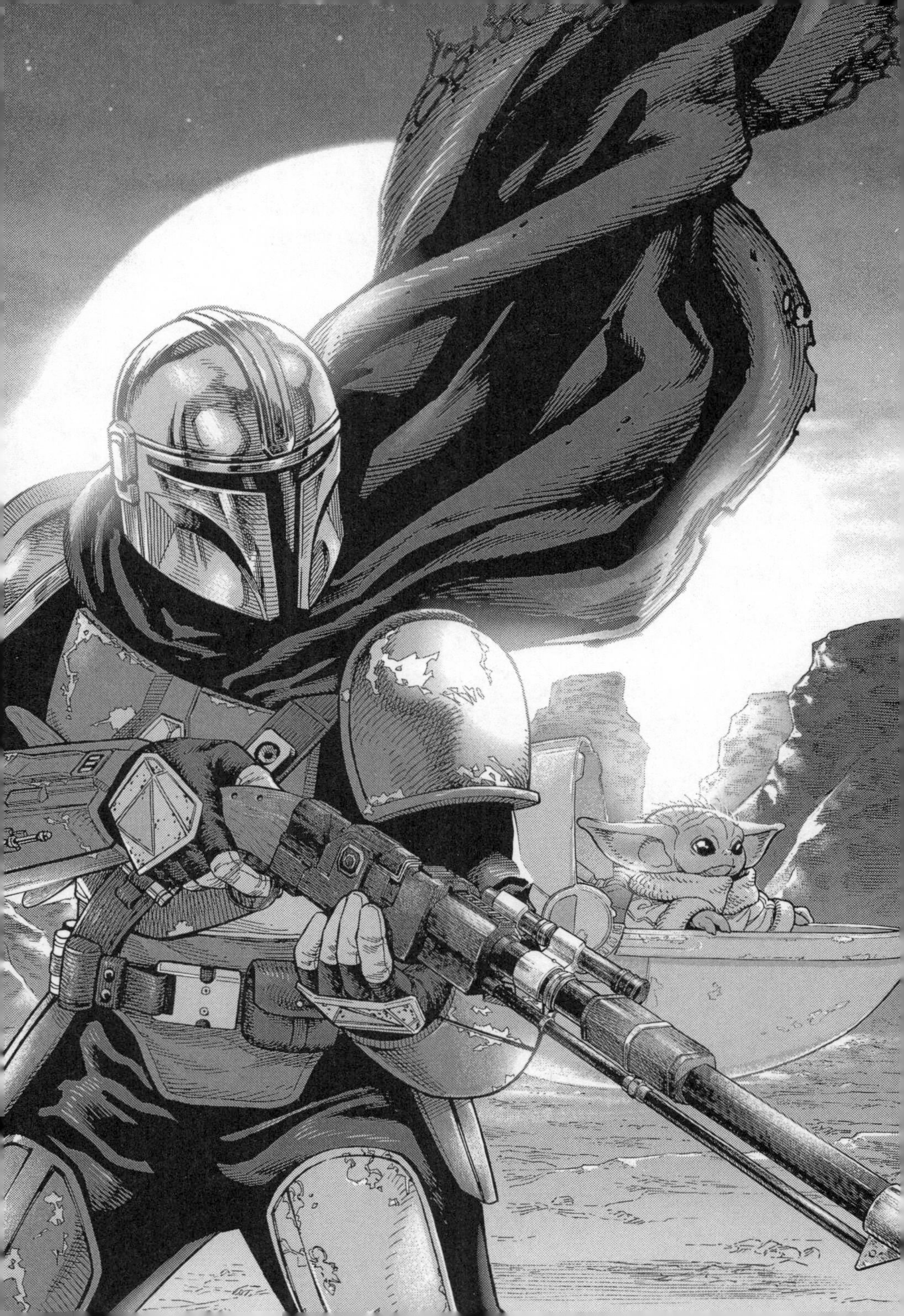

STAR WARS
THE
MANDALORIAN

THE MANGA

VOLUME 1

VIZ Media Edition

ADAPTATION BY
YUSUKE OSAWA

Based on the series created by
Jon Favreau and written by Jon Favreau,
Dave Filoni, Christopher Yost,
and Rick Famuyiwa

TRANSLATION **CALEB COOK**

RETOUCH & LETTERING **BRANDON BOVIA**

DESIGN **JIMMY PRESLER**

EDITOR **DAVID BROTHERS**

FOR LUCASFILM

SENIOR EDITOR **ROBERT SIMPSON**

CREATIVE DIRECTOR **MICHAEL SIGLAIN**

ART DIRECTOR **TROY ALDERS**

LUCASFILM STORY GROUP **MATT MARTIN,
PABLO HIDALGO,** AND **EMILY SHKOUKANI**

CREATIVE ART MANAGER **PHIL SZOSTAK**

Star Wars: The Mandalorian: The Manga
© & TM 2023 LUCASFILM LTD.

Printed in the U.S.A.

Published by VIZ Media, LLC
P.O. Box 77010
San Francisco, CA 94107

10 9 8 7 6 5 4 3 2 1
First printing, September 2023

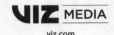
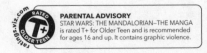

viz.com

YOU'RE READING THE WRONG WAY!

Star Wars: The Mandalorian—The Manga reads from right to left, starting in the upper-right corner. Japanese is read from right to left, meaning that action, sound effects, and word balloon reading order are completely reversed from English order. This is the Way.

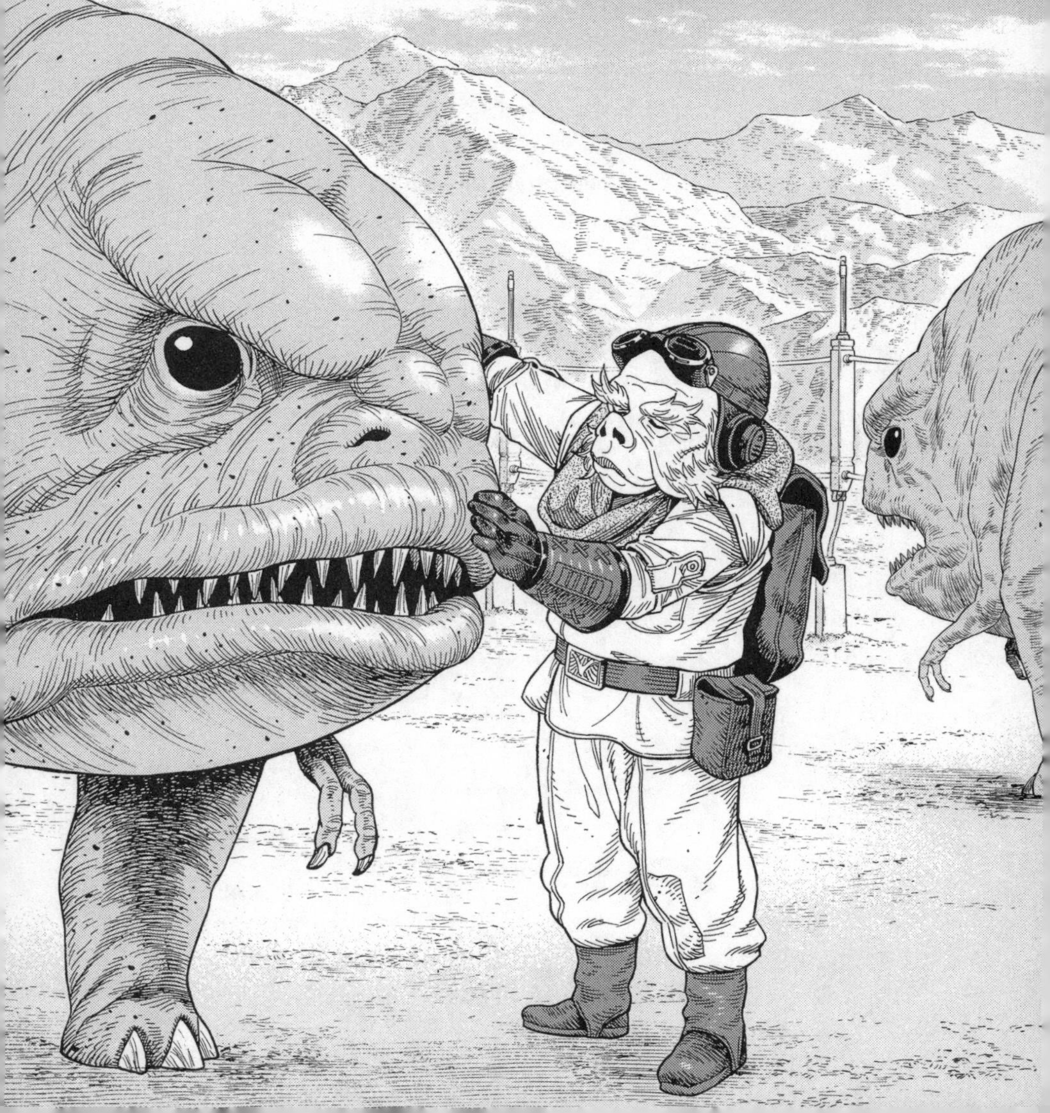